United States Fleet Carriers of World War II 'In Action'

United States Fleet Carriers of World War II 'In Action'

Richard Humble

BLANDFORD PRESS
POOLE · DORSET

First published in the U.K. 1984 by Blandford Press,
Link House, West Street, Poole, Dorset, BH15 1LL.

Copyright © 1984 Talos Books Ltd.

Distributed in the United States by
Sterling Publishing Co., Inc.,
2 Park Avenue, New York, N.Y. 10016.

British Library Cataloguing in Publication Data

Humble, Richard
    United States fleet carriers of World War 2 'in action'.
    1. Aircraft carriers—United States—History
    I. Title
    623.8′255′0973   V874.3

ISBN 0 7137 1309 7

Typeset by Polyglot Pte Ltd Singapore
Printed in the United Kingdom by BAS Printers,
Over Wallop.

Contents

Eve of battle, Philippine Sea, 1944:
USN Curtiss SB2C Helldivers silhouetted in
the sunset over a carrier.

Frontispiece
December 1944: Task Group 38.3. Langley (CVL.27)
leads *Ticonderoga* (CV.14), representing the
'Independence' and 'Essex' classes which decisivly swung
the Pacific War in America's favour.
(See pages 121 and 143.)

1
Uncertain Genesis

On the afternoon of 2 June 1942 a forlorn handful of American warships — three fleet carriers, eight cruisers and fifteen destroyers — made rendezvous in the central Pacific. Given the enormity of their mission it was hardly surprising that the Americans had christened the rendezvous 'Point Luck'. They needed all the luck they could get, for this was all that was left of the US Pacific Fleet: an unbalanced, spatchcocked force. After the massacre of the American battle fleet at Pearl Harbor in the previous December, there was no battleship support at all; one of the carriers had its innards held together by a patchwork of hasty welds after recent battle damage and another had yet to experience its first fleet action. The men at 'Point Luck' knew that the massed Japanese fleet was moving east in a naval offensive intended to win the war: eleven Japanese battleships against none, eight carriers against three, 23 cruisers against eight. In the coming battle, which would decide whether or not the entire Pacific Ocean would become a Japanese lake, the Americans only had one advantage, and that uncertain: surprise. They were lying in ambush, pinning their hopes on a smashing, unexpected blow at the four carriers of the Japanese spearhead force known to be heading for the Midway Islands.

Three days later it was all over, and the colossal results of the Battle of Midway were speaking for themselves. The lurking trio of American carriers had not, as had been hoped, succeeded in mauling the Japanese carrier force covering the thrust at Midway. Instead they had annihilated it — all four Japanese carriers were sunk in exchange for one American — leaving the Japanese armada with no option but to reverse course and head for home. Though Japan launched further land/sea offensives in the South-West Pacific, the direct threat to the Americans in Hawaii had been countered and broken at Midway and the overwhelming Japanese superiority in aircraft-carriers had been checked. That, as has been said of Trafalgar, was more than enough for one day.

After Midway and the ensuing battle of attrition off Guadalcanal, the fleet carrier be-

came the US Navy's master-weapon in the advance across the Pacific to the shores of Japan. If there was a single American weapon which did more than any other to win the Pacific War of 1941–45, it was the fleet carrier whose story is told in this book. Yet only twenty years before Midway none of this omnipotence had appeared remotely likely, as the battleship-oriented US Navy considered its first uncertain experiments with naval aviation. Indeed, until 1920 the American attitude to the idea of harnessing air power to sea power remained one of caution, even suspicion, and the lead in aircraft-carrier development had been taken by the biggest naval rivals of the United States: Britain and Japan. And this seems all the more surprising in view of the vital role played in the development of the aeroplane, in the first decade of the twentieth century, by American pioneers.

There can be no denying the initial American reluctance to adapt heavier-than-air flight to land and sea warfare, but this reluctance was by no means an uncharacteristic rejection of new technologies and opportunities. It was, in fact, completely typical: a global phenomenon. The armed forces of all nations have one element in common: a hard core of conservatism. The longer the armed forces in question have been in existence, the harder that reactionary core tends to grow: a natural ageing process. In addition, professional military and naval resistance to sudden change tends to become abnormally stubborn when costly armaments programmes are already in hand, or when armed forces are required by their governments to make drastic economies. At best, this service conservatism protects the country's armed forces from gambling unwisely with unproven technologies, weapons and theories. At worst, it rejects and delays valuable new ideas and inventions which threaten the accepted, familiar *status quo*.

Both these reactions, the best and the worst, came to bear on the development of practicable heavier-than-air flight between 1903 and 1914. Among all the leading world powers not a single war office, not a single admiralty, grasped the transformation in war-

fare which the conquest of the skies must bring, and hastened to be foremost in reaping the benefits. But was this really so surprising? It was not until 1908, after all, that aeroplanes really began to show any real promise. Today, we are accustomed to say that 'the Wright brothers first flew in December 1903', but they accomplished little more than hops off the ground in a straight line. It took them until October 1905 to master the skills of banking and turning in the air, and their 'Flyer' was not publicly demonstrated until Wilbur Wright came to France in the summer of 1908. Orville Wright soon returned to the United States, to demonstrate another 'Flyer' to the US War Department at Fort Myer, Virginia.

Public attention was duly seized when both brothers made a succession of record-breaking flights in August–September 1908, Wilbur at Le Mans, Orville at Fort Myer. First honours were taken by Orville, who became the first airman to stay up for over an hour ($65\frac{1}{2}$ minutes) on 9 September. On the 11th, Orville managed to break the 70-minute barrier, and the American Press began to hail him as a national hero — brimming with resounding prophecies on the military possibilities of aircraft. Six days later, however, the euphoria was dashed when the aeroplane claimed its first victim — Lieutenant Thomas Selfridge of the US Army's Balloon Corps. Selfridge died when Orville's 'Flyer' threw off its port propeller just after take-off, resulting in a crash from 100 feet. This tragedy hardly indicated that the aeroplane might someday accomplish more than a reconnoitring cavalry squadron or light cruiser, and more safely as well. Even with hindsight, no one could blame the US military authorities for being less than enthused with the 'Flyer', once its frailty and potentially lethal qualities had been so publicly demonstrated.

As Orville Wright suffered a broken leg in the crash which killed Selfridge, the spotlight inevitably shifted to France, where Wilbur was continuing to astonish the crowds and, more importantly, the Press. Wilbur's crowning achievement in 1908 was a world record endurance flight on 31 December of

76.43 miles (123 km) in 2 hours 20 minutes. Wilbur's new record at Le Mans dwarfed that of his countryman Glenn Curtiss, who, on 4 July 1908, had won the trophy offered by *Scientific American* for the first one-mile flight in the United States. But these early endurance flights consisted of measured circuits around a chosen flying field, officially scrutinised throughout, in the calm flying conditions demanded by the fragile stability of all early aircraft. Quite apart from the obvious high risk to the lives of pilots and their passengers it was therefore still reasonable, by the New Year of 1909, to find military authorities still refusing to commit themselves to such a limited-range, fair-weather contrivance as the aeroplane undoubtedly still was.

Twelve months later, however, it was a very different story. The publicity won by the Wright brothers in 1908 had lifted the floodgates, prompting the first cross-country flights in France, by Henri Farman and Louis Blériot, and the British *Daily Mail* prize offer of £500 for the first English Channel crossing by aeroplane. After a near-miss by Hubert Latham on 19 July 1909, the first Channel crossing was achieved by Blériot on 23 July, his left foot still in bandages from an injury sustained on a 25-mile cross-country flight from Étampes to Orleans ten days earlier. At the end of August 1909 the world's first aviation week was staged at Rheims, with the prizes for the fastest single lap and fastest three laps going to Glenn Curtiss, beating Blériot with a speed of 46.5 mph. Within two months the British cities of Blackpool and Doncaster were competing to stage the first aviation meeting on English soil. It was at the Blackpool meeting that the aeroplane's 'fair-weather only' image was first shown to be a false one, when Latham triumphantly flew his *Antoinette* monoplane in a gale gusting 90 mph, returning to earth unscathed.

The impetus of heavier-than-air aviation, thus released, redoubled in 1910, starting with the 185-mile cross-country race from London to Manchester. This was a long-standing *Daily Mail* prize which, when first announced in November 1906, had been generally ridiculed as science fiction. The race finally took place at the end of April 1910 and was won by Louis Paulhan of France in a time of 4 hours 18 minutes, excluding stops for meals, rest and refuelling. Britain's Claude Grahame-White came second. But on 2 June 1910 the Hon. 'Charley' Rolls achieved a notable 'first' for Britain: the first *double* Channel crossing, England to France and back, in 90 minutes. By the time of the second aviation week at Rheims in July 1910, aeroplanes had achieved a fleeting new endurance record of 211 miles (Olieslager of Belgium)

and a new altitude record of 4680 ft (Latham of France). Rolls, however, was killed when his Wright biplane broke up in the air at Bournemouth on 12 July.

Opponents of the aeroplane were already shaking their heads over the mounting toll of fatal air crashes, but, like all statistics, they were easy for hostile propagandists to manipulate. There were in fact 34 fatalities between 17 September 1908, the crash which killed Lieutenant Selfridge, and 9 February 1911, during which time over 1000 individuals learned to fly. This certainly contrasts favourably with the 90 people killed in mountaineering accidents in 1910 alone. And all too many of these fatal crashes were caused by foolhardy stunts insisted on, despite the airmen's protests, by promoters of air displays bent on giving the crowds their money's worth.

By the summer of 1910 the most far-sighted European airmen were already trying to show that the aeroplane had a much more practical future than merely relieving goggling crowds of their money. At the second Blackpool meeting of August 1910, Grahame-White staged mock 'army manoeuvres' in which he flew over 'enemy territory', safely out of rifle range from the ground, and returned with a reconnaissance report of 'enemy movements'; flew out a 'wounded officer' and returned carrying 'medical supplies'; and embarked a photographer to take pictures of 'enemy dispositions'. Modest though it was, Grahame-White also achieved the first official delivery of specially-franked air mail, carrying it 12 miles from Blackpool to Southport beach. His efforts were rewarded by the British War Office obtaining two Bristol 'Box-kite' biplanes for trial in the official Army manoeuvres of September 1910. The entire course of the manoeuvres was transformed by the reconnaissance reports brought back by the aircraft, which also made the first successful transmission of an air-to-ground radio message from an aeroplane, using a primitive set with a 1-mile range.

In September and October 1910, while European aviators strode ahead to achieve the first crossings of the Irish Sea and the Alps, the muted American rôle in world aviation was emphasized by Grahame-White's triumphant tour of the eastern United States. He dominated the scene at Boston, Baltimore and Washington, where he landed and took off from the White House gardens and Executive Avenue, New York and Philadelphia. Curtiss, the leading American pilot, twice refused point-blank to compete with Grahame-White, candidly declining the humiliation of defeat which he felt was a foregone conclusion.

American colours were only upheld in

September 1910 on the other side of the Atlantic by a colourful maverick and freelance meddler in Central American revolutions: John B. Moisant, from Chicago. Sent to Europe to buy aircraft for Nicaragua, Moisant took six lessons in a Blériot machine and announced that he would be the first to fly from London to Paris, carrying a passenger for greater éclat. He made it in the end, achieving the fifth Channel crossing by aeroplane and the first with a passenger, Blériot mechanic Albert Filieux. But the first London-Paris flight was an amazing odyssey lasting 22 days, from 16 August to 6 September 1910, with no less than seven intermediary landings on English soil before London was reached. As they battled doggedly towards their goal, Moisant and Filieux were plagued by bad weather, breakdowns, the need to wait for a new propeller from Paris, and crash damage, though one premature landing was caused by both men having forgotten to refill the fuel tank. In English eyes at least, Moisant put himself beyond the pale when he finally landed on the New Beckenham cricket field and ruined the pitch. It was a flamboyant piece of amateurism and Moisant deserved the publicity it brought him, but his flight (or rather flights) hardly compared with the professionalism of the leading European aviators. Only seven months later, on 19 April 1911, Pierre Prier eclipsed Moisant's laborious achievement by flying non-stop from London to Paris in 3 hours 56 minutes.

The first Paris-London flight nevertheless gave Americans what they desperately wanted: a famous flyer. By late October 1910 Moisant was back in the States, ready to cross swords with Grahame-White at Belmont Park racecourse, Long Island. Two aspects of the Belmont Park aviation meeting revealed the true state of the insecure American attitude towards aviation. The first was the refusal of every American insurance company to cover spectators against injury, such cover being readily offered by Lloyd's of London. The second was a scandalous piece of rule-bending by the American officials at Belmont Park, hell-bent on salvaging Yankee pride at all costs.

Inevitably, the most prestigious event at Belmont Park was an out-and-return speed race round the Statue of Liberty and back, all competitors to take-off by 4 pm. Two days before the race, on 28 October, American hopes had been crushed when Grahame-White walked off with the Gordon Bennett speed race, and on the 29th Moisant had wrecked his Blériot in a crash. On the 30th, when Grahame-White was declared the provisional winner of the Statue of Liberty race, Moisant paid $10,000 dollars for another competitor's reserve aircraft and covered the course 43 seconds faster. Though Moisant had taken off 6 minutes late (in the Gordon Bennett, a British competitor had been swiftly disqualified for being only *25 seconds* late), a protesting Grahame-White was blandly informed that the time limit had just been put back to 5 pm. When Grahame-White demanded the right to a second flight he was refused, and Moisant was declared the winner amid American rejoicing. It took two years of arguing by the Fedération Aeronautique Internationale before the shame-faced Americans backed down, upheld Grahame-White's protest and gave him his $10,000 prize money (plus $600 interest).

The great races of May–July 1911 proved that not even the British, let alone the Americans, could challenge the French superiority in the air established with Blériot's first Channel crossing. These events were the 874-mile Paris-Madrid race, in which 28 competitors started, but only Jules Védrines finished; the 950-mile Paris-Rome race via Marseilles and Genoa, with twelve starters of whom two finished; and the so-called 'Circuit of Europe', France-Belgium-Holland-Belgium-England-France, a 1025-mile ordeal, which lasted three weeks. The 'Circuit of Europe' was chiefly remarkable for the first massed air crossing of the English Channel when eleven aircraft crossed with ease within 45 minutes, watched from the cliffs at Calais by a stunned Louis Blériot.

The 'Circuit of Europe' was followed at the end of July 1911 by the 1010-mile 'Circuit of Britain' which, though part of the public celebrations of King George V's coronation, was by far the most serious aviation contest yet held. Not only were the stages of the race deliberately made more demanding, with a wide variety of thirteen 'legs' ranging from 20 to 190 miles, but competitors were forbidden to carry on in replaced aircraft in the event of breakdowns or crashes. All vital airframe and engine components were officially stamped beforehand and strict rules were agreed on to limit the number of parts which could be replaced during the race.

There were seventeen starters for the 'Circuit of Britain': ten British, four French, one Austrian, one Swiss, and one American, C. T. Weymann, who actually started the 'Circuit of Britain' as favourite. Weymann's Nieuport monoplane was the fastest aircraft in the race, and only a fortnight before the start on 22 July had regained the Gordon Bennett Trophy for the United States. But Weymann soon learned that there was all the difference in the world between flying speed circuits and the exacting demands of cross-country flying. He had to land ignominiously within minutes of starting when his map blew over the side, and was forced to drop out of the race before reaching Harrogate, the first goal, because of a smashed undercarriage. The race developed into an epic duel between the Frenchmen Védrines and Conneau, who had dominated every European distance race held that year. Conneau returned to Brooklands in a splendid combined flying time of 22 hours 28 minutes, with Védrines only 70 minutes behind him. The only other competitors to complete the course, the Britons Valentine and Cody, struggled home three days and four days later respectively.

Yet, though totally outclassed in direct competition with the leading European airmen of the day, American aviation nevertheless achieved an outstanding couple of 'firsts' in 1910–11. For it was an American pilot, flying an American machine, who first proved that it was possible to add the range and speed of aeroplanes to the range and speed of warships — not only by taking-off from a ship and landing safely ashore, but by landing on a ship as well.

This vital first step in the development of naval aviation was undertaken in the hope of at least doubling the reconnaissance range of US Navy cruisers patrolling the Atlantic coast. It was the result of an announcement that in due course ships of the Hamburg-Amerika Line approaching the United States would launch aeroplanes from platforms on the foredeck to hasten the delivery of mail to New York. Though welcomed in civilian circles, the prospect was less enthusiastically received by American military and naval authorities. Germany was already working flat-out to build a battle fleet fit to rival that of Britain, and the US Navy was expanding its own fleet in reply. Four new American battleships were completed in 1910 and two more were launched in the same year. The mounting distrust of Germany's imperial ambitions led to the suspicion that the Hamburg-Amerika Line's proposed air mail service could well be covert planning for a future German air attack on the United States. Given the unbelievable speed with which aviation had developed since the Wright brothers' demonstration flights in 1908, this was by no means a fantastic idea. It was also in 1908 that H.G. Wells had published *The War in the Air*, in which a German airship fleet crosses the Atlantic and bombs the American battle fleet to destruction as a preliminary to the bombardment and subjugation of New York. If German shipborne aircraft were really going to be able to approach American soil, it was clearly vital that the US Navy should have the means of detecting them out at sea, using shipborne aircraft of its own.

Such was the spirit of these pioneer years that both the threat and the answer to it were developed cheek by jowl, in the United States, with *The World* newspaper sponsoring the Hamburg-Amerika Line's attempt to beat the US Navy and make the first successful shipboard aeroplane launch. After Wilbur Wright rejected the whole idea as impracticable and far too dangerous, Glenn Curtiss and his embryo team of exhibition pilots were approached. Two Curtiss pilots took up the challenge, J. A. D. McCurdy for Hamburg-Amerika and Eugene B. Ely for the US Navy. It was a near-run thing. McCurdy was ready first, and made his attempt on 12 November 1910, but a carelessly-placed oilcan broke a propeller-blade as he ran up his engine for the start. The next day was a Sunday, which the Navy men spent completing the wooden-planked launch platform, 24 ft wide and 83 ft long, sloping down from the bridge to the bow of the light cruiser USS *Birmingham* at Norfolk, Virginia. Early on 14 November Ely's biplane was hoisted aboard, prudently fitted with flotation-bags, and *Birmingham* steamed out into Chesapeake Bay.

It was a murky, overcast day with drizzling bad visibility, and no attempt could be made until mid-afternoon; but at last Ely's machine rolled down the platform, the modest push of its 50 hp engine assisted by the 10 knots at which *Birmingham* was steaming. As pessimists had feared, Ely's plane plunged from the bow end of the platform and hit the surface, sending up a flurry of spray from its flotation-bags and propeller-blades. With brute force and a lot of luck, Ely nevertheless managed to haul his machine off the water and gain altitude. Though the tips of the propeller blades had been chewed up by the impact with the water, the undercarriage had held up and he managed to land safely ashore.

Ely had thus proved that shipborne aircraft launches within flying-range of land *were* feasible, but the US Navy's immediate reaction was understandably modest. They assigned Lieutenant Theodore G. Ellyson to become the Navy's first trainee pilot in December. There were little enough grounds for doing more. In this heyday of the big gun, long before aircraft could carry bombs or torpedoes capable of damaging enemy warships, there was no point at all in drastically reducing the fleet's fire-power by the wholesale fitting of launch platforms to its warships. The Navy also wanted time to evaluate the latest idea of fitting aircraft with floats for take-off and landing on water. Ely was nevertheless permitted to attempt the most ambitious experiment in aviation since the first English Channel crossing: the first wheeled landing on a ship.

The grey dawn of American naval air power: Eugene Ely's Curtiss Pusher is serviced before the first take-off from a ship on 14 November 1910. The scene is Norfolk Navy Yard, where the modest 83 ft flying-off deck has just been completed atop the foredeck of the light cruiser *Birmingham*. Less than 48 hours have passed since Ely's rival, another Curtiss pilot J. McCurdy, failed to beat the US Navy by taking off from the liner *Pennsylvania*, an attempt backed by *The World*.

Birmingham steaming slowly out of Hampton Roads into Chesapeake Bay, after a day of gloomy, drizzling weather had moderated enough for the take-off attempt to be made. The forward elevators of the Curtiss can cearly be seen, apparently in 'full up' position ready for the flight.

The new venture was carefully planned, in view of the obvious high risks to both aircraft and ship. The best bet seemed to be an 'uphill' touchdown on an angled platform extending over the ship's stern. To reduce Ely's approach-speed to the minimum, the ship would be steaming into wind at the moment the attempt was made. To bring him to a rapid halt after touchdown, a row of 22 parallel crosswires was laid up the landing platform for the undercarriage to catch. To prevent these crosswires wrecking the aircraft, the ends of the wires were weighted with sandbags intended to slide along the deck as soon as a wire was caught, to provide a gradual rather than an instant deceleration. The platform was quickly built aboard the cruiser *Pennsylvania*. The attempt was

The moment of truth: with its 50 hp engine going flat out, Ely's aircraft leaves *Birmingham*'s flying-off deck. The flat calm conditions and the ship's lack of speed are painfully apparent, as is Ely's downward course, but though the tips of the Pusher's propeller blades were chewed up in the heart-stopping brush with the surface seconds later, Ely hauled the aircraft back into the air and landed safely ashore.

set for January 1911, in San Francisco Bay.

During these formative years, many pilots as skilled as Ely died as a result of trivial mishaps or miscalculations. If Ely had not been an exhibition pilot, with more than a touch of flamboyant confidence in his undoubted skills, he might well have wrecked his aircraft, killed himself and set back the advent of shipboard aviation by a decade. For on 18 January 1911 *Pennsylvania*'s captain decided that it would be too dangerous, given the poor weather, for the landing attempt to be made with his ship under way. *Pennsylvania* remained at anchor, and with her stern to the wind. Thus, Ely was not only now unable to make his approach at only a few miles per hour faster than that of his touchdown point, but his landing speed was increased by the tailwind. With no emergency crash barrier to stop him on deck, it was, by later standards, a sure recipe for disaster, but Ely's superb judgement was rewarded. On his very first attempt his angle of descent and the moment he chose to cut his engine were perfectly timed. Though the tailwind carried him only inches off the deck clean over the first eleven

June 1916: over five years after Ely's historic 'firsts', the US Navy languidly experimented with catapults for launching seaplanes from warships. Here, a test load is catapulted from a rig aimed aft over South Carolina*'s fantail — a clumsy device, and useless for operational purposes because it inevitably silenced the ship's after guns. When the US Navy went to war in April 1917, only two other light cruisers had been fitted with catapults and the British lead in naval aviation, both catapulted and deck-launched, seemed unassailable.*

arresting crosswires, the twelfth brought him to a safe standstill in 30 ft. Ely then repeated his feat of 14 November by having his aircraft turned around for a second shipborne take-off, this time with 20 ft more runway and into a headwind, again landing safely ashore.

Ely's three flights proved that wheeled-undercarriage aircraft were capable of operating from warships. They are today justly remembered as the opening event in the history of naval aviation — but they were accorded no such importance in 1911. Ely got nothing from the US Navy but a letter of thanks and his only tangible reward was $500 raised by private subscription. By the end of the year he was dead, killed in an accident. Twenty-five years passed before he was posthumously awarded the Distinguished Flying Cross, belated recognition of his unique contribution to US naval air power. Yet it must be remembered that the polite caution of the naval authorities toward Ely's flights was only to be expected. He was not the first innovator to have his exploits almost immediately eclipsed by new developments, and 1911 turned out to be the year of the floatplane's debut. Only a month after Ely's first shipboard landing, a floatplane flown by Glenn Curtiss was launched from *Pennsylvania*, and hoisted aboard from the water alongside, at the end of the flight. Cynics had always predicted that air/sea flying would soon result in forceful contact between aircraft and water, but here was a real prospect of such contact being used to genuine advantage.

For the next five years, on both sides of the Atlantic, the floatplane was seen as offering the best of both worlds. The first British air launch from a warship, of a Short S.27 floatplane perched on a wheeled trolley, took place in January 1912. While avoiding the obvious dangers courted in deck landings, the floatplane gave fleets their first taste of aircraft reconnaissance: the floatplanes were stored, rigged, launched and retrieved by specially converted 'mother ships', the first seaplane-carriers.

In these years, 1911–16, it was not really surprising that British developments in naval aviation moved rapidly ahead, out-stripping the determinedly cautious American approach after the promising start made by Eugene Ely and Glenn Curtiss. Even without the tremendous impetus to British aviation imparted by Britain going to war in August 1914 while the United States remained neutral, British aviation in 1914 was more advanced than that of the United States; it had been toughened and stretched by four years of mainstream competition with the top French aviators. Nor were American military and naval chiefs motivated, as were their British counterparts, by growing uneasiness at Germany's overwhelming superiority in airships and the need to develop an effective heavier-than-air reply.

Though Italy, not Britain, was the first power to use aeroplanes in war, dropping lightweight bombs on Turkish troops during the Libyan war of 1911, the British were the first to set up a truly effective naval air arm. This was the Royal Naval Air Service (RNAS), developed from the naval wing of the Royal Flying Corps established in May 1912. By August 1914 the RNAS had floatplanes capable of dropping a light, 14-inch torpedo, the Short S.184, and of dropping bombs on German airship sheds, Short S.74 and S.135. Like Ely's first deck landing, the first British torpedo drop, made on 28 July 1914, was more of a pointer to the future than a solid gain for the present. The 14-inch torpedo had too light a warhead to do more than scratch the paint on contemporary armoured battleships and battle-cruisers, and aircraft capable of carrying the more lethal 18-inch torpedo were not developed before late 1918. The bombing of German airship bases in 1914 was a very different matter, because of the unique nature of the target. Each airship contained thousands of cubic feet of ultra-flammable hydrogen gas, easy to ignite even with puny bombs hardly bigger than hand-grenades. This was speedily demonstrated by RNAS pilots in October and November 1914 in raids from bases in Belgium and eastern France against the airship

bases at Cologne, Düsseldorf and Friedrichshafen. During the Düsseldorf raid on 6 October, a single Sopwith Tabloid armed with two 20 lb bombs blew up the Zeppelin *Z.IX* in its shed. At Friedrichshafen on 21 November, three Avro 504s armed with four 24 lb bombs apiece destroyed the gas-manufacturing plant.

The striking success of these first essays in long range bombing led to the attempt, on Christmas Day 1914, to use the new seaplane-carriers in a raid on the Zeppelin sheds at Cuxhaven on the North Sea Coast. The ships employed were the former cross-Channel steamers *Empress*, *Engadine* and *Riviera*, with basic hangar structures added to their after decks to accommodate three seaplanes per ship; they were too small for flying-off platforms to be added forward. For all that, they accomplished the first 'carrier strike' in naval history, crossing the North Sea to launch seven seaplanes only 12 miles north of Heligoland. Low cloud and mist obscured the airships sheds at Cuxhaven and three aircraft returned to the ships, to be safely retrieved. The other four arrived over Cuxhaven and, unable to find the Zeppelin sheds, dropped their bombs at ships in the harbour before heading back to the rendezvous with the carriers. But in the meantime the carriers had withdrawn after being sighted by a Zeppelin, rather than court certain destruction in the event of fast German warships making a sortie, leaving the submarine *E.11* to retrieve the returning aircrews. Three seaplanes were destroyed after their crews had been taken off by *E.11*; the crew of the fourth had the bad luck to alight beside a Dutch fishing boat, and was taken into internment in neutral Holland.

However, the days were long gone when even a triumph like the first cross-Channel flight had left the British Admiralty unimpressed. Though the Cuxhaven raid was a failure, it was taken as an example of what *could* be achieved, given more and faster carriers and improved aircraft with greater range and a heavier weapons payload. The British pressed ahead with the completion of four more seaplane carriers: *Ark Royal*, converted from a collier, and *Ben-my-Chree*, *Manxman* and *Vindex*, all converted from Isle of Man packet steamers. Meanwhile, the French Navy had had the converted torpedo depot-ship *Foudre* in service as a seaplane-carrier since late 1912, and the Japanese had been operating the converted merchantman *Wakamiya* since the end of 1913. But the US Navy had undertaken no similar ship conversions, preferring instead to develop a catapult for launching seaplanes from warships under way without the main armament having to be masked by a flying-off deck. First tested

ashore at Annapolis in July 1912, over *three years* passed before the first catapult was mounted in an American warship, the light cruiser USS *North Carolina*, in October 1915. The first launch from her took place on 5 November 1915.

The American catapult, although a most important extension of a warship's all-round vision, was never treated as anything more than a purely experimental device. By the time American neutrality had finally been broken down by the unrestricted German submarine offensive and the United States entered the war on 6 April 1917, only two other American light cruisers had been fitted with catapults. Neither the US Navy nor the US Army had been tuned up for war by the laying of contingency plans and the rôles for both services were therefore necessarily strictly conventional. Once placed on a war footing, the US Army eventually reinforced the flagging French and British armies on the Western Front. The US Navy's war rôle was more straightforward; its most modern battleships deployed to Scapa Flow to form an extra battle squadron for the British Grand Fleet, while the cruisers and destroyers escorted Atlantic convoys. So far from using aircraft to hunt for German U-boats or surface raiders in the latter rôle, the US Navy Department ordered the removal of all three aircraft catapults to prevent interference with conventional operations at sea.

By the spring of 1917, the British Admiralty had made a series of decisions which made the Royal Navy the world's leading practitioner of naval aviation. The Gallipoli campaign of 1915 maintained the impetus created by the anti-Zeppelin raids of the previous year, proving beyond doubt that carrier-borne aircraft had far more to offer than air reconnaissance alone. In August 1915 Short S.184s from *Ben-my-Chree* carried out the first successful aerial torpedo attacks, against Turkish supply ships in the Sea of Marmora and in the Narrows of the Dardanelles. However, the Gallipoli campaign also confirmed that seaplanes suffered from a number of shortcomings. Their heavy floats made it impossible to gain altitude quickly, and low-level strafing and harassing raids on Turkish troops were best entrusted to aircraft with much lighter wheeled undercarriages. This built-in sluggishness of the seaplane became the decisive factor in the attempt to beat the Zeppelins in the North Sea theatre. By 1917, it was obvious that only the latest, high-performance fighter scouts, unencumbered by floats and operating somehow from flight-decked, high-speed carriers able to keep up with the fleet, would have a chance of intercepting and shooting down Zeppelins.

The immense potential of naval aircraft in fleet actions had been briefly demonstrated in the greatest sea battle of the war: the Battle of Jutland on 31 May 1916. As the British and German battle-cruisers closed on each other at the outset of the action, one of *Engadine*'s seaplanes was launched to report by radio on the Germans' strength, course and speed. Three such reports were made before a broken fuel pipe forced the seaplane down, but a rising swell made further flights impossible before the fleets engaged each other. This further seaplane weakness, revealed in what the British regarded as the greatest missed opportunity of the war, the escape of the German fleet after inflicting heavy losses on the British battle-cruiser fleet, contributed another facet to the argument in favour of developing carriers capable of operating scout aircraft with wheeled undercarriages.

The British Admiralty's solution to the problem was a roundabout, painful return to a revolutionary solution which had been proposed by Flight-Commander H. A. Williamson, RNAS, in the summer of 1915. This was for a carrier which would have an unbroken flight-deck running from bow to stern, with bridge accommodation in an 'island' superstructure positioned on the starboard side. The purpose of the 'island' layout was to enable the ship to be conned from a conventional raised bridge without flying operations being impeded or endangered by a central superstructure, but his design was rejected as both outlandish and unnecessary. For the next two years the Admiralty continued to convert from existing types of ship until it was accepted that the arrangement of a flying-off deck forward and a landing-on deck aft, separated by a conventional superstructure amidships, was as impracticable as it was dangerous.

The last big conversion before Jutland had been the fitting of a bow flying-off platform to the old Cunard liner *Campania*, and in 1916 this was extended aft by retrunking the fore funnel into two tunnels, and moving the bridge back between the two. *Campania* had a length of 622 ft, double that of converted Channel packets like *Engadine* and *Ben-my-Chree*, and could carry up to ten aircraft. Experience gained with *Campania* indicated that converting from liners was a promising expedient, and in August 1916 another liner hull was purchased for completion as a carrier. This was the 15,775-ton *Conte Rosso*, laid down for Italy but left uncompleted since the outbreak of war; it was now planned to complete her with a flying-off deck forward and a landing-on deck aft. However, as her speed was not expected to exceed 20 knots, there was an urgent need for a carrier which

The lesson which the US Navy did not have to learn the hard way: Britain's *Furious* in 1918, with her original bow flying-off deck supplemented by a landing-on deck aft. The problems and dangers caused by retaining the central superstructure proved insuperable, leaving a simple choice between flush-deck and 'island' designs for carriers.

could provide air reconnaissance for the fastest ships of the fleet at speeds of 30 knots and more. As in the case of *Conte Rosso*, there was a suitable ship ready to hand: the uncompleted light battle-cruiser *Furious*, designed for 32 knots and launched in August 1916.

Even before they joined the Fleet, *Furious* and her half-sisters, *Glorious* and *Courageous*, had been diagnosed as unusually misconceived white elephants. They had been intended by Admiral Lord Fisher, mastermind of Britain's Dreadnought Navy, to operate at over 30 knots in German inshore waters, using their speed to stay out of trouble. They were really super-cruisers armed with battleship-sized guns: two twin 15-inch turrets in both *Glorious* and *Courageous*, and two single 18-inch guns in *Furious*. But Fisher's pet doctrine that 'Speed is Armour' had been undermined by the experience of Jutland, when three British battle-cruisers had been blown out of the water, and it was clear that the three light battle-cruisers lacked any viable tactical rôle; hence the decision, in late March 1917, not to install the forward 18-inch turret in *Furious* but to build an aircraft

hangar topped by a flying-off deck instead. This work was quickly completed and *Furious* was commissioned on 26 June 1917, with an air group of three reconnaissance seaplanes and five Sopwith Pup fighter scouts. The seaplanes were intended to carry out reconnaissance flights, while the Pups, unencumbered by heavy floats, intercepted prowling Zeppelins. However, it was clear that the Pups could be used for one flight only, because they could not land back on *Furious* and would have to ditch in the sea and be lost, unless *Furious* always remained within flying range of the British coast.

To the air group commander, Squadron Commander Ernest Dunning, this prospect was unacceptable. He was convinced that the natural docility of the Sopwith Pup at low flying-speeds and the high speed of *Furious* could be blended to permit deck landings. As Ely had done back in 1911, Dunning favoured an approach from astern at a speed only slightly greater than that of the ship, and side-slipping in to the centreline of the flight-deck as soon as the superstructure had been passed. The problem lay in safely halting the aircraft after touchdown, because the Sopwith Pup was not fitted with brakes. Ely's solution was a crosswise row of arrester-wires. In contrast, Dunning had a handling party stationed at the estimated 'safe' touchdown point on the flight-deck, ready to grab at special toggles fitted to the aircraft.

It was a perilously 'make-do' arrangement which demanded exceptional flying skills, leaving no safety margin for overshoot landings or indeed any other mishap. Fast work by the handling party got Dunning down safely at his first attempt, on 2 August 1917, but five days later he misjudged his approach and overshot his touchdown-point. The Pup's engine faltered as he opened up and tried to take-off again, only to crash down on one wheel and cartwheel over the starboard side to his death.

Tragic though it was, Dunning's death was certainly not in vain. He had proved that fighter scouts could operate from a carrier's deck, but only if the process were entirely re-thought: a short bow deck was obviously far too dangerous for landings as well as take-offs. *Furious* was therefore returned to the dockyard to have her after 18-inch gun turret removed and a 284 ft landing-on deck built abaft the funnel. The new deck was fitted with the first British attempt at an arresting system, replacing Dunning's handling-party. Fore-and-aft wires were strung along the landing-on deck, intended to receive the skids of a sled-like fixed undercarriage. Hooks fitted to these skids would snag the wires on either side and halt the aircraft by friction, and as an additional safety measure a flexible rope crash-barrier was hung at the forward end of the landing-on deck to stop overshooting aircraft from smashing into the

as the only operational British carrier for the last year of the war.

The new landing-on deck was ready for trials by April 1918, but it soon became apparent that the retention of the central superstructure and funnel rendered *Furious* grossly unsafe for deck landings. Aircraft coming in to land from astern were twisted and buffeted by wind eddies and hot funnel gases at the most crucial moment of final approach. By the end of May 1918 only three out of thirteen attempted landings on *Furious* had been accomplished without crash damage or pilot injury, a wholly unacceptable ratio. Once again there was nothing for it but to suspend deck landings by aircraft. For the rest of the war *Furious* served only to launch aircraft which returned to ditch in the sea as close as the pilots could manage. The after flight-deck of *Furious* proved of far more use to small coastal airships ('blimps') alighting at speeds too low for aircraft landings, between anti-U-boat patrols.

Though the creation of the Royal Air Force on 1 April 1918 ended the autonomy of the RNAS, the Royal Navy remained irretrievably 'air-minded' for the rest of the war. Great things were hoped for from the new Sopwith Cuckoo aircraft which could carry an 18-inch torpedo, but nothing could be done with them until *Argus* had joined the fleet, and *Argus* did not even commission until October 1918. By the summer of 1918, however, the Grand Fleet could put to sea with a total of nearly 100 shipborne aircraft, all carried on turret-mounted platforms or towed lighters for single missions ending in ditching. One such mission was entrusted to *Furious* on 19 July 1918: a raid on the Tondern Zeppelin sheds by seven Sopwith Camel fighters armed with bombs. The attack gained complete surprise and destroyed Zeppelins *L.54* and *L.60* in their shed; a captive balloon was also destroyed in a smaller shed. Three of the Camel pilots landed in neutral Denmark, three ditched in the sea and were recovered, but the seventh was never seen again. Though the Tondern raid was not repeated, it was seen as the shape of things to come. Only the signing of the Armistice on 11 November 1918 saved the German High Seas Fleet in Wilhelmshaven from a massed torpedo attack by the Cuckoos carried by *Argus* — an attack which would have anticipated the Japanese strike at Pearl Harbor by at least 22 years.

funnel. Gangways were built on both sides of the superstructure to enable aircraft to be man-handled forward and returned to the flying-off deck.

But these were only stop-gap measures, prompted by the need to take early action against the Zeppelins. It was decided that *Conte Rosso*, when fully converted as the carrier HMS *Argus*, would have no superstructure at all. Her funnel trunkings were to be trained aft through 90 deg. to vent over the stern, leaving an unbroken flight-deck from stem to stern. Moreover, Williamson's 'island' design, rejected by the Admiralty only

two summers before, was now adopted for the plans of the first aircraft-carrier to be built 'from the keel up'. This was HMS *Hermes*, laid down in January 1918. In hopes of saving time before the completion of *Hermes* another uncompleted capital ship was to be converted as a carrier, also with an 'island' flight-deck: the battleship *Almirante Cochrane*, laid down for Chile in January 1913 but left uncompleted since the outbreak of war. She was launched as HMS *Eagle* on 8 June 1918. As *Argus* could not be completed until the autumn of 1918 and *Hermes* and *Eagle* at least a year later, this left the hybrid *Furious*

The First American Carrier

There could be no denying that the US Navy's rôle during these exciting months had been very much that of a poor relation. Not only was the strongest element of the American battle fleet no more than a lone battle squadron in the massive ranks of the British Grand Fleet, but the lead established by the British in naval aviation seemed unassailable by 1918. Yet this British lead was not as unbeatable as it seemed. Even without the underlying resilience in the famed Hoosier saying, 'When they hand you a lemon, make lemonade', there was much comfort for American naval air enthusiasts. To start with, the British had done all the time-wasting trial-and-error work by 1918, saving the US Navy the need to do likewise and offering it the chance of starting with the most modern developments. Moreover, Anglo-American naval relations were extremely cordial in 1917–18. During a lengthy visit to Washington by the British Naval Director, Stanley Goodall, the American Bureau of Construction and Repair was given full details of the plans of *Hermes*. Goodall was also unstinting in his recommendations when the US Director of Naval Aviation requested formal specifications for a prototype American aircraft-carrier in June 1918. These recommendations were hardly less influential than the plans of *Hermes*, for they enshrined all the misconceptions which the Americans built into their first generation of carriers built after World War I.

The foremost error was the failure to see that the carrier was an entirely new type of warship, with both its hitting-power and its own defence entrusted to the aircraft it operated. In 1918, enemy surface forces, not enemy aircraft, were seen as the biggest menace carriers were likely to face. British

'CV.1' — America's first carrier, *Langley*, seen in about 1923 with three battleships and four destroyers in the background. The aircraft ranged on deck are Vought VE-7s, and the paling enclosure, a feature copied from early British carrier practice, is to stop aircraft being blown over the side. This enclosure could be easily struck, and the radio masts and twin smokepipes lowered, to leave the flight-deck completely clear for flying operations. The US Navy's much-loved pioneer carrier, flush-decked *Langley*, had the same nickname as Britain's *Furious*—'The Covered Wagon'.

experience indicated that a carrier escorted by light cruisers, like *Furious* on the Tondern raid, was most likely to be brought to action by enemy cruisers as it pushed deep into enemy waters to launch and recover its aircraft. Much cruiser lore had therefore been applied to the design of *Hermes*, as was obvious from her lines, and she had been given a 'light cruiser-sized' battery of six 5.5-inch guns.

As Goodall put it to the Americans: 'An armament of four 4-inch guns is insufficient, and a larger number of guns — preferably 6-inch — should be carried, *together with one or two anti-aircraft guns* (author's italics). Although such a ship should not by any means be regarded as a fighting ship, it should be sufficiently powerfully armoured to be able to brush aside light vessels of the enemy, so that its machines can be flown off in comparatively advanced conditions.' Goodall added that the current proposed speed of 30 knots

should be considered a minimum. This recommendation was again made with high-speed cruiser operations in mind, rather than in recognition of the fact that the faster a carrier could steam into wind, the quicker and easier it would be for her aircraft to take-off and land. In short, it was not yet appreciated that even the modest ability 'to brush aside light vessels of the enemy' was counter-productive, restricting the carrier's vital raison d'être, which is the ability to operate the maximum number of aircraft of all types: reconnaissance, fighter, bomber and torpedo. Moreover, the mountings, ammunition hoists and magazines required for even a 6-inch gun battery were bound to make heavy demands upon the space available which could be allocated for the aircraft hangar.

The American General Board accepted the Goodall recommendations, however, and in October 1918 agreed on the specifications for the US Navy's first carrier: CV.1. The

Langley demonstrates the ease with which carrier-launched biplanes could operate — not only without catapults, but without the carrier having to make any forward way at all if the breeze was strong enough over the bow. The aircraft is a Douglas DT-2 torpedo-bomber (unarmed). The date is around 1925. Crewmen can be seen watching the launch from the safety of the catwalk tucked below the edge of the flight-deck.

With plenty of deck to spare, an unladen DT-2 unsticks from *Langley*'s flight-deck in another practice take-off. The holes in the deck (left foreground) are the sockets for the palings.

'battleship format' of Britain's *Eagle* was seen as preferable to the more space-restrictive 'cruiser format' of *Hermes*, and the initial American specifications were for a carrier of 24,000 tons — *Hermes* displaced 10,850 tons, *Eagle* 22,600 tons — with a speed of 35 knots, over 10 knots faster than either *Hermes* or *Eagle*, and a battery of ten 6-inch guns. Five months later, in March 1919, this was modified to 34,800 tons, four 8-inch and six 6-inch guns, four 4-inch anti-aircraft guns and four torpedo-tubes. The latter refinement was another example of how in 1919 the carrier was still cast very much in a conventional rôle: to engage enemy warships at ranges which could even dwindle to torpedo range, 1 to 3 miles. However, the March 1919 specifications were most remarkable for envisaging twin islands, one to port and one to starboard of the flight-deck, each topped by a tubular cage mast of the type mounted in US battleships.

The dramatic increase in tonnage resulted from the size of hull needed to carry engines powerful enough to deliver 35 knots. Four of these big new carriers were envisaged by July 1920. They were intended to operate with the

33-knot 'Lexington' class battle-cruisers which displaced 43,500 tons, and were armed with eight 16-inch guns. The first four were laid down in August-September 1920. The first five 'South Dakota' class battleships were also laid down in 1920. The six 'Lexington' and six 'South Dakota' class battleships amounted to a new 16-inch gunned American battle fleet which, when complete, would give the US Navy parity with Britain and superiority over Japan. The Japanese were known to be planning a similar 16-inch gunned battle fleet, having also laid down the first two of four 'Amagi' class battle-cruisers, with ten 16-inch guns, in 1920. Japan's first carrier, laid down in 1919, was fast taking shape. This was *Hosho*, a 'cruiser format' lightweight of 7470 tons, and a most effective marriage of low displacement with high aircraft capacity. *Hosho* had a modest battery of four 5.5-inch guns and could carry 21 aircraft, six more than the heavier *Hermes*, but with the same top speed of 25 knots. *Hosho*'s most distinctive feature was a small, bobbin-shaped conning tower without conventional vertical funnel trunking. Her smoke was vented through three hinged smoke-pipes on the starboard side, which could be lowered horizontally to leave the flight-deck clear for flying operations.

Japan's promptness in producing a carrier underlined the US Navy's total lack of naval

aviation; but though the Navy Department's determination to give the new American battle fleet a powerful carrier arm was correct, the politicians thought otherwise. In the debates on Fiscal Years 1920 and 1921, Congress reluctantly voted funds for the new battleships and battle-cruisers but vetoed the proposed carriers on grounds of excessive cost. The only political concession won by the US Navy was for the conversion of the fleet collier *Jupiter* (5500 tons) into an experimental carrier. This short-sighted political compromise, rating a new generation of super-battleships as preferable to carriers, shows how the pre-1914 Dreadnought battleship mania had emerged from the World War I virtually intact. However, as things turned out, it was all for the best. Instead of a quartet of bizarre giants whose cost must soon have been redoubled by the need for drastic reconstruction, the US Navy got an inexpensive test-bed carrier on which invaluable experience was rapidly gained. Moreover, as events quickly proved, the design work on the heavy carriers derived from the 'Lexington' battle-cruisers was by no means wasted.

The name chosen for *Jupiter* was *Langley*, after Samuel Pierpont Langley whose flying experiments in the 1890s, with those of Octave Chanute and Otto Lilienthal in Europe, had directly inspired the Wright brothers. Designated CV.1, the USA's first fleet carrier, *Langley* was taken in hand for reconstruction by the Navy Yard at Norfolk, Virginia (where the world's first fighting ironclad had been built in 1861–62) in March 1920. The job took almost exactly two years, with *Langley* recommissioning in her new form in March 1922. The reconstruction was by no means limited to the removal of upper-works and derricks and their replacement with a wooden flight-deck 534 ft by 64 ft. Far more internal reconstruction was required than in the case of Britain's *Argus*. The six deep holds in which, as *Jupiter*, she had once carried coal for the fleet, had to be converted for aircraft and fuel stowage. They could not be turned into aircraft hangar-decks on the British pattern but remained holds, from which the aircraft were lifted onto the flight-deck elevator by crane. There were two such aircraft accommodation spaces in *Langley*, created by merging holds 2/3 and 5/6; the forward hold was used as a tank for aircraft fuel ('avgas', short for 'aviation gasoline') and the fourth for stores and aircraft weapons. Aircraft rigging and maintenance was carried out in the open space between the deckhead of the holds and the flight deck.

Other features of *Langley* showed their derivation from contemporary British and Japanese practice. She was given fore-and-aft arrester-wires and a navigating bridge tucked under the forward flight-deck, as in the British *Argus*, and her engine smoke vented through a single portside hinged smoke-pipe (a second was subsequently added) suggestive of *Hosho*. However, *Langley*'s two masts, instead of being lowered horizontally outboard, telescoped to leave the flight-deck unobstructed for flying operations, an all-American innovation. The installation of two catapults for aircraft launching was also an American innovation, but these were removed in 1928 after it had become apparent that even the heaviest aircraft in service had no difficulty in making unassisted take-offs. Catapults did not in fact become an essential carrier feature until after World War II with the much increased weights of jet aircraft.

Though not as ugly as *Argus*, which was known in the British Fleet as 'the Flat-Iron', in profile *Langley* looked what she was, a straightforward conversion with the unappealing lines of her original design completely undisguised. *Langley* rapidly became a much-loved ornament of the US fleet, which gave her the affectionate nickname of 'the Covered Wagon'. Interestingly, Britain's *Furious* was given the same nickname after her third conversion, in which the superstructure was removed to create an unbroken flush deck, in 1922–25. However, despite her looks, *Langley* was the world's second

The real thing: with smoke belching from its exhaust, a DT-2 struggles to reach take-off power with a torpedo slung under its belly — a tough job for the 400 hp Liberty engine even at full boost. This shot is a reminder of *Langley*'s invaluable pioneering work with flight-deck arrester gear in the middle 1920s. This is the original system, with rows of hooks on each undercarriage leg to snag fore-and-aft arrester wires and bring the aircraft to a halt by friction. The wires lay flat for take-offs, safely out of reach of the hooks, and were raised from the deck by 'fiddle bridges' to receive aircraft landing-on. Transverse arrester wires, as used in Ely's first deck landing in 1911, proved vastly superior.

aircraft-carrier completed with an unbroken flight-deck for both landings and take-offs; *Argus* was the first. Though briefly commissioned in 1920 for a series of test landings, *Eagle* was not fully completed until September 1923. As for the only two 'purpose-built' carriers in existence, *Hosho* beat *Hermes* to her first commission later in 1922, though the Japanese carrier was soon back in dockyard hands to have her modest island removed. By midsummer 1922, therefore, *Langley* had given the US Navy carrier parity with Japan, and even, albeit briefly, with Britain.

Langley's greatest contribution can not be judged on a ship-for-ship comparison with rival navies. It was the number of aircraft she could carry and operate, over double that of any other carrier of her day. Just as more books can be stacked on a shelf than can be laid end to end on the same length of floor, so the unique aircraft stowage arrangement in *Langley*'s holds gave her a total of 55 aircraft, an air group which has never been bettered for a carrier of her tonnage. The uncompromising rectangle of *Langley*'s flight-deck — not tapered at the bows, as in *Eagle* and *Hermes* — assisted in the ranging of more aircraft on deck. Though the first squadron to join *Langley* in 1922 was of Vought VE-7SF fighters, she was soon gaining invaluable experience in operating different combinations of fighters, bombers and torpedo aircraft.

It was in *Langley* that the art was perfected of tying down aircraft ranged on deck, rather than fencing them in with a palisade to prevent them being blown over the side, which was a clumsy British expedient used since the first experiments with *Furious* in 1917. As the only alternative was striking aircraft below immediately after landing, the result was greater flexibility in flying opera-

tions. At the same time, *Langley*'s low speed of 15 knots made the perfection of a safe arrester system essential, which was turned to great advantage. By 1929, fore-and-aft arrester wires had been abandoned and the parallel crosswires, first used by Eugene Ely back in 1911, had been adopted by the US carrier arm as a result of the experience gained in *Langley*. As the new system enabled aircraft to be prepared forward on deck, protected by a crash barrier, while other aircraft came in to land, the result was yet more flexibility in carrier operations.

Ironically, *Langley* was the only 1920s carrier destined never to serve in wartime as a carrier. Her career as a carrier lasted fifteen years, until her forward flight-deck was removed in the winter of 1936–37 to convert her into a seaplane tender. In World War II the 'Covered Wagon's' brief service was limited to aircraft ferrying, a far cry from the rôle envisaged at the time of her reconstruction in 1922. Yet in those fifteen years no other carrier can be said to have amassed as much experience, confidence and foreknowledge in carrier operations as did *Langley*, to the obvious benefit of her mighty successors. Viewed in the light of what came after, *Langley* deserves remembrance as the most successful experimental carrier of all time.

2
First Generation: The Pre-war Giants

Britain's first carriers had been clumsy attempts to meet the demands of World War I, but the first three American carriers carried the stamp of a bewildering political about-turn in the fourth year of peace. *Langley* had, as we have seen, come into existence because of the insistence of Congress on building new battle-cruisers and battleships in preference to new carriers. However, before *Langley* had even been completed, the United States had summoned an international conference at Washington which ended, on 6 February 1922, by sanctioning heavy carrier construc-

tion in preference to that of new battle-cruisers and battleships.

The Washington Conference called by President Harding in November 1921 reflected the moral ascendancy in international affairs enjoyed by the United States in the immediate aftermath of World War I. It was attended by representatives of the United States, Britain, France, Italy, Belgium, the Netherlands, Portugal, China and Japan, and was thus virtually an extraordinary working committee of the newly-formed League of Nations, pledged to the maintenance of world

peace. Three of the four main items on the agenda at Washington covered territory in dispute between China and Japan, and the status of the Pacific and Asian colonies and trading facilities enjoyed by the leading European powers. The fourth item, however, was the fast-growing menace posed by the new battleship building race between Japan and the United States, into which the other leading navies were being helplessly drawn in emulation — Britain had laid down her first 16-inch gunned battle-cruisers that year. Given the domestic financial and political

problems facing all the recent combatants in 1921, this early resumption of international naval rivalry was an intolerable prospect. The outcome was a treaty limiting naval armaments which, looking back from the thermonuclear era, must be regarded as the most successful arms limitation treaty of the twentieth century.

The main target of the Washington Naval Treaty was the capital ship — the battleship and battle-cruiser — which was defined as any warship displacing more than 10,000 tons

Opposite
Lexington (CV.2) under construction in February 1925, already completed up to the hangar deck. A prominent feature is the bulbous bow, designed to reduce hull resistance at speeds over 30 knots. She had originally been laid down as name-ship of a class of six . 16-inch-gunned battle-cruisers on 8 January 1921, but work on these ships was halted on 2 August 1922 in conformity with the Washington Naval Treaty. The confidence and speed with which *Lexington* and *Saratoga* were completed as carriers owed much to British experience with such conversions and to the US Navy's own experience with *Langley*. Nothing on the scale of *Lexington* and *Saratoga* had ever been attempted by any navy, and they remained the biggest and most graceful carriers in the world for over two decades.

with guns larger than 8-inch. A ten-year ban, loosely referred to as a 'building holiday', was imposed on all new capital ship construction, while a total capital ship tonnage of 1,715,700 tons was shared out on a ratio of Britain 5 : the USA 5 : Japan 3 : France 1.67 : Italy 1.67. This gave the US fleet battleship parity with that of Britain, each with 525,000 tons, and superiority over that of Japan, with 315,100 tons. France and Italy, Britain's only potential European naval rivals after the surrender and scuttling of the German fleet, were left with 175,000 tons each. To prevent the completion of the high-speed monsters under construction in Japan, the United States and Britain, rigid ceilings on future battleship tonnage and armament were imposed: a maximum displacement of 35,000 tons and a maximum main armament calibre of 16-inches.

Having fettered future battleship construction, the Washington Treaty then turned to the aircraft-carrier as a means of 'recycling' the giant capital ship hulls already under construction. The Treaty began by making the first formal definition of what an aircraft-carrier *was*: a warship specifically designed for

the carrying, launching and recovery of aircraft. Carriers were to carry no more than ten low-angle guns, with a maximum calibre of 8-inches, and carrier tonnage was limited to 10,000–27,000 tons. As with capital ships, total carrier tonnages were allocated to the signatory powers on a ratio of Britain 5 : the USA 5 : Japan 3 : France 2.2 : Italy 2.2. This gave 135,000 tons each to Britain and the United States, 81,000 tons to Japan and 60,000 tons each to France and Italy. However, with the secondary aim of avoiding crippling unemployment in the shipyards, Britain, the United States and Japan were

Tugs take charge of *Lexington* after her launch on 3 October 1925, six months after *Saratoga*. To the left of the gaping centreline elevator wells can be seen the dark row of boiler uptakes, scheduled for enclosure in a single gigantic flat funnel. Just aft of the distinctive 'pinch' in the forward hull are the circular magazine hoists for the 8-inch gun mountings. The site of the island is level with a point just aft of the forward elevator well. Even at this uncompleted stage, the sharp converging taper of the forward flight-deck, in harmony with the lines of the bow but cutting down the number of aircraft which could be ranged forward, is plain to see, as is the fully-enclosed bow, a legacy of the ship's battle-cruiser derivation, which would not be reintroduced to American carrier design until after World War II.

given a special concession. This was the option of converting two existing hulls to carriers with a maximum tonnage of 33,000 tons. The immediate result of the Washington Treaty was a significant change in the relative strength of the carrier navies.

With *Argus* already in service, *Hermes* and *Eagle* approaching completion and *Furious* scheduled for full conversion as a flush-decked carrier, Britain did not take up the carrier conversion option offered by the Treaty. Instead, a new design, abiding by the Treaty restrictions, was drawn up for two of the uncompleted British 16-inch gun battle-cruisers. This created the battleships *Nelson* and *Rodney*, both launched 1925, in which tonnage and speed were sacrificed for a main armament of nine 16-inch guns. *Nelson* and *Rodney* were well inside the 35,000 ton Treaty limit but had a top speed of only 23 knots, and even to the most charitable eye they looked as if their sterns had been amputated with a blunt breadknife. They were floating demonstrations of the immense obstacles which the

Treaty had placed in the path of battleship designers, and hence of the Treaty's undoubted immediate success.

Both Japan and the United States, however, went for the option of converting uncompleted capital ships into heavy carriers. Japan's first choice was to scrap the slower 'Tosa' class battleships *Tosa* and *Kaga* and convert two of the four 'Amagi' class battle-cruisers, *Amagi* and *Akagi*, whose two sister-ships had only been laid down in November and December 1921. This programme was wrecked by act of God: the Great Tokyo Earthquake of 1 September 1922. In this catastrophe *Amagi*, still on the stocks, suffered basic structural damage and it was decided to break her up. The replacement chosen for *Amagi* was the battleship *Kaga*, reprieved from the breakers. *Kaga* and Britain's *Eagle* were the only two carriers converted from battleships but *Kaga*, laid down nine years later than *Eagle*, was over 4 knots faster ($28\frac{1}{3}$ knots). Thanks to her battle-cruiser derivation, *Akagi* had a 3-knot speed advantage over *Kaga*, but not enough to prevent the two ships from operating in harness as the First Carrier Division of the Japanese Combined Fleet.

Kaga and *Akagi* both mounted the heaviest guns permitted by the Washington Treaty, 8-inches, ten in *Kaga*, six in *Akagi*. In the deluded anticipation of likely surface action, they were given the heaviest waterline

armoured protection of any of the 'first generation' carriers: armoured belts with maximum thicknesses of 11 inches in *Kaga* and 10 inches in *Akagi*. Like *Argus* and *Langley*, *Kaga* and *Akagi* were designed as flush-deckers without islands, but their most startling feature was an attempt to improve on a British idea for carrier conversions from capital ships. This consisted of a landing-on deck covering the after two-thirds of the ship, with elevators to the hangars below, and a short flying-off deck covering the forward third of the ship on the hanger-deck level, on to which aircraft could be wheeled straight through the forward hanger doorway. The idea was to get more aircraft launched in less time, using the forward end of the main flight-deck in alternation with the shorter, lower flying-off deck. This procedure was always risky at best, even with the light biplanes of the 1920s, and was rendered impossible in any conditions which sent seas breaking over the bows. But the Japanese designers took it one stage further, adding a *second* flying-off deck which gave *Kaga* and *Akagi*, when first completed, the profile appearance of low flights of steps. It was soon apparent that the gain in operating efficiency was between negligible and nil, and the wasted hangar space forward meant that the ships could only carry 72 aircraft. In 1935, after eight years of increasingly unsatisfactory service, both returned to the dockyards for costly reconstruction as 'full-length' carriers.

In splendid and near total contrast, the American *Saratoga* and *Lexington*, launched in April and October 1925 respectively, suffered from no such design restrictions on the carrier's basic rôle. Indeed, they were as remarkable in their way as the first British Dreadnought battleship launched only 25 years before, outclassing every other carrier in existence. *Saratoga* and *Lexington* were faster than their Japanese rivals, they could operate more aircraft, and their design was so sound that they went to war in December 1941 without major reconstruction since their completion.

Even before the Washington Conference met, the restless attitude of Congress to the cost of the new battle fleet had made the future uncertain enough for contingency plans to be laid for converting at least one of the 'Lexington' class battle-cruisers. Planning got under way in July 1921, and it gave the design of CV.2 and CV.3 a useful nine-month start before the ships were actually ordered in the spring of the following years. Given that no carriers on this scale had ever been attempted by any navy, the design was remarkable for its audacity, its confidence and its far-sightedness. A single level, 888 ft long flight-deck was elegantly 'hung', with pronounced overhang fore and aft, on a hull with a waterline length 38 ft shorter. The enormous hangar decks below could accommodate 90 aircraft, and proved capacious enough for the bigger, heavier monoplanes of World War II. The designers of Japan's *Kaga* and *Akagi* had copied horizontal funnel venting of the diminutive *Argus*, but in *Lexington* and *Saratoga* the uptakes of all sixteen boilers — for which no less than five funnels had been envisaged in the original battle-cruiser plans — were swept together into one gigantic, 79 ft tall, flat-sided funnel aft of the starboard island. Those boilers could deliver 180,000 hp through turbo-electric engines driving four shafts, giving a speed of 34 knots, which made the new American giants the fastest warships of their displacement in the world.

Displacement, in fact, proved the biggest headache for the designers of *Lexington* and *Saratoga*. No matter how they sliced it, there was no way of reducing the ships' displacement down to the 33,000 tons prescribed by the Washington Treaty, and their actual displacement was 36,000 tons. Thus *Lexington* and *Saratoga* were in breach of the Washington Treaty from the outset, but a face-saving formula was quickly found. A clause in the Treaty allowed existing capital ships a margin of 3000 tons extra displacement in which to incorporate improved anti-aircraft defence. The Navy General Board claimed that this

3000-ton margin also applied to post-Treaty carriers, which explained away the embarrassing 3000-ton surplus. Nor was this specious ploy used by the United States alone: Japan did exactly the same for *Kaga* (38,000 tons) and *Akagi* (36,500 tons). These depressingly early exercises in the subtle art of 'treaty-bending' showed the vulnerability of the Washington agreement, which, ultimately, could only be enforced by the very calamity the Treaty was intended to avert: war.

Despite their overall excellence, *Lexington* and *Saratoga* contained one serious design flaw: the inclusion of an 8-inch battery in four twin mountings, with two superimposed turrets positioned fore and aft of the island and funnel. This was a mistake. Apart from the space taken up below decks by the hoists and magazines which fed the turrets, the latter could not in practice function as intended. The 8-inch guns added nothing to the ships' anti-aircraft defences that could not be achieved by more and lighter high-angle weapons, and they could only be fired in safety at targets well out on the starboard beam. The guns could obviously not be fired across the flight-deck at targets to port when flying operations were in progress; and even

when all aircraft were struck below the radial blast of the guns, when trained inboard, had a shattering effect on crew positions on the port side of the ship and in the island. The 8-inch guns had only one function: to beat off enemy cruisers and destroyers in low-angle fire. It was hardly to be expected that such enemy units would always be so obliging as to attack only from the starboard beam! This built-in error was not diagnosed, and rectified in *Saratoga*, before the outbreak of war in December 1941. It is at least arguable that more anti-aircraft fire-power, provided by the pre-war replacement of the 8-inch battery by 5-inch AA guns, could well have saved *Lexington* from her fiery end in the Coral Sea in May 1942.

Close-up of *Lexington*'s after 8-inch turrets on a gunnery shoot in January 1928, shortly after commissioning. Turret Three is firing, prudently trained fully to starboard. The lateral blast from these heavy guns made firing on any other bearing highly dangerous. It was this factor, rather than the uncertainty over whether or not carriers should 'double' as conventionally-gunned cruisers, which made the 8-inch battery the biggest flaw in the design of *Lexington* and *Saratoga*. Of the two ships, only *Saratoga* would survive to have her 8-inch turrets replaced with dual-purpose 5-inch anti-aircraft guns, the correct weapon against the carrier's true foe: enemy carrier aircraft.

Fine shot of *Saratoga* about 1927–29, with her full air group ranged on deck and the destroyer *Tracy* (DD.214) in attendance. The aircraft are Martin T4M torpedo-bombers, Vought 02U Corsair scouts, and Boeing F2B fighters. The latter types, employed in the Navy's Light Bombing Wing, accumulated invaluable early experience of dive-bombing.

Lexington and *Saratoga* were fitted with a waterline armoured belt of 6 inches, equivalent to that of a heavy cruiser. Like *Langley*, they were originally fitted with a 155 ft long centreline catapult, driven by a huge flywheel, but the catapults were removed as unnecessary in 1934. The ships' sustained capacity for high-speed steaming, plus their generous dimensions, enabled them to cope easily with the stream of ever-faster, ever-heavier naval aircraft produced by Vought, Curtiss, Boeing and Grumman throughout the interwar years. As the following table of aircraft operated by *Lexington* and *Saratoga* shows, this adaptability continued without a break into World War II.

With *Langley*, *Lexington* and *Saratoga* as their experimental bases at sea, American naval aircraft remained the best in the world until the mid-1930s, and were renowned for their toughness and agility. Indeed, the Curtiss P-6E Hawk and its successor, the F11C-2 Goshawk, developed for the US Army Air Corps and US Navy respectively, had a profound influence across the Atlantic. The Goshawk's impressive performance as a

TABLE 1

COMPARATIVE DATA TABLE OF US NAVY CARRIER FIGHTERS 1928–1945

Type	In Service	Length ft in	Span ft in	Height ft in	Gross Weight lbs	Max. Speed, mph
Boeing F2B-1	1928	22 10	30 1	10 $1\frac{1}{4}$	2830	158.4 at sea level
Boeing F4B-1	1929	20 $1\frac{3}{8}$	30 0	10 4	2725	165.5 at sea level
Boeing F4B-4	1931	20 $4\frac{11}{16}$	30 0	9 10	3085	184 at 6000 ft
Curtiss F11C-2 Goshawk	1932	22 $7\frac{6}{16}$	31 6	8 11	4132	202 at 8000 ft
Grumman FF-1	1933	25 0	34 6	11 1	4643	201 at 8000 ft
Grumman F2F	1935	21 $4\frac{7}{8}$	28 6	8 6	3795	233 at 7500 ft
Grumman F4F Wildcat	1940	28 $9\frac{3}{8}$	38 0	11 $10\frac{3}{8}$	7002	331 at 21,300 ft
Chance Vought F4U Corsair	1943	32 10	41 0	12 2	12,039	393 at 25,000 ft
Grumman F6F Hellcat	1943	33 $6\frac{3}{8}$	42 10	13 0	12,800	371 at 18,800 ft

fighter/dive-bomber led to the purchase in autumn 1933 of two machines for appraisal in Nazi Germany. Exhaustively tested by World War I ace Ernst Udet, they convinced the future leaders of the still-clandestine German air force of the virtues of dive-bombing, and led to the birth of the famous *Stuka*. In US Navy service, the Goshawks of Fighting Squadron 1 — noted for its 'High Hat' fuselage insignia — were the first carrier-based unit to perfect dive-bombing attacks with an aircraft which could double as a fighter. The portly Grumman biplane fighters of the early 1930s were years ahead of their Japanese and British naval counterparts, with retracting undercarriages and enclosed cockpits.

From about 1935, however, a relapse into

The eyes of the fleet: 02U Corsair scouts over *Saratoga* in May 1929. The circle between the 'tramlines' on the flight-deck indicates the optimum touchdown point for incoming aircraft.

Flying-off: *Lexington*, steaming into wind, launches a 'strike' of Martin T4M torpedo-bombers in the 1929 Fleet manoeuvres. The flight-deck crews have already spotted the next two aircraft 'prop to tailfin' and a third is being wheeled into position behind them.

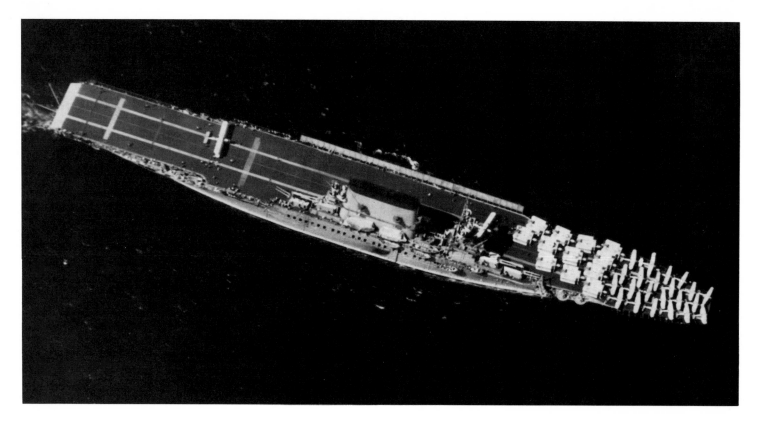

Landing-on: off the centreline to port but safely down, another T4M comes 'home' onto *Lexington* in the 1929 manoeuvres. Its predecessor is being wheeled forward prior to having its wings folded for ranging alongside the other strike aircraft in the group. Notice how, in these early days, the two fighter squadrons have been left hemmed in right forward, incapable of any kind of emergency launch until the T4Ms have been struck down to the hangar deck — a weakness which combat experience in the Pacific War would mercilessly reveal.

caution and conservatism replaced the innovatory spirit which had characterized the previous decade, and which had made it seem inevitable that the Americans would be first in the field with naval monoplane aircraft. It was the Japanese Navy which received the world's first naval monoplane fighter, the Mitsubishi A5M Type 96, in 1937. In the United States, the Navy clung stubbornly to the obsolescent biplane concept, allowing the Army to forge ahead with encouraging monoplane fighter designs: the Seversky P-35, Curtiss P-36 and Curtiss P-40 of 1936–39. Though the US Navy had already accepted monoplane torpedo-bomber and dive-bomber types, the Douglas TBD-1 Devastator (1937) and Douglas SBD Dauntless (1939), the American carrier arm did not get its first monoplane fighters until the first batch of Grumman F4F Wildcats was delivered in February 1940. By the time the Wildcat was in full service it had been outclassed by the superb Japanese Mitsubishi A6M *Zero-sen*. Even so, the Wildcat was a much better carrier fighter than any contemporary British design. Supplied to the

British Fleet Air Arm, in whose service it was known as the Martlet, the F4F performed yeoman service from October 1940 to the last year of the war, as well as bearing the brunt of the Japanese onslaught in the Pacific.

Though *Langley*, *Lexington* and *Saratoga* were an incongruous trio, the value of their services to American naval aviation in the interwar years can hardly be over-stated. They permitted the US Navy to experiment with using the aircraft-carrier, in separate task groups and task forces, as a weapon in its own right rather than as a versatile accessory of the battle fleet. (There is a direct parallel here with the similar German experiments, in the late 1930s, with tanks massed in armoured divisions instead of being doled out in 'penny packets' as mere infantry support weapons.) Between 1928 and 1941 the Americans discovered that the term 'fleet carrier', as applied to the large carrier with an air group over 25 strong, was ambiguous. If kept on a leash and tied to the battle fleet, the 'fleet' carrier could never do itself full justice, but, if allowed to operate independently in a task group, at first one carrier plus escorts, or a larger task force of two or more carriers operating together plus escorts, the carrier showed that it had more range, speed and striking-power than any conventional battle fleet.

Much ironical ink has been spilled to argue that the American carrier exercises of 1928–41 gave the Japanese 'the blueprint for Pearl Harbor'. This melodramatic notion, though

certainly not entirely without truth, is a most exaggerated one. As the main forward base of the US Pacific Fleet, over 2000 miles from the nearest base on the American mainland, Pearl Harbor's importance was always glaringly obvious. Japanese Naval Intelligence naturally kept an eye on Pearl Harbor from the moment the Americans made it a fleet base in 1919. As the Hawaiian Islands form one of the major international crossroads of the North Pacific, there was never any particular difficulty in observing the place, even without the large numbers of Japanese living in the islands. It is true that American, not Japanese, naval staffs planned the first 'carrier attacks' on Pearl Harbor, but Pearl Harbor was only one of many simulated objectives in a programme of exercises to test the flexibility of the US Pacific Fleet; and, given the novelty of the carrier element in the late 1920s, it should not be surprising that the results of these exercises were not taken at full face value.

With no combat precedents to indicate otherwise, the US Naval Planning Board naturally considered attack and defence in terms of conventional fleet gunnery action, with carrier and land-based aircraft playing a backup role. Exercises in 1928 (FLEET PROBLEM VIII) provided the first embarrassing hint of less orthodox alternatives, when aircraft from *Langley* gained complete surprise in an 'attack' on Pearl Harbor, arriving over the target before the defending fighters had time to get airborne or the fleet to

put to sea. However, in the following year's programme (FLEET PROBLEM IX) the subject was the defence of the Panama Canal, not Pearl Harbor. *Saratoga* operated with the 'enemy', *Lexington* with the 'defenders'. The results could hardly be considered decisive. *Lexington*'s aircraft failed to prevent *Saratoga* from claiming a successful 'attack' on the Canal, but the umpires ruled that defending battleships had already 'sunk' *Saratoga*. Before the exercise ended, *Lexington*'s aircraft found and 'sank' *Saratoga*, but defending Navy land-based bombers 'sank' their own carrier *Lexington* in error. If any conclusions were to be drawn from all this, the main one was that the new 'flat-tops' seemed as vulnerable as they were potent. The two main planks of defence strategy remained the battle fleet and land-based aircraft.

Nothing, however, could undermine the faith of the new-generation 'carrier men' of the US Navy — the only navy, be it noted, to stipulate that a pilot's wings were an essential qualification for carrier command. In early 1932, Admiral H. E. Yarnell, the first American flag officer to base a tactical scheme on his own flying experiences with carriers, achieved a notable 'first' for the carrier arm. He staged another simulated air attack on Pearl Harbor, this time using *Lexington* and *Saratoga* in a joint carrier task force. This operated in complete independence, commanded by Yarnell in person and escorted by only four destroyers. Against Yarnell's task force, the

Naval Planning Board deployed the best land/sea/air defence which the available assets permitted: a battle fleet and submarine flotilla, a complete division of troops and heavy mobile coastal artillery, 100 land-based bombers and increased anti-aircraft batteries. Allowing for the maximum safe operational range of the carrier aircraft of the day, it was assumed that the attacking task force would be unable to get within air-launching range — 100 miles or less — without being detected and engaged.

Yarnell based his attack plan on four proven facts. The first was that the ocean is a big place in which a compact fast task force is much harder to locate than a full-sized fleet. The second was that rain squalls and low cloud, used intelligently, make excellent cover for a task force, again, much more so than for a larger fleet. The third was that in winter time, Oahu's Koolau Range (2800 ft) forces clouds carried by the prevailing north-east winds to mass and unload their moisture in dense banks out of which aircraft approaching from the north-east can suddenly emerge to arrive in clear skies over Pearl Harbor. The fourth was that, by Christian custom, garrison forces and a fleet observing harbour routine — even when on a supposed war footing — will inevitably not be ready for an 'instant attack' first thing on a Sunday morning.

Yarnell was given an unexpected bonus in the form of unusually bad weather during his

Fighters fly-off from *Lexington*, demonstrating how the lightweight biplanes of the 1920s and 1930s could operate without catapults even when the carrier was not making speed into wind (note the boats secured to booms). In this, of course, the enormous length of the flight-decks in *Lexington* and *Saratoga*, 888 ft, was an invaluable aid.

final approach, which naturally added to the defenders' sense of security from air attack. By nightfall on Saturday, 6 February 1932, exploiting this cover, the men of *Lexington* and *Saratoga* braced themselves for a night run to a flying-off position 60 miles from Oahu. Yarnell ordered a single, 'mixed-arms' strike, 152 aircraft in all, launched simultaneously by *Lexington* and *Saratoga* to arrive over Pearl Harbor at dawn in overwhelming strength. Fighters 'strafed' the lines of parked aircraft on their runways, while the bombers went for shore installations, barracks and the fleet anchorage. Surprise was total, and not a single fighter went up to engage the attackers.

It was clear enough that a vital point had been made: that given good planning and the right circumstances, a carrier task force could raise Cain with a battle fleet of much greater conventional force. However, the battleship men had an equally good case, claiming that Yarnell's theoretical sinkings must be erased because the fleet was at sea — able in theory, as the 1929 FLEET PROBLEM IX had shown, to catch his carriers and sink them. Moreover, even if all the battleships had been caught at anchor, it was argued that Yarnell's aircraft would have been unable to sweep the

Fine bow study of *Saratoga* taken by a departing aircraft in 1933, with the rest of the fighter group ready to follow. The wake clearly records the big carrier's sharp turn into wind for the launch, necessary for this big group, given the short take-off run required of the first aircraft away. To the right of the picture the destroyer *Hulbert* (DD.342) sprints to maintain station on the port wing of the turning task group.

Opposite top
Lexington and complement on parade off Long Beach, California in September 1936, ponderously surveyed by a Goodyear 'blimp'.

February 1932: *Lexington* returns to Lahaina Roads, Maui, after the Pacific Fleet manoeuvres which included a simulated massed carrier strike at Pearl Harbor. In this highly successful 'blueprint' for the notorious Japanese attack nearly ten years later, *Lexington* and *Saratoga* launched a combined force of 152 aircraft which gained complete surprise in a dawn 'attack' on 7 February 1932.

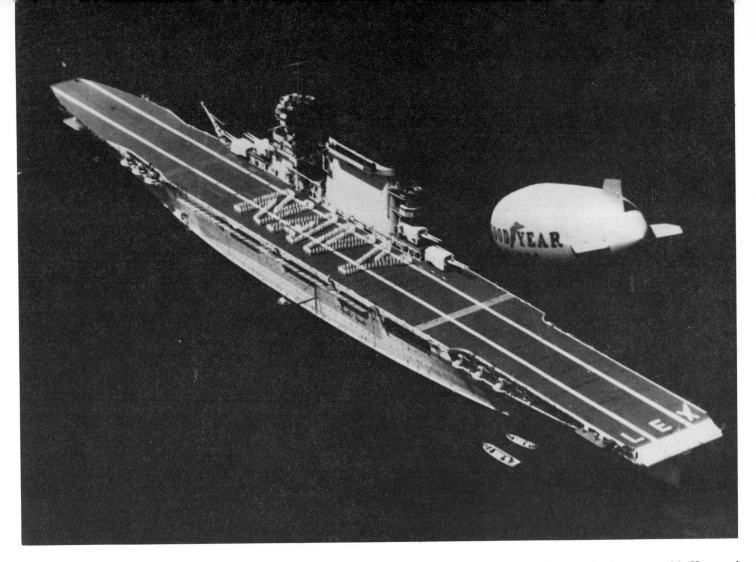

board if met by the massed anti-aircraft fire-power of the fleet. Certainly, the ability of capital ships to beat off attacking aircraft with gunfire remained an article of faith, in both the American and British navies, until it was brutally disproved by the experience of World War II. It had already been used to discount the much-publicised sinking of unmanned, immobile target battleships by General 'Billy' Mitchell's bombers in 1921–23, the first time that aircraft had proved themselves capable of aiming bombs at and sinking capital ships. Only genuine war experience could show how aircraft would fare when attacking targets which shot back, and which were manned by damage-control crews.

There was another query which could only be resolved by the test of war. This was one of the most persuasive claims pressed by the battleship men: the obvious combat advantages of the battleship over the carrier. The battleship could operate and attack in all

weathers: the carrier could not. Battleships were the most heavily protected warships afloat: carriers were unarmoured containers of vast amounts of volatile fuels. The fleet exercises and war games had shown that battleships could catch carriers, given the chance; all indications were that the carrier's chances of surviving such an encounter would be nil. Indeed, on the two occasions in World War II when battleships *did* bring carriers to action, the result in each case was one-sided slaughter, dealt out by the battleships' heavy, rifled guns. The peacetime exercises did not prove that a carrier's aircraft were its best weapon of defence as well as attack: only the possibility was suggested.

Despite all these uncertainties, it was with *Lexington* and *Saratoga* — the matched giants, the biggest carriers in the world — that the US Navy learned the rudiments of carrier task force operations between 1927 and 1941. The only other navy with two carriers of compa-

rable size was the Japanese, with *Kaga* and *Akagi*; and these were not reconstructed as 'full-sized' fleet carriers until 1935–36. However, the resulting American eight-year advantage in operating large air groups was cancelled by the speed with which the Japanese developed their new and greatly superior monoplane carrier aircraft between 1936 and 1941. Yet *Lexington* and *Saratoga* were never envisaged as prototypes for a heavyweight carrier fleet. They remained one-offs, a unique double product of the Washington Treaty, criticized, indeed, from many quarters for their excessive size. Within two years of the completion of 'Lady Lex' and 'Sara' in 1927, the US Navy's designers had already begun to work on a far smaller carrier, CV.4, named USS *Ranger*. In her, the US Navy set out to settle the longstanding question of whether many small aircraft carriers represented a better proposition than a few large ones.

3
Inter-war Prototype

The first giant carriers had come into being as the result of the restrictions imposed by the Washington Treaty. Paradoxically, those same restrictions resulted in the next purpose-built Japanese and American carriers being of far more modest dimensions. Whereas *Lexington* and *Saratoga*, *Kaga* and *Akagi* had all been built to the measure of existing capital ship hulls, the Japanese *Ryujo* and the American *Ranger*, launched on 2 April 1931 and 25 February 1933 respectively, were of an entirely different derivation. Both resulted from the attempt to build the maximum number of ships out of the remaining carrier tonnage permitted by the Washington Treaty. Each ship therefore represented the designers' attempts to get the proverbial pint into a quart pot, and their many resultant flaws provide yet another instance of the Treaty's remarkable effectiveness.

As far as the US Navy was concerned, *Lexington* and *Saratoga* had together con-

sumed 66,000 tons of the permitted carrier tonnage, their excess 6000 tons being conveniently disguised. This left 135,000 tons for new carrier construction; and in 1927, the year *Lexington* and *Saratoga* were commissioned, the US Naval Planning Board got down to the problem of how those 135,000 tons should be apportioned.

Discounting the experimental *Langley*, the array of existing carriers in 1927 presented a wide range of specimen displacements — from the 36,000 tons of the four American and Japanese giants down to the 7500 ton range of Japan's *Hosho*. In the middle lay the three British carriers converted from light battle-cruisers, *Furious*, *Glorious* and *Courageous*, all in the 22,500 ton range; *Eagle*, also of capital ship derivation, was slightly heavier, 22,600 tons. The only two purpose-built carriers, Japan's *Hosho* and Britain's 10,850-ton *Hermes*, were both far down among the lightweights and had consequently modest

air groups. For their next purpose-built carriers, therefore, Japanese and American naval designers sought to enlarge on *Hosho* and *Hermes* without going too far. The objective was to balance the lowest possible displacement with the largest possible air group.

Japan's *Ryujo* was the least satisfactory of the new ships. Another demonstration of the still-powerful British influence on Japanese carrier design, *Ryujo* was an attempt to go one stage further than *Hermes*. The Japanese chose the flush deck of Britain's *Argus* and *Furious*. However, they tried to produce a carrier which would have a 50 aircraft air group but was below 10,000 tons displacement, and which would therefore be exempt from the Washington Treaty's tonnage ceiling on carrier construction. It could not be done. The Japanese designers might have made the task easier for themselves if they had tried to use a broader hull than in the 'long and lean' format established with *Hosho*, but *Ryujo* was

Ranger's starboard profile, showing her modest island structure, with the crash barrier and clumsy after smokepipes in vertical position. The complete absence of gun turrets fore and aft of the island added considerably to marshalling space available on the flight-deck. Two of her eight single 5-inch guns are clearly visible forward, one apparently depressed for a barrel clean.

Opposite
Ranger (CV.4) as she looked when completed in June 1934, showing how the hangar deck and flight deck formed a box superstructure essentially separate from the main hull, not enclosed in the main hull as with *Lexington* and *Saratoga*. This remained a standard American feature until the giant carriers of the 1950s. Looking at the clean cruiser-like lines of *Ranger*'s hull, it is hard to believe that she actually had an extreme beam 4 feet greater than that of the 'Lexingtons'.

An undated photograph of *Ranger* in war paint, showing the typical imprint of World War Two combat experience: the addition of quadruple 40 mm AA mountings, with one tucked in the bow under the forward edge of the flight-deck and another planted forward of the island. *Ranger*'s slow speed made her unsuitable for fleet carrier operations in the Pacific, and the bulk of her wartime service was in the European Theatre of Operations in 1942–43.

given a narrower beam than any other carrier, other than *Hosho* and *Argus* which had beams of 59 ft and 68 ft respectively. Increasing the air group necessitated building a second hangar deck above the first, and the result was a dangerously top-heavy ship. In 1935, reconstructions were undertaken to atone for this, modifying the bridge structure and raising the forecastle by a complete deck, but *Ryujo* was never a successful type. Though her two-shaft turbine drive delivered double the horsepower of *Hosho*, *Ryujo*, at 29 knots, was only four knots faster.

The US Navy's *Ranger*, launched two years after *Ryujo*, was a strange mixture. She was well ahead of her Japanese counterpart in many respects, yet in others was depressingly similar because of her fundamental obsession with economy. *Ranger*'s most impressive feature was the superimposition of her hangar decks above, and essentially separate from, the main hull, resulting in an extreme beam measurement of $109\frac{1}{2}$ ft, actually 4 ft greater than that of *Lexington* and *Saratoga*. This innovation, to be repeated in every American fleet carrier built over the next twenty-odd years, freed aircraft accommodation from the confines of the hull sides. The result was an air group of most impressive strength for a carrier of *Ranger*'s modest size: 86 aircraft. Like *Ryujo*, Ranger dispensed with the 'cruiser-sized' low-angle battery considered essential for *Lexington*, *Saratoga*, *Kaga* and *Akagi*. Instead, *Ranger* carried the same high-angle battery as *Ryujo*, eight 5-inch guns, though in single mountings instead of twin mountings, as in the Japanese ship). Although she was given an island superstructure, *Ranger*'s funnel venting was an unsuccessful reversion to the hinged smoke-pipes of *Langley* and *Hosho*, three on each side — the last American carrier so equipped. And *Ranger*'s two-shaft turbines delivered 53,500 hp, 13,129 less than those of *Ryujo*, resulting in a comparable speed of $29\frac{1}{2}$ knots.

Fighter pilots in *Ranger*'s briefing room await their first sortie in French North African airspace on the eve of Operation 'Torch', launched on 8 November 1942. These are officers of 41 Squadron, which covered the Western Force landings on the Atlantic coast of French Morocco.

TABLE 2

COMPARATIVE DATA TABLE OF AMERICAN AND JAPANESE
WASHINGTON TREATY LIMITED CARRIERS

	Lexington	*Ryujo*	*Ranger*
Displacement (tons)	33,000	10,600	14,500
Length Overall (ft)	888.00	590.33	769.00
Max. Beam (ft)	105.50	68.25	109.50
Draught (ft)	24.25	23.50	19.75
Machinery	4-shaft turbo-electric	2-shaft turbines	2-shaft turbines
Max. Speed (kts)	34	29	29.50
Armament	8 × 8-inch LA	8 × 5-inch HA/AA	8 × 5-inch HA/AA
	12 × 5-inch AA	4 × 25 mm AA	(later 24 × 40 mm AA)
		24 × 13 mm AA	
Aircraft	90	48	86
Complement	3300	900	2000

As Table 2 shows, *Ranger* was therefore 100 ft shorter and nearly 5 knots slower than *Lexington*, but 4 ft wider across the beam and able to launch nearly as many aircraft. As for *Ryujo*, *Ranger* was superior in every department other than speed. With regard to gun armament, *Ryujo* and *Ranger* both show carrier designers starting to forget surface firepower and give precedence to anti-aircraft fire-power. This was an inevitable result of the 1920s fleet exercises in which carriers took part for the first time, and it was not a trend followed only by the Japanese and Americans. By the early 1930s the carriers with the best anti-aircraft batteries were the last two British conversions from light battle-cruisers, *Courageous* and *Glorious*, the latter conversion being completed in January 1930. These were the first carriers to dispense entirely with low-angle gun armament, each ship mounting sixteen 4.7-inch high angle AA guns, exceptional by the standards of their time.

Fortunately for the US Navy, *Ranger* did not become the first unit of a predominantly small-carrier fleet. The original idea of laying down five carriers of similar type between 1929 and 1933 was killed by the cash starvation of the Great Depression; by the extension, only months after the Wall Street Crash, of the Washington Treaty limitations by the London Naval Treaty of April 1930; and by a growing realisation of the inadequacies of the small carrier for fleet work. Only *Ranger* was eventually laid down in September 1931, as much to stave off unemployment in the Newport News shipyard as to increase the potential of the American carrier arm.

Ranger was a prototype carrier type found wanting even before her completion in June 1934. She was the only American carrier completed before the outbreak of war which did not serve against the Japanese in the Pacific. From 1941 to 1944, *Ranger* remained with the Atlantic command and was relegated to training duties for the last eighteen months of the war. But it would be wrong to dismiss *Ranger* as a total failure. Her very existence prevented badly needed modern fleet carriers from being held back in the secondary Atlantic theatre, secondary, that is, in the US Navy's wartime scale of priorities. In August 1943 *Ranger* was 'loaned' to the British Home Fleet with the heavy cruisers *Augusta* and *Tuscaloosa* as consorts, an invaluable reinforcement at a time when the Home Fleet, confronted by a German battle squadron of exceptional strength, was momentarily left with no operational carriers. In late September 1943, the imminent withdrawal of the German 'pocket-battleship' *Lützow* from Arctic Norway to German home waters offered *Ranger*, the Cinderella of the American carrier arm, a chance of getting to the ball at last. But *Ranger*'s air crews, only 40 per cent of whom had flown a single combat mission, were cheated of their first fair crack at an enemy warship. British air reconnaissance took so long to confirm that *Lützow* had sailed that the quarry had escaped out of air strike range before *Ranger* could be sailed to intercept on 27 September 1943.

Ranger's sole moment of glory came on 4 October 1943 when she carried the weight of a Home Fleet strike at German shipping in the Norwegian port of Bødö. Escorted by fourteen fighters, 30 Dauntless dive-bombers and Avenger torpedo-bombers carried out a spirited and highly successful low-level attack in two waves, sinking or destroying five ships totalling 20,753 tons. As the Home Fleet withdrew later in the day, *Ranger*'s fighters added to the little carrier's laurels by shooting

Jokes help relieve the tension as zero hour approaches. Lieutenant Wardell, 41 Squadron's Executive Officer (right, facing camera) was shot down during the 'Torch' landings but escaped unhurt. Notice the recognition chart of British, French, German, Spanish and Italian aircraft insignia displayed at the left.

down two shadowing German reconnaissance aircraft. This was *Ranger*'s only combat operation before she returned to American waters at the end of November 1943. In this single operation *Ranger* fulfilled her designed mission more completely than many battleships whose entire careers were spent in the secondary, coastal bombardment role.

It would also be going too far to describe *Ranger* as the forerunner of the light fleet carriers (CVLs) ordered in the first six months of the Pacific War. *Ranger*'s trouble was the mistaken attempt to fit a large air group into a small carrier, with the result that the required hangar space could only be provided at the expense of machinery space and hence speed. The wartime CVLs carried modest air groups of about 45 aircraft, permitting 4-shaft propulsion and speeds over 40 knots. As a final word on *Ranger*'s design, its many positive features led to a second pre-war attempt at a light fleet carrier which took shape as USS *Wasp*, launched in April 1939 six years after *Ranger*. *Wasp* was not laid down as CV.7 until

As 'Torch' gets under way, one of *Ranger*'s Grumman F4F Wildcat fighters begins its take-off run. AL flight-deck crewman is holding one of the restraining wheel chocks on the right. Compare the radar array atop the island with the airborne photograph on page 29. Surface-to-air radar surveillance was one of the key links in the carrier's defence system.

work had been completed on her two immortal predecessors: *Yorktown* and *Enterprise* (CV.5 and CV.6), the ships which carried the main weight of US carrier operations in the decisive first year of the Pacific War.

4
Second Generation: Saviours of the Pacific War

There was a new spirit of purpose behind the two carriers included in the US Navy's construction programme for 1934. These ships reflected Franklin D. Roosevelt's wide-ranging 'New Deal' for American national recovery from the Depression. Roosevelt was very much a 'Navy-minded' President; his first major political post had been that of Assistant Secretary of the Navy between 1913 and 1920, an often-forgotten parallel with the early career of Winston Churchill. The new carriers provided much-needed employment in the shipbuilding industry and, indeed, were funded by the Public Works Administration, but this was never the sole motivation. Far more important was the determination to achieve the ideal fleet carrier format

consistent with treaty restrictions, building on the experience gained with *Ranger*. For this reason CV.5 and CV.6 were both assigned to Newport News, the yard where *Ranger* had been built between 1931 and 1934. They were launched in April and October 1936, CV.5 as *Yorktown*, CV.6 as *Enterprise*.

The new carriers represented a fundamental change in planned additions to the American carrier fleet: from five 'smalls' to two 'mediums'. Displacement was raised to the 20,000 ton range to accommodate more powerful machinery. The result was the delivery of 120,000 hp, over twice *Ranger*'s 53,500 hp, on double the shafts, yielding an excellent 34 knots. An increase of $40\frac{1}{2}$ ft in overall length to $809\frac{1}{2}$ ft and $3\frac{1}{4}$ ft in

beam to $83\frac{1}{4}$ ft raised the maximum air group capacity to 100 aircraft. The superimposed hangar deck design of *Ranger* was repeated and enlarged, this time including three centreline elevators. The unsatisfactory hinged smoke-pipes of *Ranger* were abandoned for good, and conventional venting was provided

Yorktown (CV.5) as completed in 1937. The aircraft are Grumman F3F fighters, representing the last generation of American naval biplanes, with closed cockpits and retracting undercarriages. The debt owed to *Ranger*'s design is obvious, but *Yorktown* reverted to conventional boiler uptakes, venting through a vertical funnel astern of the island. *Yorktown*'s greatest weakness lay in having the same scanty AA battery as in *Ranger* (eight single 5-inch guns) but her 4-shaft turbines gave her all the speed she needed for fast fleet operations.

Wasp (CV.7) was the last American Treaty-restricted carrier: an attempt to eliminate *Ranger*'s faults without abandoning the light fleet carrier concept. *Wasp* had the same island/funnel structure as the two 'Yorktowns', but her 2-shaft turbines could barely deliver 29 knots.

by a trim funnel aft of the bridge structure in a lengthened starboard island.

Yorktown and *Enterprise* were completed in 1937 with several features intended to assist flying operations but which were soon found to be strikingly out of touch with operational reality. One such feature was the grouping of arresting-wires at both ends of the flight-deck in the belief that aircraft could land-on at both bow and stern. By the late 1930s, however, the days when aircraft could land down-wind in safety, on land, let alone on the strict limitation of a flight-deck at sea, were long gone, and the bow arrester-wires were never used, nor were the space-consuming single catapults mounted athwartships on the hangar deck. In this case the idea was to supplement the main aircraft launches over the bow with launches on the beam, thus despatching the air group more quickly. There was nothing wrong with the technique: an athwartships catapult was the only way of launching spotter planes from capital ships and cruisers. But it made little sense when applied to carriers, because the prime function of a carrier's hangar deck was to accommodate, service, and bring to take-off readiness the maximum number of aircraft in the shortest possible

time. Being able to get at most two or three more aircraft launched from the hangar deck while the main force took off from the flight-deck was never worth the interference with aircraft handling inevitably caused by the hangar deck catapult. The device was never used in action, nor were the two forward catapults mounted up on the flight-deck. Fully armed and fuelled piston-engined aircraft proved capable of unassisted take-offs right through World War II.

These minor flaws did little to detract from the overall excellence of *Yorktown* and *Enterprise*, in which all the best features of *Ranger* were incorporated while the worst faults were discarded. They were the direct prototypes of the 'Essex' class fleet carriers which entered service in 1942–43 and which, modernised and reconstructed almost beyond recognition, were still in service 40 years after their first commission.

The 'Yorktowns' differed in one very important respect from their British contemporary *Ark Royal*, which was launched in April 1937 and commissioned in November 1938. *Ark Royal* represented the British belief that 'the bomber will always get through', and that a measure of armoured-box protection was necessary for the hangar deck even if this meant reducing the size of the air group. The unprotected 'Yorktown' and 'Essex' classes, on the other hand, represented American faith in the doctrine that a carrier's best

protection was the largest possible fighter strength, to shoot down enemy bombers before they could attack. This utter confidence in the defensive capacity of naval aviation was to prove unfounded. Time and again in the Pacific War the effects of bombs drilling through wooden-planked flight-decks to explode below exacted a dreadful toll. When the protected British fleet carriers finally arrived in the Pacific in the spring of 1945, the way in which they stood up to Japanese bombs and *kamikazes* earned unfeigned American admiration.

The building and completion of *Yorktown* and *Enterprise* did not dispel the lingering hope that the small carrier format — despite the acknowledged failings of *Ranger* — could be made to work. The reason for this was the extension of the Washington tonnage restrictions at the London conference in 1930. After *Yorktown* and *Enterprise*, the US Navy was left with only one further small carrier of *Ranger*'s displacement to make up the total American allocation of carrier tonnage. Under the assumption that an improved small carrier would be preferable to none, CV.7 was ordered in 1935, despite the requirements of the Bureau of Aeronautics.

The contract for the new carrier went to Bethlehem's Quincy Yard in Massachusetts, where *Lexington* had been built. The care put into CV.7's design was reflected in her construction time; she was not launched as USS

A fine portrait of *Wasp* at sea on trials in 1940, with her 'roller-blind' hangar ventilators closed. The lack of quick-firing AA weapons is obvious.

Wasp until April 1939, commissioning a year later. *Wasp* was the last 'Treaty-restricted' American carrier, and as such her designers made a gallant attempt at reconciling impossible requirements. It could be said that *Wasp* was far more of a miniature 'Yorktown' than an up-graded 'Ranger'. At 14,700 tons, *Wasp* displaced 200 tons more than *Ranger*, being slightly broader in the beam and some 18 ft shorter in overall length. *Wasp*'s venting system was the conventional bridge/funnel island, and she carried a comparable air group of 84 aircraft. *Wasp*'s basic machinery was the same as *Ranger*'s, 2-shaft geared turbines, and there was no improvement in speed.

The unnecessary hangar deck catapult of *Yorktown* and *Enterprise* was also installed in *Wasp*, but the new carrier also included a much more useful innovation, an outboard elevator, supplementing the two conventional centreline elevators. With the outboard elevator extending over the water from the carrier's side, aircraft could be wheeled through the appropriate opening in the hangar side to help deliver aircraft to the flight-deck in a wider distribution, thus reducing congestion as the aircraft were ranged on deck. Making its debut in the diminutive, pre-war *Wasp*, the outboard elevator was the first of a long series of modifications to the basic carrier format which, interrupted by World War II, continued through the angled flight-deck of the 1950s to the 'ski-jump' extension introduced

in the 1970s. *Wasp*'s outboard elevator lacked the solid quadriform outline of later types. The outboard elevator was T-shaped, tailored to the outline of an aircraft's wings and fuselage, and hinged to allow it to be folded upward against the ship's side when flying operations were not in progress.

The 1930 London Naval Treaty had extended the Washington Treaty limitations to 1936, but by the time work began on *Wasp* it was already clear that the interlude of naval limitations by mutual consent was dead in all but name. In November 1934 Japan had laid down her latest carrier, *Soryu* (15,900 tons, 73 aircraft, 34 knots), only weeks before making a formal denunciation of the Washington and London Treaty limitations on 19 December 1934. The latter step was a formality because, even allowing for the recognised percentage of cheating of announced tonnage figures, the new *Soryu* put Japan well over her maximum carrier allotment of 81,000 tons, nor would any Japanese carriers after *Soryu* be completed before the treaties expired. The resultant grave implications for the future balance of sea power in the Pacific were matched on the Atlantic front. On 15 March 1935, Adolf Hitler formally announced Germany's repudiation of the military, air, and naval restrictions imposed by the Treaty of Versailles. Germany, under Nazi rule since January 1933, was making a renewed bid for sea power. The new German fleet was to include

not only the newest type of capital ship but submarines and aircraft-carriers as well. The first German carrier, *Graf Zeppelin*, was ordered in 1935 on the conclusion of a naval agreement with Britain on 18 June 1935 which allowed Germany 47,000 tons of carrier construction. When *Graf Zeppelin* was launched in December 1938 she was, at 23,200 tons, the biggest carrier ever built 'from the keel up'. She dwarfed *Wasp*, launched four months later, by 8500 tons and was designed for a speed of 4 more knots.

The American reaction to this adverse tilting of the international naval balance was the passing of the Naval Expansion Act in May 1938 which authorised an additional 40,000 tons of new carrier construction. The immediate result was CV.8, USS *Hornet*, the third of the 'Yorktown' class which was launched on 14 December 1940. However, by the time *Hornet* was laid down in September 1939, Japan had already launched *Shokaku* on 1 June 1939, the first of a pair of excellent fast carriers with a displacement of 25,675 tons, a speed of 34 knots and an air group of 84 aircraft. *Shokaku*'s sister-ship, *Zuikaku*, was launched in November 1939. With such sustained competition it was obvious that *Hornet* must be regarded as no more than a stop-gap.

Portside view of *Wasp* in 1942, by this time fitted with a masthead radar array. From this angle, *Wasp* looks far more like a scaled-down 'Yorktown' than an improved 'Ranger'. Despite her low speed and weak defensive armament, *Wasp* did sterling service in both the Mediterranean and Pacific theatres during her brief wartime career.

The US Navy needed a new breed of heavy carrier, and fast. If this was not forthcoming, the only alternative would be to build a large number of lighter carriers in the hope that quantity would outweigh quality.

A decision was eventually taken to build a new class of heavy carrier, a decision which arguably did more to ensure Japan's defeat between 1942 and 1945 than the decision to develop an atomic bomb. It was, moreover, the earliest long-term American preparation for possible involvement in a future war. Planning for 'CV.9' began in July 1939, two months before the outbreak of war between Germany, Poland, Britain and France and the United States' proclamation of neutrality toward that conflict. By January 1940, six plan-

ning variants had been put forward for the new carrier, ranging from an improved 'Yorktown' of 20,400 tons to a far more ambitious 26,000-ton 'CV.9F'.

More planning went into these 'CV.9' variants than had been the case with any previous American fleet carriers. 'CV.9' and her successors were earmarked for the Pacific. Their design criteria therefore laid stress on increased fuel storage, both for the ships and for the thirstier, heavier new types of naval monoplane aircraft under development, and maximum cruising economy to cope with the vast distances involved in Pacific operations. Paradoxically, it was the disastrous summer of 1940 in Europe — the fall of France and the apparently imminent fall of Britain — which really got the development of the Pacific-destined CV.9 class carriers under way. There seemed every prospect that the German conquest of the entire Atlantic coastline of Europe, from the French Pyrenees to the Norwegian North Cape, would turn the eastern Atlantic into a German lake. The need for

a powerful US Atlantic Fleet, which could be kept strong without imperilling American naval interests in the Pacific, was paramount. On 20 July 1940, President Roosevelt signed the vital Two-Ocean Navy Bill. This was a rapid successor to the Eleven Percent Fleet Expansion Bill which had removed the self-imposed tonnage restriction of the 1938 Naval Expansion Act. The Eleven Percent Expansion Bill had ordered three 27,100 ton carriers, CVs.9, 10, and 11, and the Two-Ocean Navy Bill ordered another eight. Such was the inception of the superb 'Essex' class fleet carriers, the ships which were to carry the US Navy to victory in the Pacific War.

But it would take two more years before the first of the new breed was launched; and for these years the US Navy had no choice but to rely on the six fleet carriers it already had in service and to hasten the completion of *Hornet*. However, this total of seven American carriers, which included the lightweight *Ranger* and *Wasp*, had to be divided between the Atlantic and Pacific commands. When Japan

H-385   NO. 68.
U.S.S. HORNET (CV 8)
(AFTER COMMISSIONING)
STERN - LOOKING FORWARD

made her bid for the mastery of the Pacific in December 1941, the Japanese Combined fleet included a total of nine carriers of all types. Unrestricted by the need to deploy their forces for a 'two-ocean' conflict, the Japanese were therefore guaranteed a decisive carrier supremacy at the outset of the Pacific War.

The carrier balance, 7 December 1941

When Japan attacked Pearl Harbor on 7 December 1941, the Japanese Combined Fleet's carrier force consisted of six 'heavies' (*Kaga*, *Akagi*, *Soryu* and her improved 'big sister' *Hiryu*, *Shokaku* and *Zuikaku*) and three lightweights (*Hosho*, *Ryujo*, and *Zuiho*, the latter a conversion from a fast submarine tender completed in December 1940). The US Navy's carrier force consisted of five 'heavies' (*Lexington*, *Saratoga*, *Yorktown*, *Enterprise* and *Hornet*) and two lightweights

(*Ranger* and *Wasp*). Only three were stationed in the Pacific, *Lexington* and *Enterprise* with the battle fleet at Pearl Harbor, and *Saratoga* at San Diego, California.

Thus, even if American Naval Intelligence had been completely aware of the Japanese plan to attack Pearl Harbor with all six fleet carriers, and if *Lexington*, *Saratoga* and *Enterprise* had been concentrated at Pearl Harbor to intercept the attack, the US Navy's carrier force would still have been outnumbered by two to one. Moreover, these are the comparatively kindly odds, expressed merely in numbers of enemy carriers. When the different classes of carrier aircraft are taken into account, the Japanese Navy had an overall advantage in quality as well as quantity. The two navies were comparatively well matched in dive-bombers. The Douglas SBD Dauntless had a slightly greater range and heavier bomb-load than the sturdy, fixed under-carriage Aichi D3A 'Val'. It was a different story with level torpedo-bombers. The lumbering Douglas TBD-1 Devastator torpedo-

Stern view of the brand-new *Hornet* (CV.8) at the time of her commissioning in November 1941 — less than three weeks before Pearl Harbor. This is a particularly good demonstration of how the hangar deck and flight-deck formed a separate box structure above the main hull.

bomber was slow and woefully lacking in defensive armament; the Nakajima B5N 'Kate' was superior in every way. Moreover, the Japanese trump was the Mitsubishi A6M2 *Zero-Sen*, codenamed 'Zeke', whose American opposite number in December 1941 was the Grumman F4F Wildcat.

The Zero lacked such refinements as armour plate for the pilot or self-sealing fuel tanks; when hit, it tended to crumple like tissue-paper or explode in a ball of flame. Its engine, the 950 hp Nakajima Sakae 12, was also less powerful than the 1200 hp Pratt & Whitney Twin Wasp of the Wildcat. But the Zero's twin 7.7 mm machine-guns were powerfully supplemented by two 20 mm wing cannon, enabling the Zero to kill at a greater distance than the Wildcat with its four .50-

Hornet at sea with the Atlantic Fleet in December 1941.
She followed *Yorktown* to the Pacific after *Saratoga* was
crippled in a submarine attack on 11 January 1942, and
immediately began training for the 'Special Aviation
Project', the raid on Tokyo at long range with Army
B-25 bombers.

inch machine-guns. To make sure of a kill,
Wildcat pilots had to get in close, and this was
far easier said than done. Robust though it
was, the tubby Wildcat had a loaded deadweight of 7002 lbs to the Zero's 5150 lbs, and
the resultant advantage in power-to-weight
ratio made the Zero one of the most ma-
noeuverable and elusive fighters of World
War II. So far as generalisations can be
made, a good Wildcat pilot had an excellent chance of shooting down an average Zero
pilot, but with two pilots of equal flying ability the Zero pilot had a built-in advantage
every time. Moreover, in December 1941, as a

result of nearly five years of unbroken combat
experience in China, the Japanese Navy had
far more battle-crafty fighter pilots in its carrier air groups than the US Navy. In contrast
to the inappropriate training and combat un-
awareness of US Navy aircrews, initially, at
least, it was the quality of training and the degree of experience of its aircrews which gave
the Japanese Navy the decisive advantage.

In the light of this analysis, it is hard to see
how anything but disaster could have befallen
the American carriers and their airmen had
Lexington and *Enterprise* been despatched to
intercept the Japanese air strikes against Pearl
Harbor on 7 December 1941. As it was, the
leisurely and belated American move towards
placing all outlying Marine garrisons in the
central Pacific on a proper war footing had left
Lexington and *Enterprise* most providentially
dispersed. Both had been sent out only days

before the Japanese attack to ferry aircraft to
the Marines on Midway, the westernmost
outlier of the Hawaiian Island chain 1136
from Pearl Harbor, and to Wake, 1300 miles
south-west of Midway.

Of the two ships, *Enterprise* was closest to
the Japanese fleet. Flying the flag of Vice-
Admiral William Halsey, she was only 24
hours' steaming from Pearl Harbor, home-
ward bound after delivering the twelve Wildcats of Marine Fighting Squadron VMF-211
to Wake on 4 December. *Enterprise*'s air
group was expected to arrive over Pearl Harbor that morning, which was one reason why
the approaching Japanese first wave retained
complete surprise until the first bombs
actually fell. In fact, Ensign Manoel Gonzales,
flying a reconnaissance patrol from *Enterprise*,
had already arrived over Oahu, but the
oncoming Zeros hacked him down before he

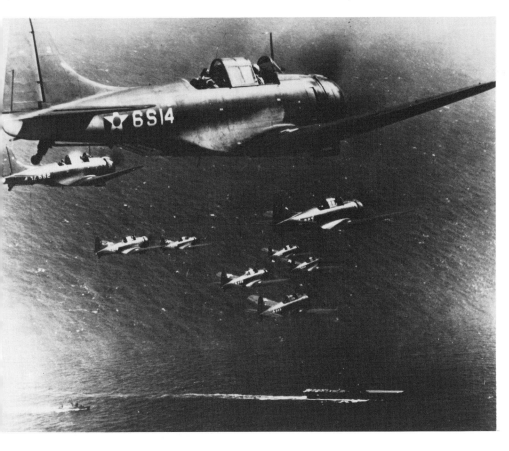

could alert Pearl Harbor. Horrified listeners in the control room of *Enterprise* picked up his last despairing message: 'Don't shoot. I'm American. Christ!'

Lexington was still over 1200 miles away, completing her delivery of a squadron of obsolete Vought-Sikorsky SB2U Vindicator dive-bombers to Marine bomber squadron VMSB-241 on Midway. Though *Enterprise* was less than 200 miles from Pearl Harbor, there was no chance of her fighters intervening. During the devastating attack by the Japanese first wave between 0753–0825 hours only seven land-based American fighters managed to take-off, and six were shot down. The Japanese second wave, also immune from molestation by *Enterprise*'s fighters, attacked at 0840 and withdrew just before 1000. By this time *Enterprise* was within easy range of a third Japanese strike, but fortunately the Japanese pilots who had shot down Gonzales had not identified his aircraft as being carrier-based. Such confirmation that an American carrier was in the offing might possibly have induced Vice-Admiral Chuichi Nagumo, commanding the Japanese force, to launch a search-and-strike force against *Enterprise*. However, he was already acutely aware that the two American carriers were 'out there somewhere', intact and able to counterattack. Content with the massive damage already inflicted at Pearl Harbor, Nagumo withdrew

after the last aircraft of the second wave had landed-on.

Only 29 Japanese aircraft had been lost out of the 354 which had taken part in the attack. This was negligible compared to the American losses: eight battleships and three cruisers sunk or damaged and 150 aircraft of all types destroyed or damaged, of which the most serious loss was all but two of the 33 PBY long-range reconnaissance flying-boats based on Oahu. Total American casualties, service and civilian, came to 2403 killed and 1178 wounded. One crumb of comfort to the Americans — a very small crumb — was the complete failure of an intended simultaneous attack by Japanese midget submarines. All five midgets involved in the attack were lost, three of them sunk by American destroyers. Three days later, *I-170*, one of the 'mother-subs' which had carried the midgets to within striking range of Pearl Harbor, was caught on the surface and sunk as she was finishing her patrol off Hawaii and starting the long passage home. The executioners of *I-170* were aircraft from *Enterprise*, winning their first battle honour of the war.

Nagumo had made his decision to withdraw in the teeth of urgings from his staff for a third strike at Pearl Harbor. This could well have destroyed the still-intact docking and repair facilities of the fleet base and, above all, the fuel storage depot with its 4.5 million barrels

of fuel oil. If the latter priceless asset had gone up in flames on 7 December 1941, the US Navy would have had no alternative to abandoning Pearl Harbor as a fleet base and pulling back the surviving units of the US Pacific Fleet to the West Coast. It may, therefore, be said that *Lexington* and *Enterprise*, though playing no tactical part in the Pearl Harbor tragedy, nevertheless won the US Navy's first *strategic* victory of the war. They did this in the classic role of an intact 'fleet in being', whose mere existence deters the enemy from achieving his full objective.

However, in the immediate aftermath of 'the Pearl Harbor attack there was certainly no American inclination to read any kind of victory into the events of 7 December 1941. If it was true that the Japanese had failed to destroy the entire US Pacific Fleet — apart from *Lexington*, *Enterprise* and *Saratoga* there was still sixteen cruisers and 40 destroyers in being — the US Pacific Fleet had unquestionably been deprived of offensive capability against the Japanese Combined Fleet. There could be no possibility of powerful American naval countermoves against the unfolding Japanese assaults on Guam in the Marianas, the Philippines or the Dutch East Indies. All other considerations apart, a total of 208 American naval and Army Air Forces reconnaissance, fighter and strike aircraft had been destroyed in the two Japanese attacks on Pearl Harbor. Until replacement aircraft could be ferried out to Oahu, the only effective air cover of the Hawaiian Islands would have to be provided by the air groups of *Lexington*, *Enterprise* and *Saratoga*, the latter carrier being immediately transferred to Pearl Harbor from San Diego.

The fall of Wake

Unjustly though predictably, one of the first results of the Pearl Harbor disaster was the appointment of a new Commander-in-Chief Pacific Fleet (CINCPAC). Admiral Husband E. Kimmel was cast in the role of chief scapegoat for his fleet's unpreparedness when the Japanese struck. Kimmel's misfortunes, however, did not prevent him from swiftly diagnosing the new strategic imperatives — or from doing everything in his power to exploit the one bright gleam on the horizon in the first week after Pearl Harbor, the superb defence against overwhelming force put up by the Marine garrison of Wake.

Although Wake's solitary Wildcat squadron was reduced to four aircraft by Japanese attacks on the first day of the war, the Marines succeeded in beating off the first Japanese landing attempt on 11 December 1941 with heavy losses to the would-be invaders. A Marine artillery battery sank the destroyer *Hayate*, the first Japanese warship loss of the war. One of the surviving four Wildcats, all of which were pressed into service as fighter-bombers, blew the destroyer *Kisagari* out of the water with an improvised 'bombload' of depth charges. Against the unending catalogue of Allied land, sea and air disasters stretching from Malaya to Pearl Harbor, the exploits of the Marines of Wake seemed to offer the chance of at least one early rally against the Japanese offensive. As soon as *Saratoga* arrived from the States, Kimmel assembled the strongest relief force he could. This he entrusted to Rear-Admiral Frank Jack Fletcher in *Saratoga* — whose reinforced air group included a replacement Wildcat squadron for the Wake garrison — with three heavy cruisers and nine destroyers.

Kimmel's spirited reaction was a long shot, in more ways than one. Wake lay 2860 miles from Pearl Harbor, deep in enemy territory, and the precise Japanese strength was unknown. The distance problem was compounded by the fact that the only available oiler to accompany Fletcher's relief force had a miserable top speed of 12 knots, and speed was of the essence. By 22 December, when the relief force was only 515 miles from Wake, the garrison's fuel was all but used up and all workshops had been destroyed, together with over half the vehicles and equipment. A fresh Japanese invasion force had sailed from Kwajalein, escorted by two of the veteran carriers of the Pearl Harbor attack, *Soryu* and *Hiryu*. US Naval Intelligence was unaware of this, and of the fact that for the moment four Japanese cruisers were lying east of Wake, wide open to attack by *Saratoga*'s aircraft. Fletcher's reconnaissance patrols, however, failed to detect this tempting target. He has been bitterly criticized for taking the whole of 22 December in steaming slowly north, refuelling his ships after their 2300-mile voyage from Pearl Harbor; but even if he had known that two Japanese fleet carriers were in the offing, he could hardly have done otherwise.

In any event, by the time Fletcher's task force headed back towards Wake on 23 December it was too late. Shortly after midnight the Japanese had established a secure beachhead on Wake and by sunrise over 1000 Japanese troops were ashore, covered by aircraft from *Soryu* and *Hiryu*. The surviving

Marines — there had never been more than 449 of them, ground and air, gallantly assisted by a handful of armed civilians — formed a last defence perimeter, but nothing could avert the inevitability of their surrender on 24 December. Even if, on 23 December, *Saratoga*'s airmen had by some miracle destroyed both *Soryu* and *Hiryu* and restored American air superiority over Wake, a full-dress opposed landing would still have had to be made to eject the Japanese.

Fletcher, however, was never required to make this decision to attempt the impossible. Since the relief force had sailed, Kimmel had been replaced as acting CINCPAC by Admiral William S. Pye, pending the formal assumption of the Pacific command by Admiral Chester Nimitz. It was Pye and not Fletcher who took the hard decision to abandon Wake, ordering the relief force to withdraw on 23 December. As with Fletcher's decision to spend 22 December refuelling, Pye's recall order has always been open to condemnation on the grounds of caution; and there can be no denying that the US Navy was left with a bitter sense of shame at having left the Marines of Wake in the lurch, but it must be judged the right decision, tragic though the circumstances were. If Fletcher had been ordered to press on with the relief attempt, the outcome would almost certainly have been the loss of one of the priceless capital ships on which the Pacific Fleet was now forced to rely: the fleet carriers. Nor was Fletcher's vain foray a complete waste of time — far from it. Invaluable lessons were learned in this first American carrier operation of the war, such as the need for constant long-range air reconnaissance and for high speed supply ships to accompany carrier task forces.

First carrier raids, February–March 1942

Admiral Chester Nimitz took over as CINC-PAC on 31 December 1941, just over three weeks after the attack on Pearl Harbor. His orders from the Commander-in-Chief US Navy (CINCUS; later COMINCH), Admiral Ernest J. King, amounted to 'hold what you've got and hit them when you can.' The immediate objective was to keep open sea communications with Australia by holding a line stretching south from Midway to Samoa, Fiji and Brisbane while, hopefully, the separate American/British/Dutch/Australian ('ABDA') command beat off the multi-fingered Japanese clutch at the Dutch East Indies. The first clear sign that the amazingly ambitious Japanese offensive plans included the isolation of Australia came on 20–23

January 1942 when Nagumo's carriers covered the conquest of New Britain and New Ireland, east of New Guinea. Rapidly setting up a new air/naval base at Rabaul in New Britain, the Japanese prepared to invade New Guinea.

Meanwhile, in the first week of the New Year, *Yorktown* had joined the Pacific Fleet via the Panama Canal and was immediately put to work with her sister-ship *Enterprise* escorting a troop convoy to Samoa. *Yorktown*'s arrival gave Nimitz the fleet carriers for four separate task forces, but this was immediately cut to three. On 11 January 1942, *Saratoga* was badly damaged by a torpedo from a Japanese submarine, 500 miles southeast of Pearl Harbor. It was necessary to send her 'Stateside' for extensive repairs at Bremerton Navy Yard, Puget Sound. While these repairs were being made the opportunity was taken to upgrade her anti-aircraft battery, replacing her obsolete 8-inch turrets with 5-inch dual purpose (DP) guns in twin mountings. This prolonged repair and refit kept *Saratoga* out of the dramatic carrier operations of April, May and June 1942 but made her a far more effective fighting unit when she rejoined the Fleet in July.

Thus, Nimitz was again left with only three single-carrier task forces for his first attempts to hit back at the Japanese. Task Fource 8 (TF.8) was commanded by Halsey, in *Enterprise*; TF.17 was commanded by Fletcher, who transferred to *Yorktown* after *Saratoga*'s mishap; and TF.11 was commanded by Rear-Admiral Wilson A. Brown, in *Lexington*. It was hardly to be expected that hit-and-run raids carried out by single-carrier air groups had a chance of halting the Japanese advance, but Nimitz never believed that they would. His immediate objective, after the traumatic shock of the Pearl Harbor attack, was to give his carrier men maximum combat experience in the shortest possible time — and to foster in his fleet a sense of being the equal of their enemy in all but numbers.

American carrier men looked back on these first missions as glorified training exercises but they had another, a deadly serious purpose. This was to give as much practical help as possible to the reeling Allied commands in the Philippines and Dutch East Indies by distracting the Japanese and showing that the US Pacific Fleet was still in the ring and a force to be reckoned with. To this end Nimitz directed his first carrier attacks against as wide a spread of targets as possible, from Marcus and Wake over 2500 miles south to New Britain and the Coral Sea.

The raids began on 1 February 1942, the first targets being Kwajalein Atoll in the northern Marshalls, which had been the

Japanese base for the assault on Wake two months before, and the Gilbert Islands to the south. Halsey's *Enterprise* group tackled Kwajalein and Fletcher and *Yorktown* attacked the Gilberts, while Brown's TF.11 hovered east of Wake in a role intended to be both supportive and diversionary. Though it was admittedly prudent at this time to hold TF.11 back as a floating reserve, it is also certain that more would have been achieved if *Lexington*'s air group had been added to one of the two raids. Both strikes encountered fierce resistance from Japanese shore-based aircraft, and the handful of Japanese shipping sunk and damaged was naturally exaggerated by the American press.

Much was learned right from the beginning — such as the disconcerting tendency of doomed Japanese aircraft to try to crash deliberately on to the biggest American warship within reach, and the tendency of returning pilots to exaggerate the damage they had

caused. Ship recognition, it was found, stood up badly to the excitement of combat, with minesweepers being claimed as destroyers and destroyers as cruisers. Tighter radio discipline was needed to reduce the chaotic babble crowding the frequencies in and immediately after action — less excited chat and more sober talk, expressed as economically as possible. Another urgent need was the electronic boon of IFF (Identification Friend or Foe) transmitters for American aircraft. Without IFF, it was virtually impossible for radar and fighter-directing personnel to tell the difference between 'friendlies' and hostile 'bogeys' in the milling blips on the screen.

Lexington's turn came three weeks later, when Brown led TF.11 against Rabaul — the first American carrier probe into the South-West Pacific. Once again, vigilant Japanese air reconnaissance heralded heavy land-based bombing attacks on the American task force. There was a hectic sequence of combats in

Aircraft ferry run: *Lexington* leaving San Diego, California, on 10 November 1941. Stacked right forward are sixteen obsolete Vought Sikorsky SB2U Vindicators, destined for the Marine garrison on Midway. This was the delivery mission which kept *Lexington* well outside the range of Nagumo's carrier aircraft when the Japanese struck at Pearl Harbor. The work put in by 'Lady Lex' in the last weeks of peace are attested by the weather-beaten state of her paintwork. She also wears a false bow-wave, a trick intended to fool attacking submarines that the target was travelling faster than it actually was.

which *Lexington*'s Wildcats showed the vital defensive function of a carrier's fighters, downing five 'Kates'. *Lexington*'s defensive success was genuine enough but it took all the sting out of the planned strike at Rabaul. It was small beer compared with the massive Japanese air attack on Darwin only two days before, undertaken by 135 land-based and carrier-based aircraft with four Japanese fleet carriers participating under Nagumo's command. The Darwin raid left five ships sunk,

Nimitz's cautious sequence of hit-and-run carrier strikes at the Japanese perimeter bases began on 1 February 1942 with attacks on the Gilbert and Marshall Islands. These are Dauntlesses of *Enterprise*'s air group, being armed for the strike at Kwajalein in the Marshalls. The slotted metal strips let into the flight-deck assisted the tying-down of aircraft for extra security.

three beached, extensive damage to the port installations and casualties of 240 dead and 150 wounded; but far worse was to follow. On 27 February the old *Langley*, one-time CV.1, was staunchly ferrying a much-needed consignment of crated P-40 fighters to Java when she was sunk off Tjilatjap, the victim of land-based bombers. By the next morning the last hope of staving off the fall of Java had vanished with the annihilation of the 'ABDA' cruiser/destroyer fleet in the Battle of the Java Sea.

None of these disasters diverted Nimitz from his cautious step-by-step policy of building up the expertise of his carrier task forces while trying to keep the Japanese guessing; he refused to throw away his carriers in futile interventionary gestures. Nimitz's next strikes were launched across the northern end of the prescribed defensive perimeter by Halsey with *Enterprise* against Wake on 24 February and Marcus on 4 March. The raid on Marcus, 3600 miles west of Pearl Harbor, was the deepest penetration yet of the theoretically 'Japanese-held' Central Pacific — another demonstration of the carrier's unique long-distance reach. However, within days the Marcus raid was followed, like Brown's foray against Rabaul, by another ominous Japanese advance. On 8 March, unopposed Japanese forces seized Salamaua and Lae on the mainland of New Guinea. From this new base area preparations were ordered for the capture of Port Moresby, less than 200 miles away across the towering, jungle-clad Owen Stanley Mountains. The latest Japanese thrust, now clearly aimed at the severance of the American-Australian supply sealane through the South-West Pacific, had begun.

The next American carrier strike was aimed squarely at the new menace: a combined raid on Salamaua and Lae on 10 March by *Lexington* and *Yorktown* under Fletcher, the first American carrier operation to put up a strike force 100 aircraft strong. The latest venture built on the experience gained by Brown's frustrated attack on Rabaul, doubling both the weight of the strike force and the fighter cover. Moreover, the operational flexibility of the aircraft-carrier was exploited to the maximum, making geography work in favour of the attackers. The strike was not launched directly from the seaward, as at Rabaul, but came in overland, across the Owen Stanleys, after a circling approach by the carriers

through the Coral Sea into the Gulf of Papua.

The Japanese had only committed a small force in the capture of Lae and Salamaua 48 hours before; indeed, the infantry battalion used in the landing was withdrawn with its troopships to Rabaul. As a result, the American attack force found that the cupboard was mostly bare, sinking only a transport and a minesweeper, but the promptitude of the attack, so soon after the Japanese landing, had one immediate result. To secure the Lae base area and step up air attacks on Port Moresby (the apparent source of the 10 March attack), the Japanese built up a handpicked wing of top-ranking Navy pilots at Lae, including the famous Zero ace Saburo Sakai. Forcing the Japanese Navy to dissipate its air strength in shore defence on the eve of its latest advance, inevitably at the expense, in the long run, of the Japanese carrier fleet, was the first indication that Nimitz's strategy was paying off. It was the second 'invisible victory', though barely recognized at the time, of the American fleet carriers. There was nothing invisible about the next American carrier attack, the fame of which went round the world: the raid on Tokyo of 18 April 1942.

The 'Doolittle Raid' on Tokyo

Apart from the obvious propaganda value to be reaped from bombing the Japanese capital, the whole point of the raid on Tokyo was that it would have been suicide for a conventional carrier force, which would have had to remain in the launching area to recover its aircraft

before withdrawing. For precisely this reason, it was the last move expected by the victory-drunk Japanese High Command. The raid was only made possible by the temporary marriage of long-range US Army Air Forces twin-engined bombers to the Navy's proven carrier manoeuvrability. North American B-25 Mitchell bombers could just take-off from a carrier steaming flat out into wind, but could never land-on again. After bombing their targets, the aircrews were to fly on to China and land in, or bale out over friendly territory. This would enable the launch carrier to retire at full speed as soon as the aircraft had taken off.

The plan was first mooted in the despondent days of January 1942 and *Hornet*, latest carrier arrival from the Atlantic, was held back on the West Coast to test the feasibility of launching B-25s from a carrier flight-deck. The project was relished by *Hornet*'s Captain Marc Mitscher, a veteran aviator who had been the first pilot to land on *Saratoga* after her commissioning in 1927. The bombing force commander was Lt-Col. 'Jimmy' Doolittle, America's outstanding post-1918 aviator and a winner of the Schneider Trophy for high-speed seaplanes, while the task force command was entrusted to Halsey. The project was given the green light after *Hornet*'s successful launch of two B-25s on 2 February 1942, but the bomber pilots still needed a month of intense training in the art of making short take-offs with bombed-up aircraft. *Hornet* finally sailed from San Francisco on 2 April with the attack force of sixteen B-25s lashed to her deck, ostensibly on a routine ferry mission to Pearl Harbor. Though *Hornet* was able to carry the entire attack force, this was only possible by keeping her own aircraft below, and she was therefore defenceless. *Enterprise* was attached to the task force to provide such air cover as might prove necessary. The two carriers made rendezvous north of Hawaii on 13 April.

The mission began on 15 April with the task force, designated TF.16, making a 1000-mile run west to a final refuelling rendezvous. Early on 18 April, TF.16 was approaching the planned launch point 500 miles east of the Japanese mainland when it was spotted. Luckily, the B-25s had been readied for launching later the same day. With surprise gone, Halsey and Doolittle agreed that no time should be lost in getting them airborne, even though this would mean adding some 200 miles to the flight.

As she headed into a 40-knot gale, *Hornet* was pitching violently and taking water over the forward end of the flight-deck on every downward lurch. No one who watched that launch ever forgot it. Doolittle, in the first B-25, only had 467 ft of flight-deck in which to reach flying speed. Each pilot had to try to time his run with an upward pitch, knowing full well that the smallest error or accident would result in disaster. When Doolittle led his men off at 0725 that morning, Halsey recalled that 'there wasn't a man topside in the Task Force who didn't help sweat him into the air.' But although 'one pilot hung on the brink of a stall until we nearly catalogued his effects', those frantic weeks of training had been well spent. It took precisely one hour and one minute to get all sixteen B-25s safely airborne, and another minute to change TF.16's course due east for a withdrawal at 25 knots.

After the sighting of TF.16 the Japanese believed that a carrier attack would probably be carried out the following day, but they neither imagined that twin-engined bombers could be flown from a carrier nor that a carrier strike on Tokyo would be launched from a distance nearly three times greater than that from which the Pearl Harbor attack had been launched in December 1941. Tokyo was therefore taken completely by surprise when Doolittle's bombers swept in to attack, thirteen of them hitting Tokyo and the other three scattering incendiaries over Kobe, Nagoya and Osaka. The American force was actually sighted by the aircraft taking the Japanese Prime Minister, General Hideki Tojo, on an inspection trip but not one of the B-25s was intercepted over Japanese soil, and all escaped to reach Chinese air space. Out of the 80 aircrew who made the raid 71 survived crash landings or parachute descents, and pursuit and capture by the Japanese.

In the exultant aftermath of the 'Doolittle

The men of the 'Doolittle Raid': US Army aircrew en route for Tokyo aboard *Hornet* in April 1942. In the foreground are Doolittle (left) and Captain Marc Mitscher of *Hornet* — the latter, a veteran Navy aviator, with his wings worn with particular pride in such company.

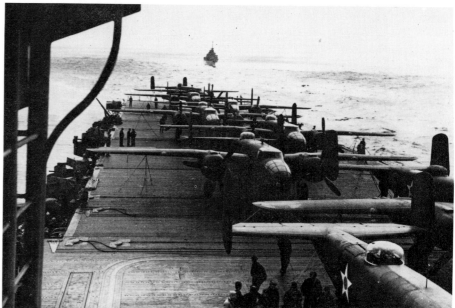

Opposite
The sixteen B-25s of Doolittle's raiding force, lashed down on *Hornet*'s flight-deck against the gales and high seas of the North Pacific. They rendered *Hornet* completely incapable of self-defence in the air. Combat air patrols were accordingly provided by her sister-ship *Enterprise*, flying the flag of Halsey as task force commander.

Raid', President Roosevelt, asked where on earth the bombers could have flown from to attack Tokyo, smilingly answered 'Shangri-La' — the mythical timeless land of James Hilton's *Lost Horizon*. The tag stuck, as was right and proper, because it perfectly summed up the eternal advantage of the carrier task force, that of operating from 'no fixed address'. The name *Shangri-La* was in due course assigned to one of the later 'Essex' class fleet carriers, CV.38, launched in February 1944. On the Japanese side after the raid, there were no such pleasantries. Slight though the aggregate damage had been, the fact that the Emperor's Palace had been exposed to enemy bombardment was intolerable to the Japanese mentality. Revenge and expiation became the order of the day for the Japanese Army and Navy High Commands. The result was a sequence of strategic blunders which, in less than two months, brought Japan's days of glory to an abrupt halt in the Battle of Midway.

The C-in-C of the Japanese Combined Fleet, Admiral Isoroku Yamamoto, had always known that the time must come for the US Pacific Fleet, unsupported by battleships after Pearl Harbor, to be brought to decisive action. As early as February 1942, Yamamoto's HQ staff began work on a plan to take Midway, a base which, as Yamamoto rightly calculated, the Americans could not afford to abandon as they had abandoned Wake. A Japanese attack on Midway would leave Nimitz with no option but to engage the greatly superior Combined Fleet in an all-or-nothing battle. However, the speed of the Allied collapse in Malaya, the Philippines and the Dutch East Indies had prompted a fatal over-confidence which the Japanese themselves later called 'Victory Disease'. Its first symptom was the attempt to isolate Australia by moving against New Britain and New Guinea before accounts had been settled with the US Pacific Fleet.

The shock of the Tokyo Raid led to the immediate acceptance of Yamamoto's Midway plan, code-named 'MI', but it did not cause the suspension of all operations in the South-West Pacific until 'MI' could be executed with the maximum force available. 'MI' was to go ahead *after* New Guinea had been cleared with the capture of Port Moresby — plan 'MO' — and after a foothold

Above
One of Doolittle's B-25s begins its take-off run, carefully timed to coincide with one of *Hornet*'s upward pitches. 'Tramlines' painted on the flight-deck helped pilots to correct yaw as they headed down the deck, approaching flying speed at full boost.

Below
Airborne. 'There wasn't a man topside who didn't help sweat him into the air', wrote Halsey later. 'One pilot hung on the brink of a stall until we nearly catalogued his effects.' An interesting detail, at right, is the old-style 'tin hat' still being worn at action stations in April 1942, before its replacement by the famous GI 'battle bowler'.

had been established in the Solomon Islands. In addition, the Japanese Army was still advancing north in Burma, over 4000 miles from New Guinea. This amounted to the most ambitious strategic over-reach since Napoleon had invaded Russia with one wing of his army while besieging Cadiz with the other.

As a further consequence of the decision to go ahead with 'MO', the use of Nagumo's carrier striking fleet in separate divisions, as had been done to make certain of Wake and to cover the subsequent conquest of the Dutch East Indies, would be further protracted. Nagumo's most dramatic flourish since Pearl Harbor had been a westward rampage through the Bay of Bengal (5–9 April), sinking two British cruisers and the carrier HMS *Hermes* and launching damaging air strikes on Ceylon and the Indian east coast. However, Nagumo's command had not been restored to the full concentration of six fleet carriers which had attacked Pearl Harbor, and his force remained dissipated for 'MO'. Only a single fleet carrier division, comprising *Shokaku* and *Zuikaku*, plus the light carrier *Shoho*, were assigned to cover the attack on Port Moresby. The odds against the American fleet were thus temporarily reduced to manageable proportions.

Another major Japanese mistake was their assumption that both 'MO' and 'MI' would enjoy the advantage of surprise, like the Pearl Harbor attack. In fact, US Naval Intelligence was steadily increasing its expertise in assessing probable future Japanese moves from radio intercepts. By mid-April the Combat Intelligence Unit in Pearl Harbor was able to assure COMINCH that the latest Japanese foray in the Indian Ocean did not herald a new Japanese offensive against Ceylon or India, nor were there any indications of an imminent invasion of Australia. The Japanese build-up for 'MO' had been detected, and CINCPAC had been assured that the next big push would be south-east of Rabaul. By 20 April, Nimitz was satisfied that Port Moresby was the main objective and that the Japanese would undertake a seaborne invasion through the Coral Sea. With *Hornet* and *Enterprise* still returning from the Tokyo Raid, Nimitz could only deploy *Lexington* and *Yorktown* for operations in the Coral Sea. Thus, for the first time, a forewarned US Navy carrier task force set out to frustrate a major Japanese invasion, still against superior odds but with the advantage of surprise. The confrontation in the Coral Sea produced the first carrier versus carrier battle in history.

This is Yokosuka Naval Air Base, one of the subsidiary
targets, seen from one of the B-25s during the 'Doolittle
Raid' — the supreme demonstration of carrier versatility
in the bitter spring of 1942. The raiders met with no
opposition because the Japanese had never counted on
twin-engined Army bombers being launched from
carriers. The actual damage inflicted by the Doolittle
Raid was trivial; what mattered was the traumatic shock
to Japanese morale, and leading to the confirmation of
the grandiose 'MI' plan to liquidate what was left of the
US Fleet at Midway.

Opposite
The last five left to go, seen from *Enterprise*. If any of
the B-25s had developed a fault before launch it would
have been ruthlessly ditched overside, but happily no
such drastic measure proved necessary.

Hornet returns in triumph to Pearl Harbor after the
'Doolittle Raid', the state of her paintwork speaking
volumes for the violence of the North Pacific seas.
Though the Raid was the first real gleam of American
success in the Pacific War, there was still a price to pay.
It prevented a full concentration of the US carriers
against the next Japanese in the South-West Pacific,
leaving only *Lexington* and *Yorktown* to fight the Battle
of the Coral Sea in the first week of May.

Search-and-strike: Dauntlesses, armed only with light bombs, are spotted 'prop to tailfin' aboard *Enterprise* (*above*) and *Yorktown* (*right*). On the leading aircraft the perforated dive-brakes, lowered when in the full bombing dive, can be clearly seen. These search missions were vital; during the first carrier-*versus*-carrier actions of May–June 1942, the Americans still had to learn the art of keeping the enemy's true position fixed and homing attack forces to the target.

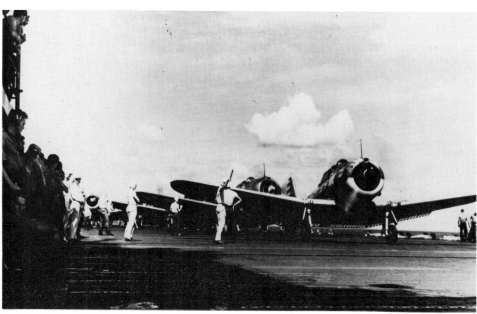

Battle of the Coral Sea

The 'MO' operations were entrusted to the 4th Fleet, based on Truk and Rabaul and commanded by Vice-Admiral Shigeyoshi Inouye, who in December had directed operations against Wake and Guam. For 'MO', 4th Fleet was reinforced by a scatter of units which had recently seen service in the Dutch East Indies and Indian Ocean. The value of these reinforcements was offset by the three objectives which 'MO' was confidently expected to achieve: first, the actual seaborne conquest of Port Moresby; second, the establishment of a seaplane base in the Louisiade Archipelago, 150 miles south-east of the 'tail' of New Guinea; third, the establishment of a seaplane base on Tulagi in the central Solomon Islands, 700 miles south-east of Rabaul. The capture of Port Moresby would push the Allies clean out of New Guinea, complete a chain of Japanese bases from Truk to New Guinea and lay open Australia's Queensland coast to direct air/sea attack. The new seaplane bases would broaden the foundation of subsequent Japanese advances south-east towards the Allied forward base at Nouméa in French New Caledonia, Fiji and Samoa. Their seizure at the outset of 'MO' would, it was hoped, distract the Allies and make it easier for the Port Moresby invasion force to achieve its objective.

The Japanese assumed that such American naval forces as might attempt a counterattack against 'MO' would be assisted by the 200-odd land-based aircraft operating from New Guinea and Australia. Japanese intelligence, however, believed that *Saratoga* was the only American carrier available for such a counterattack; she was, in fact, 7800 miles from Nouméa, completing her refit in Puget Sound. This fundamental miscalculation resulted in two Japanese fleet carriers being considered a sufficient allocation to the five 'MO' task forces, as follows:

Plan 'MO'

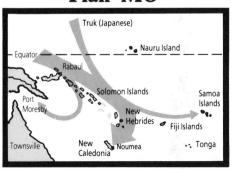

From Rabaul

Port Moresby Invasion Group (Rear-Admiral Kajioka) One cruiser, six destroyers, eleven transports plus minesweepers and oilers.

Tulagi Invasion Force One destroyers plus minelayers and transports.

From Truk

Covering Group (Rear-Admiral Goto) Light carrier *Shoho* and four heavy cruisers.

Support Force (Rear-Admiral Marushige) Seaplane-carrier *Kamikawa Maru* and two light cruisers.

Carrier Striking Force (Vice-Admiral Takagi) Fleet carriers *Shokaku* and *Zuikaku* plus two heavy cruisers.

The plan was to begin with the capture of Tulagi on 3 May 1942. The Moresby Invasion Force would then sail, covered by the warships of Goto and Marushige as it headed south through the Jomard Passage into the Coral Sea and 'round the corner' of New Guinea on its final approach to Port Moresby. Meanwhile, Marushige's force would set up the Louisiade seaplane base. It was expected that the Allies would detect these opening moves, and that a single American carrier task force would enter the Coral Sea to intervene. Any such intervention would be neatly caught in the rear by Takagi's two fleet carriers, which would enter the Coral Sea from the east after a wide circling approach south-eastward round the Solomon Islands.

In the light of recent experience, the plan was sound, though intricate. The Japanese had operated in this fashion with outstanding success for the past six months. But there was no provision for the unexpected. 'MO' calls to mind the Duke of Wellington's famous criticism of French strategy in the Peninsular War: that it was a very pretty harness until something snapped, when it became useless. Wellington preferred to use ropes, coping with setbacks by tying a knot and going on. 'MO' broke down under the unexpected stress of encountering double the enemy force which had been expected, and through lacking the flexibility and combat experience to cope with this predicament.

Forewarned by the decryptographists of the Pearl Harbor Combat Intelligence Unit, Nimitz acted on the assumption that the Japanese operation would start on or soon after 3 May, with Port Moresby as the ultimate Japanese objective. Therefore, he had time to concentrate his two available carrier task forces for a penetration of the Coral Sea from the east, even though, in mid-April, they were separated by some 4000 miles.

Fletcher's TF.17, with *Yorktown*, three cruisers, six destroyers and the fleet oiler *Neosho*, had been operating from Nouméa since the Salamaua/Lae raid in March. On 14 April, Nimitz sent TF.17 east to Tongatapu for 'upkeep' — replenishment, refuelling and repairs in preparation for battle. TF.11, with *Lexington*, two cruisers and four destroyers, had begun three weeks upkeep at Pearl Harbor at the end of March. On 3 April, TF.11 had been taken over by Rear-Admiral Aubrey W. Fitch, who took his force south-west from Pearl Harbor on 16 April. In total contrast to the intricacies of 'MO', Nimitz's plan was starkly simple. TF.17 and TF.11 were to rendezvous and operate in the Coral Sea from 1 May under Fletcher's overall command. Fletcher was left to assess the situation and act as he saw fit, his brief being to use his combined task forces as a 'flying wedge' to frustrate the latest Japanese move and inflict maximum damage on the Japanese fleet in the process.

Phase 1, 1–3 May 1942

According to plan, the two American task forces made rendezvous about 250 miles south-west of Espiritu Santo in the New Hebrides at 0630 on 1 May. As he took over tactical command of Fitch's force, Fletcher knew that the heavy cruiser *Chicago* and another destroyer were on their way to join him from Nouméa, but that another two days must pass before his final reinforcements joined up. These were the Australian cruisers *Hobart* and *Australia* and one American destroyer of TF.44, commanded by Rear-Admiral J. C. Crace, Royal Navy. Heading north from Sydney, TF.44 was under orders to join Fletcher in the Coral Sea by 4 May. Fletcher's immediate concern was refuelling, TF.17 from *Neosho*, TF.11 from *Tippecanoe*. TF.17 finished refuelling first, having had over 3000 miles less to steam on its approach to the rendezvous, but, even so, the process took up the whole of 2 May.

This was the day that the Tulagi Invasion Force sailed from Rabaul. It was detected by Australian-based aircraft flying over the Solomon Sea; Fletcher received these reports on the evening of 2 May, but they seemed to have little relevance to the expected Port Moresby Invasion Force. He therefore left TF.11 to complete fuelling, gave Fitch a rendezvous for the 4th, and set off north-west with TF.17 to bring the Solomons area within range of his own aircraft. By 0800 on 3 May the *Yorktown* and *Lexington* task forces were over 100 miles apart.

Fletcher was still out of carrier air reconnaissance range when, at 1900 on 3 May,

Coral Sea, Day 1, 7 May 1942: *Lexington*'s Dauntlesses are ranged forward after their triumphant return from sinking *Shoho*, the first Japanese carrier sunk in the war. Aircraft right forward already have their wings folded, ready to be struck down to the hangar deck.

Opposite top
Coral Sea, Day 2, 8 May 1942: *Shokaku* under attack, frantically zig-zagging at full speed to avoid *Yorktown*'s aircraft. Three bomb hits started a bad fire which prevent *Shokaku* from operating aircraft and effectively knocked her out of the battle; but this was speedily avenged by the explosive fate of *Lexington*.

Opposite below
Coral Sea, Day 2, 8 May 1942: *Lexington*'s ordeal begins. As shellbursts from her AA guns pepper the sky, an ominous gout of smoke and spray indicates a Japanese torpedo hit. In this attack *Lexington* took two torpedo hits, both on the port side; *Yorktown* in TF.17, from which this picture was taken, managed to evade all eight torpedoes aimed at her, due to her built-in manoeuvrability and the superb ship-handling of Captain Buckmaster.

Battle of the Coral Sea, 1-8 May 1942

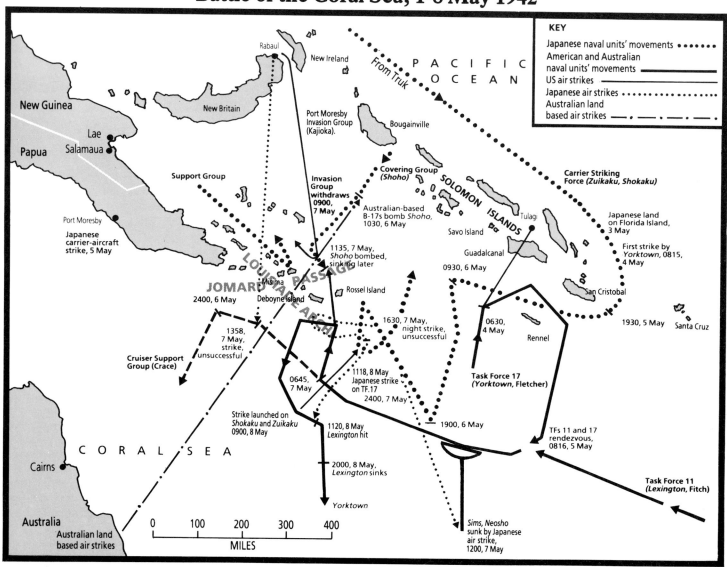

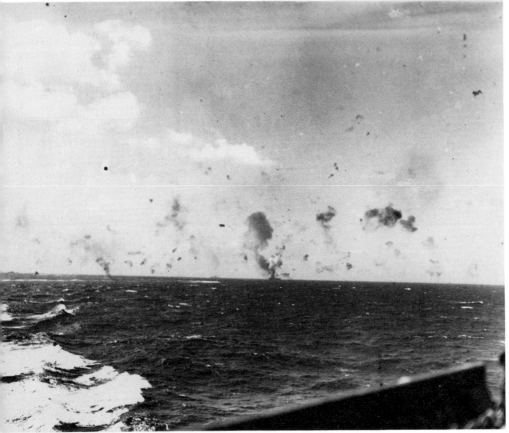

the long voyage south-east round the Solomons chain and was still north of Bougainville, northernmost island of the group. The 'MO' planners, assuming that the Tulagi invasion force would be left unmolested, had built in no defences against such a prompt American counter-strike. Neither side had counted on the fluky weather conditions prevailing in the Coral Sea that week. As it ran north, TF.17 passed under the northern fringe of a 100-mile wide cold front which screened the ships of the task force and the aircraft of the first American strike, launched at 0630 on the 4th, from Japanese air reconnaissance.

Yorktown's first strike consisted of twelve TBD Devastator torpedo-bombers and 28 SBD Dauntless dive-bombers. They went out without fighter escort; Fletcher, very much aware that TF.17 was out on a limb, prudently held back his eighteen Wildcats to fly combat air patrol (CAP) over *Yorktown*. The strike force enjoyed cloud cover until 20 miles from Tulagi, bursting out into clear sky to launch its attack from 0815. It was an exhilarating if confused attack, with excitement heightened by the absence of fighter opposition and the safe return to *Yorktown* of all aircraft by 0931. Unwittingly, Fletcher had swung a sledgehammer to crack a nut; but he was prevented from realizing this by his pilots' exaggerated reports of the damage inflicted and of the strength of the Japanese force. Bad ship recognition was again a problem, with landing-craft being mistaken for gunboats, minesweepers for troop transports and — worst of all — a minelayer for a light cruiser. In fact, the most powerful Japanese warship off Tulagi, the destroyer *Kikutsuki*, had been damaged so badly that she was abandoned, and three minesweepers had also been sunk; but it was a depressing score for an unopposed bombing attack 40 aircraft strong.

This false report of the Japanese strength at Tulagi and the damage inflicted prompted Fletcher to launch two more strikes from *Yorktown*. They went in around noon and at 1400. The result was two seaplanes and four landing-barges destroyed and a patrol boat damaged in exchange for one Devastator shot down, and two Wildcats lost in crash landings on Guadalcanal after losing their way on the flight back to *Yorktown*. The Wildcat pilots were picked up that night by the destroyer *Hammann*. By the evening of 4 May, however, Fletcher believed that *Yorktown*'s three strikes had sunk two destroyers, a freighter and four gunboats, leaving another destroyer and a seaplane-carrier damaged. He toyed briefly with the idea of sending in two cruisers to 'clean up the cripples' at dawn next day, but wisely stuck to his original plan. *Yorktown*

further land-based reports came in. Japanese forces were landing not only on Tulagi but on Florida Island in the south-eastern Solomons. Fletcher's immediate reaction was to steam through the night for a dawn strike by *Yorktown* at Tulagi, detaching *Neosho* and a destroyer. The latter were to rendezvous with Fitch and Crace at the arranged point; all ships would then head east to rejoin the *Yorktown* group 300 miles south of Guadalcanal on the 5th.

Phase 2, 4–6 May 1942

By dawn on 4 May Fletcher was poised to launch his first air strike against the Japanese invasion forces in the Solomons, and none of the 'MO' detachments could do anything to stop him. The forces of Goto and Marushige, having landed their troops on Tulagi, had fallen back to the north. They now prepared to cover the Port Moresby Invasion Force on its voyage south from Rabaul. Takagi, with *Shokaku* and *Zuikaku*, had only just started

With the Japanese attack over, repair crews get to work on *Lexington*'s damaged flight-deck. This hit, forward on the port side, exploded in an ammunition store for the 5-inch gun at left. The overall bomb damage was quickly repaired and *Lexington* began to recover her aircraft.

Opposite
The scene on *Lexington*'s flight-deck around 1500, shortly after the second big explosion. Smoke from the spreading internal fires filters ominously through the planking of the flight-deck, shrouding the Wildcats which had returned to apparent safety.

Lexington, with her air group back on board, apparently none the worse for the Japanese attacks and her two torpedo hits. This picture was taken around 1200, shortly before Commander Healy, the Damage Control Officer, reported that: 'We've got the torpedo damage temporarily shored up, the fires out, and soon will have the ship back on an even keel. But I would suggest, sir, that if you have to take any more torpedoes, you take 'em on the starboard side.' Minutes later, the first big internal explosion from accumulated gasoline fumes marked the beginning of the end.

and her group withdrew south, reaching the prearranged rendezvous with Fitch and Crace at 0815 on 5 May.

Unexpected though they had been, *Yorktown*'s attacks on Tulagi were taken by the Japanese as a welcome indication that the American mouse had entered the trap, and 'MO' proceeded according to schedule. Takagi's fleet carriers, which had increased speed when the news of the raids on Tulagi came in at noon on 4 May, rounded San Cristobal and

headed west into the Coral Sea at 1900 on 5 May 1942. The 5th and 6th also saw the Port Moresby Invasion Force sail for the Jomard Passage, Goto's force refuelling before heading south on its covering mission, and Marushige's force leaving the seaplane-carrier *Kamikawa Maru* at Deboyne island in the Louisiades before withdrawing northwest.

Fletcher spent 5 May and the morning of 6 May refuelling. There was still no clear-cut pattern to the air reconnaissance reports on

Japanese shipping movements which reached him on the 5 and 6 May, but by the evening of 6 May he could deduce, with fair certainty, that the Moresby Invasion Force had sailed from Rabaul. This would see it threading through the Jomard Passage on the 7 or 8 May. Fletcher therefore headed north-west at 1930 on 6 May to be in a postion to intercept by dawn on 7 May. He planned to entrust the destruction of the Moresby Invasion Force to his cruisers and destroyers,

keeping back only four destroyers to screen *Yorktown* and *Lexington*.

By thus dividing his forces, Fletcher planned to fulfil his mission of saving Port Moresby, and to cope with any attempt by the elusive Japanese carriers to intervene. The known prowess of Japanese surface warships was a very good reason for Fletcher to beef up his attack on the Japanese invasion force by committing all his cruisers. But what neither Fletcher nor any other carrier admiral knew — no such encounter ever having occurred before — was the inability of carrier aircraft to guarantee the safety of their own carriers in the teeth of heavy attacks by enemy carrier aircraft. A fundamental lesson learnt over the next few weeks was that a colossal volume of shipboard anti-aircraft fire of all calibres was needed to supplement the work of the carrier's combat air patrol fighters overhead. Right down to the last moments of the Pacific War three and a quarter years later, US warships would continue to augment their anti-aircraft fire-power in the certain knowledge that there could never be enough of it. That knowledge did not exist on the eve of the Coral Sea fight in early May 1942, when four destroyers with their puny anti-aircraft fire-power were considered adequate to screen a two-carrier task force. Fletcher can be criticised for not giving *Yorktown* and *Lexington* the benefit of his cruisers'

anti-aircraft fire-power, but it is hard to blame him for this omission, even with the benefit of hindsight.

By nightfall on 6 May, therefore, both the American and Japanese commanders were feeling that their respective plans were proceeding as hoped. The Japanese were in particularly good heart, because the news of the American surrender on Corregidor in the Philippines came through that day. The Moresby Force was standing on towards the Jomard Passage, with Goto and Marushige covering its flanks north-east and north-west of the new Japanese seaplane base established on Deboyne, but Takagi's fleet carriers missed a splendid chance on 6 May. As they pushed west into the Coral Sea to close the trap on Fletcher, *Shokaku* and *Zuikaku* were screened by the overcast of the cold front, while Fletcher's TF.17 lay refuelling in brilliant sunshine. Though the American and Japanese carrier task forces were only 70 miles apart at one point, neither side found the other with reconnaissance flights on 6 May. The gap opened rapidly after Takagi turned north on the evening of 6 May to reinforce the cover for the Moresby Invasion Force.

Fletcher had meanwhile sent *Neosho* south, escorted by the destroyer *Sims*, to take up position at TF.17's next fuelling rendezvous.

Carrier action, Day 1, 7 May 1942

The carrier actions of 7–8 May were governed by a sequence of mistakes and misjudgments on both sides, with bad ship recognition by Japanese and American pilots playing a baneful role. The first of these mistakes was Japanese, and derived from a reconnaissance flight to the south launched by Takagi's carriers at 0600 on 7 May.

At 0736 Takagi and his carrier division commander, Rear-Admiral Hara, heard exactly what they wanted to hear: the sighting report of a single American carrier and a single cruiser in company, bearing south-south-east. This was precisely the sort of lightweight American carrier force which the 'MO' plan had hoped to trap, and Hara ordered an all-out air strike to liquidate it. The 'carrier' and 'cruiser' were, however, *Neosho* and *Sims*, both of which were overwhelmed by Hara's aircraft, 25 level bombers and 56 dive-bombers. Heroic evasive action enabled *Sims* to survive until noon, when she was hit squarely by three 500-lb bombs, but *Neosho* was set ablaze after taking seven bomb hits. Like all tankers, she died hard, and remained afloat until 11 May when the last of her crew were taken off and she was scuttled. The fact remained that for the entire forenoon of 7 May Hara had committed the bulk of his air-strike forces to a minor target. This could have left *Shokaku* and *Zuikaku* wide open to

As *Lexington*'s fires pass out of control, severing communications and silencing her power rooms, the attendant destroyers move close alongside to port and starboard to help take off non-essential crewmen and provide power for fire-fighting.

attack by *Lexington* and *Yorktown*, had it not been for the fact that Fletcher had made exactly the same kind of mistake as Hara.

At 0645 Fletcher had ordered Crace's cruiser force to press on to the north-west, completing the interception and destruction of the Moresby Invasion Force. He himself headed north with *Yorktown* and *Lexington*, intending to bear the brunt of Japanese air attacks and so give Crace the best possible chance of success. Given the enormity of the stakes — the fatal weakening of what was left of the US Pacific Fleet which would have resulted from the loss of half its remaining fleet carrier strength — Fletcher's decision was courageous in the extreme. Though he was operating on the slenderest of margins, because of the lack of accurate information, Fletcher's courage was repaid with good luck. While Takagi's fleet carriers squandered their efforts on *Neosho* and *Sims*, the formidable Japanese land-based air forces concentrated their attentions on Crace's cruisers, which were spotted at 0810. By the end of

7 May, Crace's force had survived three heavy Japanese bombing and torpedo attacks, plus a fourth from US Army Air Forces B-17s which had mistaken Crace's ships for Japanese. These two Japanese distractions left Fletcher's fleet carriers free to destroy the western jaw of the pincers which had been intended to destroy him, enjoying, in the process, yet another generous slice of luck.

A Japanese seaplane spotted TF.17 at 0810, five minutes before *Yorktown*'s reconnaissance aircraft sighted units of the Japanese covering forces. As Crace's force had already been sighted to the west, the appearance of this American carrier task force was deeply worrying to Inouye. At 0900 Inouye ordered the Moresby Invasion force, which was preparing to run the Jomard Passage, to turn back until the American carriers had been dealt with. For the first time in the Pacific War, the mere presence of American fleet carriers had forced the postponement of a Japanese invasion.

At 0815, just 39 minutes after the *Neosho* and *Sims* had been reported by Japanese air reconnaissance as an aircraft-carrier and a cruiser, one of *Yorktown*'s reconnaissance aircraft reported 'two carriers and four heavy cruisers' 225 miles to the north-west. This was a double error, the result of a coding

mistake by the American pilot, who had intended to report 'two heavy cruisers and two destroyers'; but the ships in question were actually two light cruisers and a couple of gunboats from Marushige's Support Force. The mistake caused Fletcher to launch 93 aircraft between 0926 and 1030, keeping back 47 Wildcats for the defence of *Yorktown* and *Lexington*. He was horrified when, just after the strike aircraft had left, his scouts returned and the coding error was revealed; but he left his strike in the air, hoping that more worthwhile targets would come its way. His faith was soon rewarded.

Just after 1100 Lieutenant-Commander Hamilton, leading one of *Lexington*'s Dauntless squadrons, sighted a carrier with cruisers and destroyers in company 35 miles southeast of the original target location. This was *Shoho* and the main body of Goto's Covering Force. *Lexington*'s air group commander, Commander William B. Ault, led his whole force into an overwhelming attack from 1110 to 1125, when *Yorktown*'s aircraft joined the fray. The lightweight *Shoho* never stood a chance. She only had an air group of 30 aircraft and five of these, caught on deck, were blown clean over the side in the first attack. For the Zeros which did get airborne

Crewmen swarm over the side after Captain Sherman's
'Abandon Ship' order at 1710.

The Captain and the last men to leave were still aboard
when this enormous explosion shattered the flight-deck
at 1753.

Lexington survivors are hauled from the water.
Mercifully, there was no great loss of life during the
explosions and fires in the wake of the Japanese attack.

there were simply too many attackers; only
one American bomber was shot down, while
another was badly damaged and had to force-
land on Rossel Island in the Louisiades. In a
sky filled with American aircraft, the eighteen
Wildcat pilots escorting the Dauntlesses and
Devastators tore into the Zeros and shot eight
of them down while *Shoho*, after taking
thirteen bomb and seven torpedoes hits in
just over 20 minutes, sank just after 1135.
Over the airwaves came the exultant voice
of Lieutenant-Commander R. E. Dixon,
Lexington's other Dauntless squadron commander: 'Scratch one flat-top! Dixon to
carrier, scratch one flat-top!'

This was not the only message picked up by
TF.17, which also detected Goto's frantic

reports to Takagi. By the mid-afternoon of
7 May Fletcher knew that the Japanese fleet
carriers now had his position, while he was
still ignorant of their's. The day's operations
had carried TF.17 back into the wide belt of
poor weather shrouding the northern Coral
Sea with low cloud interspersed with dense
rain squalls, adding to the difficulty of hunting for the Japanese carriers. Fletcher's thinking would have been greatly helped if he could
have known that the Moresby Invasion Force
had been temporarily withdrawn, but he
could only assume that it was still holding its
course for the Jomard Passage and New
Guinea. He therefore decided against searching for the Japanese carriers and headed
west for the night of 7–8 May, still intent on
frustrating the Moresby invasion at all costs.

Takagi and Hara, however, decided on an
immediate strike at the American carrier
force, accepting the dangers involved in

battle-tired aircrew having to land-on after
dark. The 27 most experienced strike aircraft crews, flying twelve 'Vals' and fifteen
'Kates', were launched without fighter escort
at 1630. Conditions were atrocious, with
dense overcast and rain squalls, and as nightfall drew on the dispirited Japanese force
jettisoned its bombs and torpedoes and turned
for 'home'. The return track took the
Japanese aircraft, without fighters for defence
or weapons to attack, right over TF.17. Once
again the Wildcats of TF.17's combat air
patrol tore in to attack, shooting down eight
'Kates' and one 'Val'. This one-sided battle
completed the disorientation of the Japanese
pilots; six of them joined the landing circle of
Wildcats waiting to land on *Yorktown*, to be
driven off into the gloom by AA fire. Only
seven Japanese aircraft returned to their carriers, the remaining eleven having helplessly
'splashed' when their fuel ran out.

Thus presented with a tally of unabated losses without the enemy's ships having suffered a scratch, Takagi and Hara contemplated the most humiliating day in the history of the Japanese Navy and looked for revenge on the morrow. To prevent Takagi's hands being tied by concern for the Moresby Invasion Force (dependent on Takagi for air cover since the loss of *Shoho*), Inouye ordered the Moresby invasion to be postponed for two days. No other consideration was to take precedence over the location and destruction of the American carriers on 8 May.

Carrier action, Day 2, 8 May 1942

The alertness of the rival carrier forces by the early morning of 8 May was shown by the rapidity with which they found each other. *Shokaku* and *Zuikaku* were sighted at 0815, *Yorktown* and *Lexington* 23 minutes later. Admiral Fitch, in command of TF.17's air operations, began launching at 0900: nine Devastators, 24 Dauntlesses and six Wildcats from *Yorktown*, followed ten minutes later by twelve Devastators, 22 Dauntlesses and nine Wildcats from *Lexington*. The Japanese strike force launched by Fitch's opposite number, Hara, was already in the air: eighteen 'Kates', 33 'Vals' and eighteen Zeros. Unlike the Americans, whose two air groups operated separately, the Japanese strike force was compact and much better balanced, with the vulnerable torpedo-bombers protected by a higher percentage of fighters (a Zero strength of 26 per cent, against a Wildcat strength of only 18 per cent). The Japanese force was also much better directed to the target, the original target location followed by *Lexington*'s pilots proving to be 45 miles out. These advantages did much to compensate for the weaker overall strength of the Japanese strike, caused by the squandering of aircraft in the fiasco of the previous evening.

Once again *Yorktown*'s aircraft drew first blood, but they only attacked at 1057 after a 23-minute wait for the slower Devastators to arrive on the scene. This delay had serious consequences, giving *Shokaku* time to get more Zeros airborne while *Zuikaku* vanished into the shelter offered by a timely rain squall. When the Devastators attacked, *Shokaku* evaded all nine of their torpedoes, which were not only slow-running but had a distressing tendency not to explode on impact. The Dauntlesses fared better. Two bomb hits were scored on *Shokaku*, one destroying an after repair compartment and another, forward on the starboard bow, starting a fuel fire. *Lexington*'s aircraft had meanwhile become separated during their search for the Japanese force amid dense rain clouds. The 22 Dauntless dive-bombers from *Lexington* did not find the Japanese, their absence reducing *Lexington*'s contribution to eleven Devastators and the four reconnaissance Dauntlesses of Commander Ault's section. Despite being mutilated by the absence of its dive-bombing component, *Lexington*'s air group attacked through the overcast at 1107. Its nine Wildcats were out-numbered by *Shokaku*'s Zeros and, despite gallant efforts, failed to keep the Japanese fighters off the tails of the vulnerable Devastators. Five Devastators and three Wildcats were shot down. As with *Yorktown*'s Devastators, no torpedo hits were scored, but one of the light bombs carried by Ault's Dauntlesses did strike home, adding substantially to *Shokaku*'s damage, at the cost of two Dauntlesses shot down.

Shokaku had lost 108 men killed and, though her fires were soon under control, she was unable to launch aircraft. Takagi, therefore, detached *Shokaku* at 1300, after most of her aircraft had been transferred to *Zuikaku*. Though *Lexington*'s excited airmen reported that *Shokaku* was sinking — 'on fire and settling fast' — she had not been holed below the waterline, and she eventually struggled home to Japan after a hazardous voyage via Truk.

While the *Yorktown* and *Lexington* air groups were engaged in knocking *Shokaku* out of the battle, Takagi's airmen were inflicting the Japanese counter-strike 180 miles to the south. To American carrier men whose only sight of their Japanese counterparts had been during the unwonted fiasco of the previous evening, the deadly expertise displayed in the attacks on TF.17 on the morning of 8 May was a revelation. Apart from their superior combat experience, the Japanese airmen had three telling advantages. The first was the suicidal bravery of the scout pilot who had sighted TF.17 earlier that morning, Warrant Officer Kanno. Instead of nursing his last drops of fuel in an attempt to return to *Shokaku* and *Zuikaku*, Kanno flew alongside the strike commander's plane and guided the whole force through to TF.17's actual position. He did this in the certain knowledge that he would never regain his carrier, but would end as a lonely casualty in the sea, far away from any hope of rescue. The second advantage was TF.17's southerly position, well out of the cold front under clear skies, in excellent visibility. The third advantage was the excellence of the Japanese torpedoes, faster-running than any of the US Navy's slow practice torpedoes on whose performance American evasive manoeuvres were based.

The Japanese attacks began at 1118 and concentrated on the American carriers from the outset. With only five of his available eight cruisers on the spot, the other three having been detached with Crace, Fletcher had put TF.17 into a defensive formation with *Lexington* and *Yorktown* at the centre, with an inner ring of cruisers $1\frac{1}{2}$ miles out and the destroyers forming an outer ring half a mile beyond the cruisers. The cruiser AA fire available for the carriers' defence was thus diluted over a circle with a 3-mile diameter, but the biggest weakness was in the air. American radar had picked up the incoming attack force at a range of 70 miles — a respite of 20 minutes — yet Fitch had only eight Wildcats in the air, and his order to launch nine more came far too late. The attacking 'Vals' and 'Kates' were unmolested as they began their assaults and the counter-attacking Wildcats tended to be soaked up in dogfights with the Zeros.

The Japanese attack lasted from 1118 to just before noon and would undoubtedly have achieved far more success without the superb evasive ship-handling displayed by Captain Elliot Buckmaster of *Yorktown* and Captain Frederick C. Sherman of *Lexington*. To be sure, the more modern *Yorktown* was the handier of the two carriers, with a smaller turning circle than *Lexington*; but she also had the luck to be attacked only from the port side. This helped Buckmaster avoid all eight torpedoes launched at *Yorktown* by the 'Kates' at the beginning of the attack. *Lexington*, however, was caught by the practised 'anvil' attack launched from both sides, and, despite Captain Sherman's best efforts, 'Lady Lex' suffered two torpedo hits at about 1120 — both on the port side, one forward and the other opposite the bridge.

Yorktown's luck ran out as the 'Val' dive-bombers plunged to attack. Corkscrew manoeuvering limited the results to a single 800 lb bomb which drilled clean through the flight and hangar decks to explode four decks down. *Yorktown*'s engines, however, remained intact, and, most important of all, flight operations were unimpaired. Two small bombs hit *Lexington*, one in a ready-use ammunition box on the port side and the other on the huge smokestack structure, but the damage was contained. Unlike *Shokaku* under the American attack, *Lexington* was nevertheless left as a viable carrier when her attackers retired at noon. *Lexington*'s flight-deck was unmarred, and her four major fires were rapidly brought under control, while the 7° list to port caused by the two torpedo hits was soon tackled by shifting oil fuel to starboard. By 1320 the recovery of *Lexington*'s aircraft was already under way, and ten minutes later Commander H. R. 'Pop' Healy, Damage Control Officer, delivered a report of laconic good cheer to Captain Sherman.

'We've got the torpedo damage temporarily shored up, the fires out, and soon will have the ship back on an even keel. But I would suggest, sir, that if you have to take any more torpedoes, you take 'em on the starboard side.'

But disaster was only minutes away. Neither Healy nor any carrier man had any experience of the insidious spread of petrol fumes released by battle damage. *Lexington* was about to give the first demonstration of the carrier's vulnerability to this deadly menace. At 1247 *Lexington*'s spreading internal petrol fumes reached the Motor Generator Room, where the sparking commutator of a running generator triggered a shattering internal explosion. Healy's damage control teams threw themselves back into the fray with superb determination, and for a while it still seemed that all would be well. *Lexington*'s last aircraft were still landing-on as late as 1400, but a fatal chain reaction was already under way. The explosion released more fumes which fed greedily on the new fires which leaped up inside the ship. A series of further internal explosions resulted, with another major detonation at 1445. By 1500 the fires aboard *Lexington* had passed out of control, communications were out, and electric power and steering control had failed.

The destroyer *Morris* came close alongside to help fight the fires, but to no avail. By 1630 the engine and boiler rooms had had to be evacuated and *Lexington*, shrouded in smoke, lay dead in the water. *Minneapolis*, *Hammann* and *Anderson* came in to help *Morris* take off *Lexington*'s wounded. At 1710, Fitch bowed to the inevitable and told Sherman to evacuate the ship. The last men to leave, Sherman and his Executive Officer, Commander Seligman, were still on board when another heavy explosion at 1753 rent the flight-deck and hurled aircraft into the sea. After Seligman and Sherman had been picked up safely, the destroyer *Phelps* put *Lexington* out of her misery with five torpedoes. Another explosion tore *Lexington* as she sank at 2000, taking 35 of her aircraft with her. The only consolation was that nearly all of *Lexington*'s complement of 3,300 had been saved, although 216 officers and men had been killed in the battle during the Japanese attack.

The loss of *Lexington* transformed a battle which, down to noon on 8 May, had been tipping in favour of the Americans. The morning's air strikes had left the Japanese with only one operational carrier, *Zuikaku*, while both *Yorktown* and *Lexington* remained able to operate aircraft. The decisive factor was the crippling loss of carrier aircraft suffered by the Japanese on 7 and 8 May. On the morning of the 8th, 43 Japanese aircraft were

lost to only 33 from *Yorktown* and *Lexington*, leaving *Shokaku* and *Zuikaku* with only six 'Kates' and nine 'Vals' between them. As with the Americans and *Shokaku*, the Japanese believed that they had sunk both *Lexington* and *Yorktown*, yet Inouye recoiled from the gamble of pushing through the Moresby invasion in the teeth of Allied land-based air attacks, with Crace's force still to be reckoned with south of the Jomard Passage. At 2400 on the night of 8–9 May Yamamoto, incensed at this hesitancy, ordered Inouye to locate and sink all surviving American ships in the Coral Sea. By the time that Inouye had ordered *Zuikaku* back to the south, on the morning of 9 May, Fletcher was well on his way back to Nouméa with TF.17.

Yamamoto was now left with no choice but to confirm the cancellation of 'MO'. On 5 May Japanese Imperial Headquarters had ordered him to proceed with 'MI', the all-important blow at Midway in the Central Pacific. Protracted operations down in the South-West Pacific would inevitably have resulted in the postponement of 'MI', which, given the prevailing belief that the US Pacific Fleet had just suffered a further crippling blow in the Coral Sea, was out of the question.

The results of the Coral Sea action were read very differently by Nimitz at Pearl Harbor. By 9 May, Nimitz was well aware that if the Japanese did sail the Moresby Invasion Force again it could well get through. With *Lexington* gone, Nimitz dared not risk what was left of TF.17 by sending Fletcher back into the Coral Sea. A fortnight before the Coral Sea battle, the Combat Intelligence Unit at Pearl Harbor had detected signs of a massive Japanese attack building up in the Central Pacific, compared with which the Japanese operations against Moresby would be a sideshow. To meet this new offensive in the Central Pacific, *Yorktown*, regardless of her damage, was going to be a vital asset. All Nimitz could do after the events of 8 May was to send his only intact carrier task force, Halsey's TF.16, to hover off the northern Solomons as a backup force; but *Enterprise* and *Hornet* were not in the South-West Pacific for long. By 15 May, the Combat Intelligence Unit had confirmed that Midway would be the next Japanese objective, and within 48 hours both Fletcher and Halsey were under orders to get back to Pearl Harbor with all speed. There was comfort to be derived from the fact that Port Moresby was still in Allied hands after obvious Japanese discomfiture in the Coral Sea, but not much. If the Japanese succeeded in their attack on Midway, they would be able to go where they pleased. The supreme crisis of the Pacific War was at hand.

Battle of Midway

'MI': The Japanese Midway plan

As devised by Yamamoto's staff, Plan 'MI' remains a classic example of how to enjoy both the initiative and overwhelming force, and throw both away in an over-elaborate dispersion of strength. The plan repeated all the errors which had bedevilled 'MO', and blew them up to enormous size. 'MI' involved no less than sixteen separate groupings of Japanese warships and transports, operating on a front 3,000 miles wide; it was embellished with diversionary attacks by midget submarines on Sydney and Madagascar, respectively 4,900 miles and 18,200 miles from the true objective of Midway Atoll. Moreover, it was all based on that most dangerous of double assumptions in strategic planning: that nothing would go wrong and that the enemy would be taken completely by surprise.

The supreme objective of 'MI' was that of provoking the US Pacific Fleet to come out and fight in defence of Midway, and be wiped out in the process. The Japanese Combined Fleet certainly had ample force to achieve this: eleven battleships against none, eight carriers against three, 23 cruisers against eight, 65 destroyers against fifteen. But this overwhelming advantage in force was never concentrated to full advantage. Two of the eight Japanese carriers were assigned to the Northern Force under Admiral Hosogaya, scheduled to attack and take Attu and Kiska in the Aleutians as a last-minute diversionary move. The Aleutians attack was to begin three days before that on Midway; next morning would see Nagumo's Carrier Striking Force begin the softening-up of Midway's defences before the Invasion Force landed the day after that. Nagumo's carriers would have the support of Admiral Kondo's Covering Group of battleships and cruisers, to which was attached yet another carrier. The Japanese Main Body under Yamamoto himself would be lurking some 300 miles to the west. It included the fourth carrier which could have been added to Nagumo's force, the lightweight *Hosho*, and the three most powerful battleships in the Japanese Fleet: *Yamato*, *Nagato* and *Mutsu*. The Main Body's time would come when the American fleet responded to the news of the invasion of Midway, and came charging west from Pearl Harbor to counter-attack.

What amounted to the full battle order and operations plan of the 'MI' task forces was intercepted and decoded at Pearl Harbor on 25 May. This key interception, mercifully for the United States, the last before the Japanese

Rushed down to the South-West Pacific too late to join in the Coral Sea action, *Enterprise* (*left*) and *Hornet* were recalled to Pearl Harbor on 16 May. Apart from the bomb-damaged *Yorktown*, they were the only carriers available to counter the imminent assault on Midway by the full might of the Japanese Combined Fleet.

changed codes and sent the American crypt-analysts back to square one, gave Nimitz the most comprehensive look at the enemy's cards ever enjoyed by a naval commander on the eve of a decisive battle. Above all, the decrypt of 25 May told Nimitz that *Shokaku* and *Zui-kaku*, thanks to the damage and aircraft losses suffered in the Coral Sea, would not be sailing with Nagumo's carrier force.

Nimitz and his advisers already knew that Nagumo's carriers were the keystone of the whole 'MI' plan. There would be no landings on Midway until Nagumo's carriers — only four of them now — had neutralised Mid-way's air and land defences. If *Yorktown*, *Enterprise* and *Hornet* could do to Nagumo's four carriers what *Yorktown* and *Lexington* had managed to do to the three carriers of Goto and Takagi in the Coral Sea, the main-spring of the Japanese plan would be buckled if not broken. The three American carriers would have to strike at Nagumo's carriers with maximum force as soon as the latter were

Yorktown in dry dock at Pearl Harbor after Coral Sea, with repairmen working flat out to patch up the extensive damage inflicted four decks down by the Japanese bomb. In an amazing feat of dedication and endurance, weeks of normal repair time were crammed into three exhausting days, rendering *Yorktown* fit to join *Enterprise* and *Hornet* at the rendezvous of 'Point Luck' on 2 June.

located, and this could well be delayed until Midway was already under attack by Nagumo's airmen. The odds against defeating the whole Japanese armada were impossible; the odds against Nagumo were not. It was the only chance, but it all depended on whether or not *Yorktown* could be made fit for another all-out carrier battle.

Nimitz plans the Midway ambush

Before the all-important question of *Yorktown*'s readiness could be resolved, the return

to Pearl Harbor of Halsey's TF.16 on 26 May brought Nimitz another major problem. Weeks of strain had caused Halsey to go down with an incapacitating skin complaint requiring instant hospitalization. A new commander had to be found for Halsey's task force, at once. Even without the imminent crisis at Midway, it was a crucial appointment, for Halsey's standing in the Pacific Fleet was unique. He was the carrier man's carrier man who, at the age of 53, had gone through the aviation course and won his wings in order to skipper *Saratoga* in 1935. Since December 1941, Halsey's ebullience and aggression had never ceased to boost the morale, self-confidence and combat efficiency of TF.16. Well aware of all this, Nimitz went along with Halsey's own recommendation of the man most likely to take over TF.16 with minimum disruption and maximum effectiveness. Halsey's choice came as a surprise: Rear-

Admiral Raymond Ames Spruance, hitherto in command of TF.16's cruisers and destroyers. Not only was the silent, austere Spruance the complete opposite of the outgoing Halsey in temperament, but he was not a carrier man. Appointing a gunnery specialist who had never served a day in a carrier to command a task force in the most important carrier battle of the war was a colossal gamble. For Nimitz, however, the knowledge that Spruance would enjoy not only Halsey's full confidence but the expertise of Halsey's staff was quite sufficient. Events proved that the advancement of Spruance to command TF.16 was one of the most inspired appointments in the history of the US Navy. Spruance was confirmed in his new role in the afternoon of 26 May, 24 hours before Fletcher's TF.17 followed TF.16 into Pearl Harbor.

All attention now focussed on *Yorktown*, which went straight into dry dock for a thorough inspection. It was immediately evident that the ship's internal damage would normally require weeks of repair work, but Nimitz quietly told Lieutenant-Commander Pfingstag, the Navy Yard's hull repair expert, that *Yorktown* would have to be fit for sea within three days. After a moment's appalled reflection, Pfingstag agreed. The exhausting labour of cutting out damaged plates, girders and pipes and tacking-in makeshift replacements began at once and continued headlong, with all yard bosses and many of the repair shifts working 48 hours at a stretch. Their sweat and endurance made them the first heroes of the Midway battle.

Meanwhile, Nimitz received Fletcher and gave him the grim news of what was coming at Midway. Though TF.17 had spent 101 days at sea before, during and after the Coral Sea action, it would have to go out again at once. Spruance would sail the next morning, 28 May, with TF.16; Fletcher would follow with TF.17 on the 30th. Spruance and Fletcher would rendezvous north-east of Midway, at a pinpoint code-named 'Point Luck', on 2 June. This would place the combined force, command of which was to be exercised by Fletcher, in a perfect position to ambush Nagumo's carriers as they came in to pound Midway on or soon after 3 June. Thanks to incredible exertions by the men of the Navy Yard the carriers left on schedule: TF.16 on 28 May and TF.17 on the morning of 30 May, with *Yorktown* still disembarking her last dockyard workers as she headed down the anchorage.

Three thousand miles to the east, in San Diego, similar frantic efforts were readying *Saratoga* for sea. Nimitz knew that *Saratoga* could not arrive in time for the Midway action, scheduled for 3–4 June; but at least, even if TF.16 and TF.17 met with total disaster off Midway, *Saratoga* could provide a vestige of carrier cover for the last-ditch defence of Pearl Harbor. Though Nimitz could not spare enough 'tin cans' — destroyers — to give *Saratoga* an adequate screening force for her passage, she sailed from San Diego on 1 June and reached the safety of Pearl Harbor on 6 May, 48 hours after the battle.

First cracks in the 'MI' plan

The fatal inflexibility of the 'MI' plan made itself felt even before *Yorktown* had joined *Enterprise* and *Hornet* at 'Point Luck'. Yamamoto's master-plan included a last-minute reconnaissance of Pearl Harbor — Operation 'K' — to make sure that the US Fleet was not already at sea and to assess its strength. This was to be carried out by two long-range

flying-boats from Kwajalein, refuelling from submarines at the lonely atoll of French Frigate Shoals about halfway between Pearl Harbor and Midway. But when the tanker submarines reached French Frigate Shoals they found that American flying-boats were already using the lagoon as a temporary base, and 'K' had to be called off. All 'MI' task forces, rigidly governed by the need to maintain radio silence, were therefore left to proceed under the delusion (for want of positive information to the contrary) that all was well and the US Fleet was still at Pearl Harbor according to plan.

Worse was to follow. 'MI' also provided for a cordon of Japanese submarines to lie across the direct route from Pearl Harbor to Midway, and sound the alarm when the US Fleet came out. However, the Japanese planners had not allowed for the time needed to prepare the submarines for yet another long-range patrol so deep inside American waters, and the boats arrived on station 24 hours late. If they had arrived on time, 31 May, they would still have missed TF.16 but would most probably have sighted *Yorktown* and TF.17. As things stood, by the time Yamamoto's submarines took up station to warn of the expected American sortie from Pearl Harbor, Fletcher and Spruance had already made rendezvous and were lying in ambush 500 miles to the west.

Meanwhile, as his carriers continued on course for their bombardment of Midway, Nagumo had a particularly comforting intelligence estimate to read: 'It is not believed that the enemy has any powerful unit, with carriers as its nucleus, in the vicinity.' By nightfall on 3 June, with no news to the contrary from either the 'K' flying-boats or the patrol submarines, 'MI' seemed to be running like clockwork. This did not prevent Nagumo, as the Midway strike aircraft took off at 0430 on 4 June, from launching simultaneous reconnaissance flights to the east and north-east. Moreover, only 36 'Vals' and 36 'Kates', half the available strike aircraft, were committed to the attack on Midway; the other half was held back to be armed with torpedoes and armour-piercing bombs — anti-shipping missiles. Nagumo was planning to take no chances of being caught unawares in the event of the American Fleet reacting more quickly than had been anticipated. Nor would he have been, but for an apparently trifling mishap. Under orders to scout east for 300 miles on an arc of 165°, six of Nagumo's reconnaissance aircraft were launched on time. The seventh was delayed 30 minutes because of catapult failure in its parent ship, the cruiser *Tone*, but finally got airborne at 0500. Added to the failure of Operation 'K' and the late arrival on

station of the patrol submarines, those lost 30 minutes were to prove the last insignificant straw which broke the Japanese hopes of victory.

Phase 1: Nagumo's carriers are located

By first light on 4 June, Fletcher had brought TFs.16 and 17 back to the likeliest ambush position, 200 miles north of Midway, after a day of considerable uncertainty. This had been caused by the early sighting of the Japanese Invasion Force on the 3rd, coming in from the south-west. Were Nagumo's carriers, after all, further south — in closer touch with the Invasion Force than had been anticipated? Nimitz had taken no chance of Fletcher coming to this conclusion, momentarily intervening to signal: 'THIS IS NOT REPEAT NOT THE ENEMY STRIKING FORCE'.

With the location of the Japanese carriers still the top priority, Fletcher sent out reconnaissance aircraft at dawn on 4 May to search the sector north-west of Midway, but first contact was made by Consolidated PBY flying-boats out of Midway. The first PBY sighted two Japanese carriers at 0534, and the second sighted the massed aircraft of the Midway strike force about six minutes later. By 0603 follow-up reports from the PBYs had left Fletcher in no doubt that this was the long-awaited quarry. At 0607 he gave his orders to Spruance: 'PROCEED SOUTH-WESTERLY AND ATTACK ENEMY CARRIERS WHEN DEFINITELY LOCATED. WILL FOLLOW AS SOON AS SEARCH PLANES RECOVERED'.

Both Fletcher and Spruance knew that nothing could be attempted until TF.16 had closed to within air-strike range of Nagumo's force — but there were two ways of assessing this vital moment. One was by the book: to launch the strike at the optimum calculated distance for strike aircraft to reach the target and return with an adequate margin of fuel. The other was a gamble justified only by the desperate nature of the whole operation: to launch the moment that effective striking range was reached, and let the returning aircraft take their chances with little or no safety margin.

Spruance's first instinct was to go by the book and launch at 0900, when the range from the Japanese carriers should be down to 100 miles or less. But the Chief of Staff whom Spruance had inherited from Halsey, Captain Miles Browning, vehemently disagreed. Browning's interpretation of the calculated risk, which in the words of Nimitz's operations order governed the whole operation, was that anything was justified if only TF.16 could get in its blow before the Japanese found the American carriers. Browning urged

61

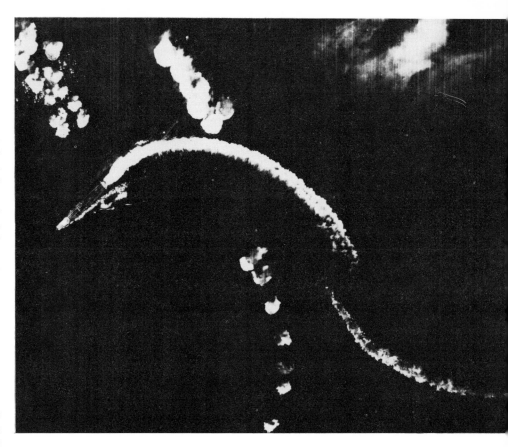

The Japanese carrier *Hiryu* twists and turns to dodge the sticks of bombs dropped by Midway-based B-17s on the morning of 4 June 1942. As the B-17s bombed from 20,000 feet it was not surprising that they failed to score a single hit. This was the fourth Midway-based air attack hurled at Nagumo's carriers that morning, all of them evaded without damage or loss. After a fifth attack, by Midway's obsolete Marine Corps Vindicators, the first American carrier-based attacks went in.

launching at 0700, not 0900; and Spruance, who had been picking the brains of Halsey's carrier experts non-stop ever since TF.16 had sailed from Pearl Harbor, had the greatness to accept the validity of his subordinate's advice. This was not all. Spruance also decided to hit with everything he had — 58 Dauntlesses, 30 Devastators and twenty Wildcat fighter escorts — holding back only the barest minimum of Dauntless scouts and Wildcats to give the carriers defensive air cover.

Setting aside the fact that no American carrier force had ever launched a strike of this strength before, two uncertain factors made Spruance's decisions all the harder. The first was that American chances of success depended on Nagumo's attention being kept focussed on Midway for as long as possible. Nagumo's attack on Midway might well be limited to a single strike if all Midway's Army, Marine Corps and Navy aircraft were caught on the ground, as had happened at Pearl Harbor and Manila in December 1941. Spruance could only hope that enough Midway-based aircraft would survive to act as a 'matador's cloak' under Nagumo's nose while, unseen to the eastward, the carrier-borne American sword was lifted, poised and driven home. The snag here was that there was no direct communications link between the three American carriers and Midway. Fletcher and Spruance would be operating in near total ignorance of how the Midway garrison and air defence force were faring, because Midway and the Fleet used different radio frequencies, messages between the two being relayed via Pearl Harbor. Thus Spruance's attack as launched was made on the strength of nothing more positive than the initial sighting reports of Nagumo's force.

Phase 2: Midway's aircraft retaliate

Nagumo's airmen sighted Midway at 0616 and their attack went in at 0634, with the Zeros brushing aside valiant attacks by Midway's 26 antiquated fighters. By 0648, having given a severe battering to Midway's ground installations, and leaving the garrison with only two operational fighters, the Japanese were on their way home. However, the attackers had been shaken by the spirited reaction of Midway's defenders and by the readiness and ferocity of the AA fire, which had claimed

bombers and lessened the precision of the attack. Worse still, no American aircraft had been caught and destroyed on the ground; Midway remained a viable air base, and at 0700 the Japanese strike force commander radioed to Nagumo: 'THERE IS NEED FOR A SECOND ATTACK'.

For the next 80 minutes, blissfully unaware that an American carrier task force was already racing into position to attack the Japanese carriers, Nagumo and his staff were left to concentrate on the problem of rearming the aircraft of the second wave for a second attack on Midway after the first strike force had been recovered. Their concentration was repeatedly shaken by successive attacks from the aircraft which Midway had hurled into the air only minutes before the Japanese attack had come in. Six Navy TBF Avengers attacked at 0705, closely followed by four Army B-26 Marauders armed, like the Avengers, with torpedoes. Their inexpert attacks, dropping from too far out, were easily evaded without a single hit being scored, and six of the ten aircraft were shot down. At 0715 Nagumo ordered the rearming of the second attack force from anti-shipping to anti-ground weapons to begin. The work was fairly under way when, at 0728, startling news came in from the reconnaissance aircraft belatedly launched from *Tone*. This reported what seemed to be ten American surface ships

240 miles from Midway, but failed to make any mention of carriers in company.

Nagumo began to vacillate, a state which, kept in being by continuing attacks by Midway-based aircraft and maddeningly vague reconnaissance reports, brought his superb force to utter ruin in little over three hours. His instincts told him to strike immediately at these American warships, but all his available strike aircraft were being rearmed from torpedoes to bombs. At 0745 he ordered them to change back from bombs to torpedoes, two minutes later demanding precise details of the American force from *Tone*'s search plane. Almost at once, however, Nagumo's attention was dragged back to Midway. At 0755, sixteen Midway-based Dauntlesses headed in to the attack. This was Marine bombing squadron VMSB-241, a group so inexperienced that its pilots were under orders to make glide-bombing rather than powered dive-bombing attacks. Once again, the defensive formation of Nagumo's carriers was broken up by violent evasive manoeuvres, saving all four ships from a single hit while eight Dauntlesses, easy targets as they came gliding in, where shot down.

As soon as the Dauntlesses had been repelled Nagumo radioed *Tone*'s search plane 'ADVISE SHIP TYPES', and at 0809 was immensely cheered to receive the reply: 'ENEMY IS COMPOSED OF FIVE CRUISERS AND FIVE

DESTROYERS'. However, after the last three attacks the Japanese carriers were so spread out that more fighters had to be launched, drawn from the aircraft strength of the second attack force, to guarantee fighter protection against further attacks. This had not even begun when, at 0814, yet another Midway-based attack began. These were the fifteen B-17 Flying Fortresses which had taken off that morning to attack the Japanese Invasion Force again, only to be diverted north as soon as Nagumo's carrier force was spotted.

The B-17s sighted Nagumo's force when it was still twisting and turning to avoid the glide-bombing attacks of the Dauntlesses. An uncoordinated splatter of bombing runs, carried out at the unpromising height of 20,000 feet to avoid the Japanese AA fire, lasted from 0814 to 0820. Again, no hits were scored — miraculously, to many Japanese observers watching their ships being deluged by bomb splashes — but again the attacks kept the Japanese force from resuming its tight box formation. As the bombs were still falling, the first aircraft of the Midway attack arrived back, only to be waved off by their carriers and left to orbit until the coast was clear.

It was at this moment that *Tone*'s search plane came through again with the worst news Nagumo had had that morning: 'ENEMY IS ACCOMPANIED BY WHAT APPEARS TO BE A

CARRIER BRINGING UP THE REAR.' Nagumo now had to make an instant decision on what to do. By the book, it was an easy decision: forget Midway and nail the American carrier. But half Nagumo's aircraft were in the air, waiting to land-on after returning from the Midway attack; and the change from bombs to torpedoes had not been carried out on all the aircraft in the carriers. Should all aircraft with anti-shipping weapons be brought up and launched at once — an under-strength strike at a vital target? Or should the strike at the American carrier be suspended until the aircraft returning from Midway had been recovered?

For the fifth time that morning, Midway's patchwork air force forced Nagumo's ships to concentrate on survival and lose another vital ten minutes. At 0820, eleven Marine Corps Vindicators attacked the battleship *Haruna* and the accompanying cruisers supporting Nagumo's carriers. This attack had only just been beaten off — again with no hits — when at 0830 *Tone*'s search plane came through like a bird of ill omen. Two more cruisers had been sighted to the west of the American force, making Nagumo's decision and action vitally important; this could be a second American task force. Nagumo was finally swayed by his chief-of-staff and his operations officer to recover the Midway force still orbiting overhead, then complete the rearming of

TF.16 heads into action at Midway. This is *Enterprise* at high speed, flying the flag of Rear-Admiral Spruance. *Enterprise*'s first strike at Nagumo's carriers began launching at 0706, but Spruance's planned 'all-arms' mass attack did not materialise; the air groups of *Enterprise* and *Hornet* attacked piecemeal, none of them with close fighter support, and suffered heavy losses.

the second attack force and launch it in full strength against the American warships. A second counter-order set in motion the rearming of the aircraft, the urgency of the job leaving discarded bombs littering the decks. The four carriers then turned into wind and at 0837 the tired men of the Midway attack force started landing-on at last. The last of them had been gathered in by 0900, and at 0917 all four of the Japanese carriers swung to the north-east in a 70° turn, now heading away from Midway and straight for the American ships.

As Nagumo saw it, the pieces were falling into place at last after a hectic but triumphant morning. At 0855 *Tone*'s search plane had reported another ten torpedo-carrying aircraft heading in Nagumo's direction but that seemed little to worry about; five American air attacks had been beaten off without loss. Nagumo was now planning to launch a full-strength attack on the American task force: 45 'Kates', 36 'Vals' and an escort of twelve Zeros. Delaying their launch until 1030 would lessen the distance to the target,

Battle of Midway, 4 June 1942

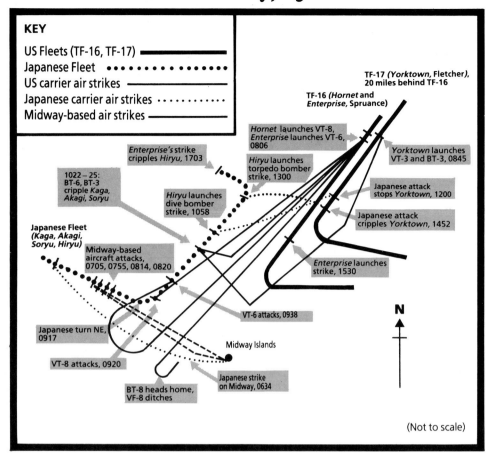

KEY

US Fleets (TF-16, TF-17)	▬▬▬▬▬
Japanese Fleet	•••••••••
US carrier air strikes	▬▬▬▬▬
Japanese carrier air strikes	••••••••••
Midway-based air strikes	▬▬▬▬▬

TF-17 (*Yorktown*, Fletcher), 20 miles behind TF-16

TF-16 (*Hornet* and *Enterprise*, Spruance)

Hornet launches VT-8, *Enterprise* launches VT-6, 0806

Yorktown launches VT-3 and BT-3, 0845

Enterprise's strike cripples *Hiryu*, 1703

Hiryu launches torpedo bomber strike, 1300

Japanese attack stops *Yorktown*, 1200

1022 – 25: BT-6, BT-3 cripple *Kaga*, *Akagi*, *Soryu*

Hiryu launches dive bomber strike, 1058

Japanese attack cripples *Yorktown*, 1452

Japanese Fleet (*Kaga*, *Akagi*, *Soryu*, *Hiryu*)

Midway-based aircraft attacks, 0705, 0755, 0814, 0820

Enterprise launches strike, 1530

VT-6 attacks, 0938

Japanese turn NE, 0917

Midway Islands

VT-8 attacks, 0920

BT-8 heads home, VF-8 ditches

Japanese strike on Midway, 0634

N

(Not to scale)

increase the chances of a quick, clean kill and reduce the time it would take to resume the job of flattening Midway. After its last displays of competence over the preceding three hours — launching and recovering the first strike at Midway while beating off five air attacks — there was nothing at 0920 to indicate that the Carrier Striking Force had just over 80 minutes to live.

Phase 3: American torpedo attacks

The early American strike at the Japanese carriers ordered by Spruance on Browning's advice got under way shortly after 0700, when the first Wildcats and Dauntlesses were launched from *Hornet* and *Enterprise*. The original plan was for the fighters and dive-bombers to orbit overhead until the slower torpedo planes had been launched, then for the whole coordinated force to head off together, but it never happened. Sheer inexperience dragged out the launch, and at 0728 a Japanese seaplane was sighted on the southern horizon. This was *Tone*'s seaplane, making its first misleading report of the American force to Nagumo. At 0745 Spruance, accept-

The last aircraft of *Enterprise*'s air group to be launched were the slow and vulnerable TBD Devastators of Torpedo 6, here shown preparing for launch at about 0800 on 4 June. Attacking without close fighter escort, they scored no hits and fell easy prey to the Zeros. Only four of the aircraft shown in this photograph came back.

Smoke belches from *Yorktown* after the Japanese dive-bombing attack just after noon. Of the three bomb hits suffered in this attack, only one mattered: the one that burst in the uptakes at the root of the stack, wrecking two boilers and blowing out the fires in the other two. With his flagship dead in the water, Admiral Fletcher had no choice but to shift his flag to the cruiser *Astoria* while the fight to save *Yorktown* went on.

Yorktown's repairmen set to work on the flight-deck, but the soot and smoke belching from the superstructure in the background indicate the source of the biggest trouble: the bomb hit in the boiler uptakes.

ing that there was nothing else for it, ordered *Enterprise*'s Dauntlesses to set off without waiting for the rest of the air group. The torpedo-carrying Devastators from the two carriers finally got away at 0806: Torpedo 8 from *Hornet* (Lieutenant-Commander Waldron) and Torpedo 6 from *Enterprise* (Lieutenant-Commander Lindsey).

Many factors made this a caricature of what a combined air strike should be. The two carrier air groups set out in virtual isolation, ignorant of what the other was trying to do. Moreover, each air group itself remained dislocated, leaving the aircraft which needed close fighter cover most of all, the Devastator

Opposite
Shell splinters rain into the sea as four 'Kates' (ringed) come boring in through *Yorktown*'s 5-inch barrage, heading straight for the carrier's port side. Two of the attacking aircraft scored hits.

squadrons, to face the Zeros alone. No less serious was the failure to estimate the true position of the target. Not knowing that the Midway-based aircraft had been able to throw five separate attacks at Nagumo, the American planners gave their pilots and navigators a target position which was too far south. Therefore, the chances of actually making contact with the Japanese depended, in the long run, on the persistence of the squadron commanders and the hunches they chose to follow.

Meanwhile, Fletcher's staff in *Yorktown*, planning to join the fray after the recovery of her search planes at 0645, was taking a different approach to the same problems. There was the same willingness to launch at extreme range, but Commander Pedersen, *Yorktown*'s air group commander, recommended sending the squadrons off separately to rendezvous on the way to the target in order to save time. For his part, Fletcher was determined not to repeat the error he had made exactly a month before in the Coral Sea, and throw his whole air group at a minor target. His final decision was to commit two striking squadrons — Torpedo 3 (Lieutenant-Commander Massey) and Bombing 3 (Lieutenant-Commander Leslie) — but to hold back the Dauntlesses of Scouting 5 and all but six Wildcats of Fighting 3 (Lieutenant-Commander Thach).

Having closed to just inside the calculated maximum range from the Japanese position, *Yorktown* started launching at 0845, barely 40 minutes after the last aircraft had taken off from TF.16. By 0906 the last of the six Wildcats were away, following the seventeen Dauntlesses and twelve Devastators in the launching sequence. Within five minutes, Bombing 3 lost nearly 25 per cent of its striking power due to a technical fault. A new electrical device had been fitted in the aircraft to arm the bombs with a flick of a switch, but when Commander Leslie flicked his it not only armed his bomb but released it. Leslie broke radio silence to warn his pilots to arm their bombs with the familiar manual technique, but not before three other pilots had also lost their bombs. Leslie, however, stayed at the head of his squadron, determined to lead it into the attack with or without a bomb of his own.

In their approach to the target the airmen from *Yorktown* were far luckier than their comrades from *Hornet* and *Enterprise*. Though equally hamstrung by radio silence, the three elements of the smaller *Yorktown* striking force kept in visual contact throughout the approach flight, stacked-up from the Devastators at 1500 feet to the Dauntlesses up at 16,000 feet. Moreover, thanks to the Japanese turn to the north-east at 0917, the *Yorktown*

strike was approaching the oncoming Japanese carriers just a little south of head-on. At 1000, Massey, at the head of Torpedo 3, sighted smoke 30–40 miles away on the north-west horizon and headed in to attack — unaware of the disaster which had already befallen the Devastators from *Hornet* and *Enterprise*, and which was to engulf his own squadron.

The Devastator squadron commanders of TF.16 had led their aircraft in very different circumstances. Waldron, at the head of Torpedo 8, had followed a hunch of his own that the Japanese would be further north than he had been told. He was right, but only just — Nagumo's carriers were sighted at 0920, bare minutes after they had made their turn to the north-east. As the only survivor of Torpedo 8 later recalled, Waldron 'went just as straight to the Jap fleet as if he'd had a string tied to them'. However, in following Waldron's lead, Torpedo 8 lost contact with *Hornet*'s ten Wildcats, which were dutifully following the course they had been given. Waldron went in to attack, vainly calling on fighters which were not there. Devoid of fighter cover but still pressing their attacks with all the determination which Waldron had drilled into them, the men of Torpedo 8 paid a terrible price. Between 0920 and 0936 all fifteen Devastators of Torpedo 8 fell victim to the

Zeros and AA fire from Nagumo's carriers. Only Ensign George Gay, supported by his Mae West and hiding under a floating cushion for fear of strafing Zeros, survived to be picked up after the battle. And not a hit was scored on the Japanese carriers to repay the gallantry expended with the lost squadron's torpedoes.

Two minutes later, Lindsey's Torpedo 6 from *Enterprise* arrived on the scene, having found empty sea and corrected course with a wide swing to the north. The Torpedo 6 pilots, coming in from the south with speeds little higher than 100 knots, found themselves faced with the task of chasing targets moving at 30 knots, overhauling them, then circling to get a decent beam shot. The result was a 20-minute approach flight, unsupported by *Enterprise*'s Fighting 6 whose Wildcats were restlessly waiting to be called in by the strike aircraft below. In the end, Fighting 6, running low on fuel, headed back to *Enterprise*. The Fighting 6 Wildcats had been waiting to be called in at the crucial moment by the operations officer of Torpedo 6, but it seems that he was shot down before he could pass the word. In any event it was another field day for the Zeros, which shot down ten Devastators out of fourteen. Lindsey, the squadron commander, was among them. Yet again, no hits were scored.

Approaching from the south-east, *Yorktown*'s Torpedo 3 sighted Nagumo's force while it was still evading the last attacks of Torpedo 6. By 1015, Massey's Devastators were still closing the outer ring of destroyers, some 14–18 miles from the widely-dispersed carriers, when the Zeros attacked for the third time in 65 minutes. The six Wildcats escorting the strike had no chance of keeping the Zeros off the Devastators' backs and it was the same sad story: Massey was shot down with ten of his squadron's twelve Devastators, and no hits were scored. Since Waldron had led in Torpedo 8 at 0920, the three Devastator squadrons of the American carrier-borne strike had met with disaster, with an untouched enemy hacking down 35 Devastators out of 41.

Despite their tragic end, for all the wrong reasons, the Devastators had made a mighty contribution to American victory. By 1020, when Nagumo ordered his carriers to launch when ready, the Japanese force was badly dislocated by the evasive manoeuvering of the past hour. More important, the covering Zeros were now short of ammunition and had been dragged down to sea level to intercept the Devastators. There was therefore no high-level fighter opposition to the American dive-bombers which arrived over the Japanese fleet at 1020. Below them, Nagumo's four carriers

were turning into wind to launch, their flight-decks and hangar-decks the juiciest of targets, crammed with armed and fuelled aircraft, fuel lines and the bombs discarded during the rearming of the aircraft.

Phase 4: Dive-bombers knock out *Kaga*, *Akagi* and *Soryu*

The confusion which had dogged TF.16's attack was not limited to the immolation of Torpedo 8 and Torpedo 6. By 1015 *Hornet*'s Bombing 8 and Fighting 8, having ranged much too far south in their search for the Japanese, were on their way home with rapidly emptying fuel tanks. This left *Enterprise*'s Scouting 6 and Bombing 6, led by air group commander Wade McClusky, to begin the first American dive-bombing attacks at about 1022. Unmolested as they went into their dives, McClusky's 25 Dauntlesses divided their attacks between the rearmost carriers, *Kaga* and *Akagi*. Three minutes later, at 1025, Leslie's Bombing 3 from *Yorktown* fell upon *Soryu*. *Hiryu*, furthest to the north, escaped untouched.

The circumstances of the dive-bombers' attack and the unique ripeness of the target made this one of the most devastating bombing attacks ever carried out by such a small number of naval aircraft. It took less than five

This sequence of photographs taken from *Yorktown*'s screening warships during the attack by *Hiryu*'s torpedo aircraft shows 'Kates' milling round *Yorktown* (*right*), a torpedo hit on *Yorktown*'s port side (*below*), *Yorktown* starting to list (*opposite above*), and again trailing on ominous black train of smoke as she takes a second hit (*opposite below*).

minutes to convert *Kaga*, *Akagi* and *Soryu* into blazing wrecks. The total number of bomb hits will probably never be known accurately, because the bombs set off a chain of explosions amid fuel bowsers and the aircraft ranged on deck, but there were at least four on *Kaga* and three apiece on *Akagi* and *Soryu*. No less important, the Japanese aircraft already in the air had nowhere to land. When their fuel ran out, those which could not land back aboard *Hiryu* would have no alternative to ditching in the sea.

The tremendous results of the dive-bombers' attack did not, however, give the Americans a hands-down victory. Some four-fifths of Fletcher's aircraft had either been shot down or were still in the air, returning from their attacks. The initiative now lay with *Hiryu* and her intact air group, burning for revenge.

Phase 5: *Hiryu*'s attack cripples *Yorktown*

Until Nagumo, abandoning the blazing *Akagi* at 1046, transferred his flag to the cruiser *Nagara* at 1130 command of the remnants of the Carrier Striking Force passed to Rear-Admiral Abe in the cruiser *Tone*. Abe wasted no time in ordering *Hiryu* to launch an immediate attack on the American carriers, and by 1058 it was away. There had been no time to rearm the aircraft back from Midway with torpedoes, which limited the strike force to eighteen 'Val' dive-bombers and six Zeros. After a flight of just under an hour they sighted their objective, *Yorktown*, whose radar had already detected the Japanese force at a range of 32 miles at 1152.

The first to return from their attack, *Yorktown*'s aircraft had begun landing-on at 1115, but matching often contradictory aircrew reports took time, and it was not until 1150 that Fletcher knew for certain that although three Japanese carriers had been left ablaze the fourth was still very much alive. By this time the Japanese were already on their way in to attack TF.17, guided on their final approach by the last American aircraft returning home. The six escorting Zeros attacked one of these groups, Dauntlesses from Bombing 3, which turned out to be unexpectedly agile and aggressive. Two Zeros were so badly damaged that they had to head back to *Hiryu*, leaving only four to escort the eighteen 'Vals'.

By the time the alert sounded at 1152,

Yorktown was, thanks to her Coral Sea experience, at a far higher state of readiness than she had been on 8 May when attacked from *Shokaku* and *Zuikaku*. *Yorktown* had a combat patrol of twelve Wildcats up and waiting, fuel lines drained of gasoline and filled with inert carbon dioxide, all surplus inflammable materials and equipment ditched overside, and repair parties and 'medics' poised to cope with damage and casualties. Thirty miles out, the Wildcats tore into the small Japanese force. Attacking twelve against 22, the Wildcats did well to intercept ten, but seven of the eight which broke through managed to attack *Yorktown*, and three of them scored hits. *Yorktown*'s long ordeal had begun.

The first Japanese bomb burst on the flight-deck aft of the island, setting fire to three aircraft in the hangar deck below. Another went through the forward elevator and burst

50 feet below, starting a fire in the rag storage locker with fuel stowage and 5-inch shells dangerously close to hand. Excellent damage control smothered the fires and had the flight-deck ready for operations in only 20 minutes, but the third Japanese bomb was the one that did the real damage. It burst three decks down in the funnel uptakes, silencing the engines and leaving *Yorktown* dead in the water. At 1230 Fletcher made the decision to transfer his flag, unable to wait for prolonged repairs to get *Yorktown* moving again. By 1324, he had transferred to the cruiser *Astoria*.

Meanwhile, 20 miles to the south, TF.16 was gathering in the last survivors of the morning's attacks. *Hornet*'s air group had suffered the worst: all of Torpedo 8 had been shot down, all of Fighting 8 had splashed when their fuel ran out, and only four aircraft

from Bombing 8 had returned. TF.16 not only lacked the aircraft but was too far away to help *Yorktown* when the dive-bombers from *Hiryu* struck. After this attack, unable to operate from the immobilised *Yorktown*, ten Dauntlesses of Leslie's Bombing 3 transferred to *Enterprise*. Even with these modest reinforcements, only a threadbare striking force was left to renew the attack on the last Japanese carrier — once she had been located. Japanese reconnaissance proved the more efficient, bringing back news of TF.16 a full two hours before Spruance was given *Hiryu*'s position.

By 1300 *Hiryu* was preparing to keep up the running with a second lone attack, this time in the knowledge that the American fleet included *three* carriers, TF.16 having finally been sighted at 1130. This time, ten 'Kates' would carry out a torpedo attack, operating in two sections and under orders to concentrate on the undamaged American carriers. Like the airmen of TF.16 that morning, however, *Hiryu*'s second strike headed for an inaccurate target position: further north than TF.16 actually was. The result of this error was that *Hiryu*'s 'Kates' found not *Enterprise* and *Hornet* but *Yorktown*, last seen blazing furiously but now with all fires out, working up to 20 knots after magnificent work by the repair crews in the boiler-rooms, and preparing to launch aircraft. The Japanese strike commander never doubted that the undamaged American carriers he was seeking had split into two task groups for greater security, and that this was one of them. At 1432 he ordered his aircraft in to attack.

The Japanese were eager to revenge the morning's losses. They got it in sweeter measure than they knew. There were strik-

ing parallels between *Yorktown*'s fate under this second attack from *Hiryu*, and that of *Kaga*, *Akagi* and *Soryu* under the morning's dive-bombing attacks. If Nagumo's carriers had had ten minutes more, the Zero combat patrol would have been in far better state to cope with the attacking Dauntlesses, and the planned strike at the American fleet would have been launched in full strength. If, four hours later, *Yorktown* had also had ten minutes more, she would have been able to add ten more Wildcats to her combat air patrol and to have worked up enough additional speed to have had a far better chance of evading the Japanese torpedoes.

The 'Kates' were escorted by only six Zeros, but these were enough to keep off the handful of Wildcats and let the strike force through with the loss of only one 'Kate'. At least the Japanese were prevented by the Wildcats and furious AA fire from repeating the deadly two-sided 'anvil' attack which had crippled *Lexington* in the Coral Sea battle, but Captain Buckmaster simply lacked the speed to avoid the four 'Kates' which attacked from the port side at 1444. Two torpedoes hit at about 1445, the first amidships, the second fair and square in the forward generator room. As in the earlier attack on *Yorktown*, it was the second hit which did the most damage, knocking out the ship's entire power supply, blacking out even the emergency lights below decks, and making it impossible to correct *Yorktown*'s increasing list by pumping. Once again *Yorktown* was left dead in the water — but this time with the helm jammed over at 15° and the ship listing 17° to port. It was the extremity of the list, and the impossibility of correcting it due to the lack of power, which persuaded Buckmaster to order 'Abandon Ship' at 1455.

By this time the surviving Japanese aircraft were on their way back to *Hiryu*. They had taken savage losses — only five 'Kates' and three Zeros survived the attack — but they were sustained by the belief that they had fulfilled their mission. 'TWO CERTAIN TORPEDO HITS ON AN ENTERPRISE CLASS CARRIER', radioed section commander Lieutenant Hashimoto: 'NOT THE SAME ONE AS REPORTED BOMBED.'

By 1515, therefore, *Yorktown* had been knocked out of the battle and her crew was abandoning ship, a lengthy process for 2270 officers and men, not completed until 1646. The Japanese believed that only one intact American carrier was now left to challenge *Hiryu*, but Spruance and his staff in *Enterprise* finally had *Hiryu*'s position and were assembling the survivors of the morning's attacks for the day's decisive strike: a *coup de grace* to complete the ruin of Nagumo's carrier force.

1703 *Hiryu* was plunged into her last fight against the Dauntlesses of TF.16. *Hiryu*'s last six Zeros attacked with a ferocity heightened by the knowledge that their last flight-deck was in supreme peril. With reckless courage, they harried the Dauntlesses all the way down, but there were too many Americans to be stopped. A scatter of near-misses astern was followed by three hits plumb on the flight-deck. The first hit was enough. It ripped the forward elevator from its mountings and sent it smashing into the front of the bridge where it remained propped like a reeling tombstone. The engine-rooms remained momentarily intact, but intense fires were searing her upper decks. *Hiryu* was out of the battle at last.

The last Dauntlesses from TF.16 to bomb, seeing the ruin of the carrier's flight-deck, switched to other targets — the battleship *Haruna* and cruisers *Tone* and *Chikuma* — but no further hits were scored. The late arrivals from *Hornet* kept up the pressure until 1832, but achieved no hits either. The confusion of these last American attacks was heightened by the intervention of two separate groups of USAAF B-17s, neither of which knew the other was there. One group of five was a reinforcement flight from Oahu to Midway, plunging into the battle at 3600 feet; the second group of four, flying up from Midway on its second mission of the day, bombed from high altitude. These last B-17 attacks went the way of the first and not a single hit was scored.

Phase 7: Yamamoto's hopes of night action dashed

At 1603 Spruance had reported the launching of TF.16's last strike to Fletcher in *Astoria*, ending his signal with a deferential 'HAVE YOU ANY INSTRUCTIONS FOR ME?' 'NONE', Fletcher replied, 'WILL CONFORM TO YOUR MOVEMENTS'. From that moment tactical control of the battle passed to Spruance. At 1909, after recovering the aircraft which had wrecked *Hiryu*, Spruance took the decision which won the battle outright. He took TF.16 east, away from the Japanese. Leaving the destroyer *Hughes* to stand by the listing *Yorktown*, Fletcher had also headed east at 1738, to rejoin Spruance, and heartily approved of his junior admiral's decision to withdraw the fleet from the threat of a night action against Yamamoto's battleships and cruisers.

Phase 6: *Enterprise* and *Hornet* knock out *Hiryu*

By 1500 on the afternoon of 4 June, TF.16's remaining strike capability was fragmentary. *Hornet*, because of her appalling losses in the morning's attacks, was a spent force. *Enterprise* was equally lacking in torpedo aircraft and had a total of only eleven Dauntlesses left from Bombing 6 and Scouting 6 combined. *Yorktown*'s final contribution to the battle, now operating from *Enterprise*, consisted of fourteen refugee Dauntlesses from Bombing 3 and Scouting 3. The resultant total of 25 Dauntlesses was all that TF.16 had left to throw at *Hiryu* — and to make certain of getting her they would all have to go, with no Wildcats to spare as escorts. It was vital to keep back all airworthy fighters for the defence of *Enterprise* and *Hornet* against whatever attacks the Japanese might still make.

Grimly aware though he was that this was the last shot in his locker, Spruance did not hesitate. Once fuelled and armed, the Dauntlesses were launched against *Hiryu* at 1530, but one of them struggled back in with engine failure, reducing the strike force to 24. But the Dauntlesses had not even taken off from *Enterprise* when TF.16 was favoured with an apparent miracle. Over the southern horizon came eleven Dauntlesses heading in towards *Hornet*. These were the missing aircraft of Bombing 8, which had prudently chosen to land and refuel at Midway instead of risking a direct return flight with insufficient fuel. No sooner had they landed on *Hornet* than they were refuelled and rearmed, taking off again as a back-up strike force at 1603. With them went the last five of *Hornet*'s Dauntlesses able to fly, raising the total to sixteen.

Hiryu was down to her last throw, too. By the time the survivors of the second strike against *Yorktown* had returned, Nagumo's last carrier was left with only four 'Kates' and five 'Vals' to send against what was believed to be the last American carrier. Rear-Admiral Yamaguchi, who had taken over operational command of what was left of the Carrier Striking Force, ordered their launch at 1630, but it could not be done. The airmen and the ship's crew were exhausted and desperately hungry after the most demanding day which they had ever known. To provide a brief respite for rest and food, the strike was put back to 1800, but it was never launched. At

thinking that the American admiral's natural desire to follow up the successes of the day would make such a night action possible — in other words, he once again assumed that the Americans would do what Yamamoto wanted them to do. He ordered Admiral Kurita's four heavy cruisers to take over the pre-invasion bombardment of Midway at 0200 on 5 May, and the four battleships of Admirals Nagumo and Kondo to join forces for an attack on the American fleet. By midnight, however, Yamamoto was realising that the plan was not viable because the 'MI' task forces were too dispersed. By the time that the battleships and cruisers would be in position, first light, and thus the certainty of renewed American carrier attacks on the unprotected Japanese warships, would be less than two hours away.

Yamamoto's bitter acceptance of the fact that 'MI' had failed came in two stages. At 0015 on 5 May he signalled Kondo, Kurita and Nagumo to rendezvous with the Main Body at 0900, 350 miles north-west of Midway, and cancelled Kurita's cruiser bombardment of Midway. Finally, at 0255, he sent out a general signal to all 'MI' task forces, informing them bleakly that the occupation of Midway was cancelled, no longer merely postponed.

Final Phase, 5–6 June: The sinking of *Mikuma* and *Yorktown*

Kurita's four cruisers had closed to 80 miles of Midway when they received Yamamoto's order to withdraw. As they did so, a panicky turn to port caused by the sudden sighting of the submarine *Tambor* resulted in a severe collision between the cruisers *Mikuma* and *Mogami*, with *Mogami*'s bow suffering heavy damage and reducing the ship's speed to 12 knots. Kurita pressed on to his rendezvous with Yamamoto, leaving *Mikuma* and two destroyers to cover *Mogami*.

It was there, on the morning of 5 June, that a PBY sighted the retreating Japanese force, noting the oil slick being trailed by *Mikuma*. The last ten Marine dive-bombers left on Midway, six Dauntlesses and four Vindicators, attacked at 0808. No bomb hits were scored but Captain Richard Fleming, flying the lead Vindicator, received a mortal hit on his bombing run and deliberately crashed his aircraft on to *Mikuma*'s after turret. This left two cripples helplessly awaiting the attentions of Spruance's carriers.

Spruance later provided the best summing-up of his thinking in his official report to Nimitz:

I did not feel justified in risking a night encounter with possibly superior enemy forces, but on the other hand, I did not want to be too far away from Midway next morning. I wished to be in a position from which either to follow up retreating enemy forces, or to break up a landing attack on Midway.

It was a doubly courageous decision, rejecting both the ancient military dictum that a beaten enemy must be kept on the ropes with repeated attacks, and the advice of Halsey's staff officers which Spruance had previously followed. Spruance, however, had 'thought himself' perfectly into Yamamoto's shoes. When Yamamoto heard at 1730 of the disaster which had overtaken *Hiryu*, he knew that there was only one way of saving 'MI' now: to fight a night action in which the overwhelming fire-power of his battleships and cruisers could be brought to bear on the American force. However, he made the mistake of

71

Left and Below
Destroyers gather round the abandoned *Yorktown*, listing heavily but still holding her own, on the morning of 5 June. It took time to assemble a salvage crew from more than 2000 *Yorktown* survivors divided between six destroyers; but by the mid-afternoon of the 5th the destroyer *Hammann* had begun to ferry repairmen back to the carrier.

Opposite
On the morning of 6 June the salvage crew got down to the job of working off *Yorktown*'s list by cutting loose the portside 5-inch mounts. This picture was taken shortly before *I-168*'s torpedoes ripped into *Yorktown*'s starboard side.

Spruance turned TF.16 south-west at 0420 on 5 May, his first intention being to snap up this tempting target, but at 0800 a PBY reported a burning carrier, two battleships, three cruisers and four destroyers 275 miles away to the north-west. Spruance did not receive this information for three hours because of the communications problem, but never doubted, when the news did come through, that the ships sighted at 0800 were his top priority. At 1115 he headed north-west in pursuit, unaware that the carrier he was chasing, *Hiryu*, which had burned all night, had gone down by 0915.

Not surprisingly, the powerful strike of 58 Dauntlesses launched at 1500, at a range of 230 miles, failed to overtake the retreating Japanese ships. All they found was the lone destroyer *Tanikaze* which, attacked by the entire strike force, not only evaded all 58 bombs but shot down one Dauntless. The crestfallen airmen of TF.16 now faced a long flight home and the perils of deck landing after dark. This was alleviated by the courage of Captains Mitscher of *Enterprise* and Murray of *Enterprise*, who burned deck lights and searchlights to help the aircraft in. Fortunately, no Japanese submarine was close enough to spot the lights before the last aircraft landed and the ships were darkened again.

While TF.16 followed this wild-goose-chase, hopes were rising that *Yorktown*, still afloat on a calm sea as daylight broke on 5 May, could still be saved. At 1000 she was taken in tow, and at 1400 on the following day the destroyer *Hammann* closed on the listing derelict. On board were Captain Buckmaster and a team of repair experts, picked from hundreds of volunteers scattered through the crowded destroyers of TF.17. Using power supplied by *Hammann*, the repair team's priority was to reduce *Yorktown*'s deadweight by all possible means and reduce the list so that she could be eased back to Pearl Harbor.

Spruance had meanwhile settled accounts with *Mogami* and *Mikuma*, launching his first strike from *Hornet* which attacked at 0950, a second from *Enterprise* at 1045 and a third from *Hornet* which hit at 1445. It was the third attack on the incredibly battered cruisers which sealed *Mikuma*'s fate, but more excellent damage control just managed to save *Mogami* and nurse her into Truk.

However, the last act in the Battle of Midway was a Japanese, not American, success. At 1330 on 6 June, the Japanese submarine *I-168*, approaching undetected by the screening destroyers, fired a spread of four torpedoes at *Yorktown* with *Hammann* close alongside. One broke *Hammann*'s back and sank her in two minutes, one missed, and the other two hit *Yorktown* amidships. It was the end. The last men were taken off and though the gallant carrier held on through the night of 6–7 June, her list gradually increased until, at 0443, she was lying on her side. Attended by ships of TF.17 with their colours at half-mast, *Yorktown* finally sank at 0501.

Midway: A balance-sheet

Even if Nimitz's ambush had failed completely and Yamamoto's armada had taken Midway, Fletcher and Spruance would have done well to emerge from the action with only

Opposite above
Smoke pours from *Yorktown*'s starboard side, torn open by two torpedoes from *I-168*. This was the attack which sealed *Yorktown*'s fate.

Opposite below
Near the end: *Yorktown*'s hangar deck dips closer to the surface. Her last signal — 'MY SPEED, 15' — can still be seen at the flag halyards. She finally rolled clean over and sank with great dignity at 0501 on 7 June

one fleet carrier and one destroyer lost. The fact that these losses were suffered in exchange for four Japanese carriers sunk and the frustration of the second Japanese invasion in a month still seems astonishing, and the American triumph was not to be measured in ships alone. The Americans lost only 307 dead, the Japanese 3500; the Americans lost 147 aircraft, the Japanese 332. Midway destroyed what had been the key Japanese weapon in the winning of an unprecedented string of naval victories since December 1941: Nagumo's Carrier Striking Force. The victory gave the US Pacific Fleet instant carrier parity with the Japanese Navy — and indeed, in the Central Pacific immediately after the battle, overwhelming carrier supremacy.

The disaster suffered at Midway forced a totally new choice of strategy on the Japanese Imperial High Command — from further expansion towards Hawaii and Fiji to a dogged defence of the gains already made. In the first month after Midway, the most important loose ends in Japan's new strategic pattern were both in the South-West Pacific: New Guinea and the Solomon Islands. Neither had been completely reduced since the Coral Sea setback in May, yet both were vital to the security of the air/sea base of Rabaul, the south-eastern bastion of the Japanese Empire's outer defensive perimeter. After

Midway, therefore, new plans were drawn. The Japanese Army in New Guinea was to prepare for the conquest of Port Moresby overland across the Owen Stanley Mountains, while a new airfield was to be constructed on the island of Guadalcanal in the central Solomons. These tidying-up operations would secure Rabaul from air attacks and bring the whole Solomons area under the Japanese air umbrella.

Allied planning after Midway also concentrated on the Japanese weakness in the southeastern Japanese perimeter. In April, two new command areas were designated: the South Pacific Area, embracing Espiritu Santo, New Caledonia, Fiji, Tongatapu and Samoa, under Admiral Ghormley; and the South-West Pacific Area embracing Queensland and New Guinea, under General MacArthur. Originally the Solomons were assigned to Mac-Arthur's command, but after planning began on Operation 'Watchtower', a joint offensive against Rabaul by the two Commands, the demarcation line between South and South-West Pacific areas was shifted west by one degree of longitude to add the Solomons to the South Pacific Command. The reason for this was that 'Watchtower' was to commence with the recapture of Tulagi and the expulsion of the Japanese from the central Solomons, a predominantly naval operation to be under-

taken by South Pacific area forces. As Tulagi lay well beyond the range of the nearest land-based fighter airfields in the South Pacific Area, air cover for the initial assault on Tulagi would have to be provided by the carriers of the Pacific Fleet, three-quarters of which were therefore despatched to the South Pacific.

These three carriers were *Enterprise*, *Saratoga*, now back in service with her greatly enhanced AA battery of 5-inch dual purpose (DP) guns, and *Wasp*, the last of the Atlantic Fleet carriers to be transferred to the Pacific Theatre. *Hornet*, however, had suffered such heavy losses at Midway that she had to be held back until her new air group could work up to full operational readiness. Japan's carrier strength in the South-West Pacific was reduced to *Shokaku* and *Zuikaku*, the last fleet carriers left after Midway. The light carrier *Ryujo* was assigned to operate with them, maintaining nominal parity with the American trio.

In terms of carrier fighters, the Japanese still held the *matériel* advantage with the magnificent Zero, but it was a dwindling advantage, and heavy inroads had been made into the Japanese Navy's reserves of expert pilots by the Coral Sea and Midway battles, and the Zero had shown itself to have considerably less 'survivability' than the Wildcat.

Aftermath: Ensign George Gay, the only survivor of *Hornet*'s Torpedo 8 from the attack on the morning of 4 June, reads the news of the Midway triumph in the Naval Hospital at Pearl Harbor. Gay was rescued by a PBY on 5 June after spending 24 hours in the water; he had watched the destruction of Nagumo's carriers, hiding from strafing Zeros beneath the cushion used by his dead rear gunner.

For their part, the Americans were, by June 1942, phasing out the death-trap TBD Devastator which had carried the brunt of torpedo operations at Coral Sea and Midway. The Devastator's replacement was an excellent new torpedo-bomber, the Grumman TBF Avenger. Faster and much better armed than the Devastator, with a power-operated rear dorsal twin turret, the Avenger could also carry double the bomb-load: up to 2000 lbs.

Wasp — the new arrival

Of the three American carriers in the South Pacific, *Wasp* was the uncertain factor. She not only lacked any Pacific combat experience — even *Saratoga* had more — but was known to have a woefully under-strength AA battery which there was not time to augment. *Wasp*'s eight 5-inch guns lacked the rapid-fire back-up of a 40 mm or even 20 mm battery, the absolute necessity of which had been rammed home at Coral Sea and Midway.

For all that, *Wasp* had already made a mighty contribution to Allied victory by the time she arrived in the Pacific. As the first large US warship to serve in the European Theatre of Operations, temporarily attached to the British Home Fleet, *Wasp* had crossed the Atlantic to fill the gap created by the detachment of British carriers for service in the Indian Ocean. When, at the beginning of March 1942, it became vital to fly out substantial reinforcements of Spitfire fighters to the island of Malta, *Wasp* was 'borrowed' for the purpose on the personal request of Churchill to Roosevelt, because there was only one fleet carrier still with the British Home Fleet, HMS *Victorious*, and her lifts could not accommodate RAF Spitfires with non-folding wings. On 13 April, *Wasp* embarked 47 Spitfires and their pilots at Glasgow and sailed for the Mediterranean next day, escorted by the battle-cruiser HMS *Renown*, two cruisers and a US/British destroyer screen. On 20 April *Wasp* headed into wind 45 miles east of Algiers and the Spitfires were flown off at extreme range, this being necessary in view of the powerful German-Italian bomber strength massed in Sardinia and Sicily.

All but one of the Spitfires landed in Malta, but so ferocious was the air bombardment of the island and the intensity of the air battles that by the time *Wasp* returned to British waters a week later, Malta had only six serviceable Spitfires left. A second supply run was essential and once again the services of *Wasp* were co-opted, this time with the old British carrier *Eagle* in company. On 8 May, *Wasp* and *Eagle* flew off 64 fighters, of which 60 arrived, and, due to greatly improved reception arrangements, survived the raids sent to knock them out. Though Malta's ordeal still had another four months to run, the vital injection of fighter strength delivered by *Wasp* had averted not only the fall of Malta but an outright Axis victory in North Africa. *Wasp*'s second delivery to Malta took place on the same day that *Lexington* was lost in the Coral Sea. Regardless of Churchill's thankful message to Roosevelt — 'Who said a wasp couldn't sting twice?' — it was the end of *Wasp*'s tour in European waters. Undergunned or not, she was desperately needed in the Pacific.

'Watchtower' and the Guadalcanal crisis, June–August 1942

In the weeks after Midway, the 'Watchtower' plan was accepted as a saner Navy alternative to General MacArthur's demands for a direct amphibious assault on Rabaul, for which there were clearly not enough land, sea or air resources. Launched by South Pacific Command forces, 'Watchtower' would be 'Task One' in a step-by-step advance on Rabaul, opening up the central Solomons by taking

Wasp in the spring of 1942, while still serving with the Atlantic Fleet at Casco Bay, Maine, with Wildcats and Dauntlesses ranged on deck.

Wasp's first Spitfire ferry run to Malta: the scene on her flight-deck the day before the Spitfires were flown off at extreme range (20 April). The Wildcats of *Wasp*'s combat air patrol are ranged forward of the Spitfires. Only twelve of the Spitfires were tied down on deck; the other 35 occupied the hangar deck below. In the week after *Wasp* made this historic delivery, ferocious *Luftwaffe* attacks on the Malta airfields wiped out all but six of the Spitfires, necessitating a second ferry run by *Wasp* in May — her 'second sting', as Churchill put it.

Tulagi and Guadalcanal. 'Task Two' would be the capture of the northern Solomons by MacArthur's South-West Pacific Command. Only then, with MacArthur's forces hemming in Rabaul from the south-east, would the time be ripe for 'Task Three': the assault on Rabaul itself.

This orderly and methodical approach collapsed in the middle of June 1942, when it was learned that the Japanese had already started to lay out a new airfield on Guadalcanal. Once the new field was operational and garrisonned, 'Watchtower' would be hopelessly jeopardized. The only chance was to stage a pre-emptive invasion to snatch Guadalcanal from the Japanese before they could build it up to a level as formidable as, say, Lae and Salamaua on the New Guinea coast. The result was a frenzied five weeks of preparation for an amphibious landing on an island about which next to nothing was known — apart from the fact that an airstrip on it had to be taken and held regardless of losses.

On 7 August 1942, General Vandegrift's 1st Marine Division, which had not expected to go into action until 1943, was dumped ashore with none of its heavy transport, only 60 days' rations and supplies, enough ammunition for only ten days of heavy fighting and the minimum of individual equipment. And that was after two postponements and a 'dress rehearsal' landing exercise in the Fijis described by one observer as 'a fiasco, a complete bust'. The only good thing to be said for the invasion of Guadalcanal was that the timing was perfect. The airstrip was virtually ready to receive aircraft but the Japanese garrison had not yet arrived, giving the Marines an unopposed landing on Guadalcanal. Across the sound, on Tulagi, it was a very different story. The 800-man Japanese

The vital work of servicing and arming the aircraft, in both these cases Dauntlesses aboard *Enterprise* on the eve of the Guadalcanal and Tulagi landings.

Above
The exhaust pipe makes a useful footrest during a cowling check while an ordnanceman uses a light bomb as a seat.

Right
Ordnancemen prepare to winch a 500 lb 'demolition bomb' on to its rack beneath the fuselage.

garrison fought to the last man and most of the 27 prisoners taken on 7 and 8 August were labourers, not combat troops.

Once the Navy had put the Marines into Guadalcanal and Tulagi it was up to the Navy to keep them there, and the naval command structure cobbled together for 'Watchtower' was far from ideal.

At the top, Ghormley was Commander South Pacific (COMSOPAC) at Nouméa. With Halsey still completing his convalescing and Spruance appointed Chief of Staff to Nimitz after Midway, Fletcher commanded the carrier-borne Air Support Force, TF.61: *Saratoga* (flag), *Enterprise* and *Wasp*, the new fast battleship *North Carolina*, six cruisers and sixteen destroyers. This left little scope to the tactical commander of the carrier force, Rear-Admiral Noyes. Close surface cover for Rear-

Admiral Richmond K. Turner's Amphibious Force of 23 transports was provided by the British Rear-Admiral Crutchley's US/Australian cruiser-destroyer force: eight cruisers and fifteen American destroyers in all. Both Turner and Crutchley — to say nothing of Vandegrift's Marines ashore — were totally dependent on Fletcher's carriers for protection against the furious Japanese air attacks which came boiling down from Rabaul on 7 and 8 August.

The Japanese raiders were twin-engined Mitsubishi G4M 'Bettys', which could carry either bombs or torpedoes, and Aichi dive-bombers, escorted by Zeros, the single-engined aircraft using a refuelling airstrip on Buka Island in the northern Solomons. In these early days, as throughout the entire ensuing Solomons campaign, invaluable

Enterprise recovering aircraft off Guadalcanal. One of her planes has just landed, while the Dauntless pilot above has just lowered his arrester-hook. Three other SBDs on the far side of the landing circuit can be seen, above and just to the left of the Dauntless's rudder. In the background, *Saratoga* is recovering her own aircraft with the inevitable 'plane guard' destroyer following astern, ready to retrieve any 'splashed' aircrew in the event of accidents.

Off Guadalcanal on D + 1, 8 August 1942, the ultimate in low-level attacks. Japanese 'Betty' bombers, based on Rabaul, streak in *below* the low-angle American flak in an attempt to cripple the invasion fleet off the Guadalcanal beaches. Until Henderson Field was ready to operate land-based aircraft, Fletcher's carriers were the only way in which attacks like this could be intercepted.

early-warning reports of Japanese air and sea movements were passed by the 'Coast-watchers' — dedicated groups of radio-equipped observers, living rough deep in Japanese territory. 'Coast-watcher' reports alerted Fletcher to the incoming raids on the afternoon of 7 August and his carriers put up 60 Wildcats to intercept.

In a wild encounter over beaches clogged with unloaded stores, eleven Wildcats were shot down for the loss of fourteen out of 43 Japanese bombers and two out of eighteen Zeros. On 7 August, the 'Bettys' came again, this time attacking with torpedoes at zero feet — 26 in all. *Enterprise* fighters nailed four and another thirteen were shot down as they

attacked through the dense cone of AA fire thrown up by the Amphibious Force. In addition to the destroyer HMS *Mugford*, damaged by a bomb hit on the 7th, the destroyer USS *Jarvis* survived a torpedo hit while one of Turner's transports was lost after a doomed 'Betty' pilot deliberately crashed his bomber into the ship. However, a despondent Fletcher was left with a carrier fighter strength which had slumped from 99 to 78 in the first 24 hours of the invasion — a loss rate which now drove him to take one of the loneliest, bravest, and most bitterly criticised decisions of the war. At 1807 on 8 August he radioed Ghormley at Nouméa, requesting permission to withdraw with the fleet carriers and leave Vandegrift, Turner and Crutchley to their own devices.

Fletcher's decision was that of a carrier specialist who had never believed in the feasibility of 'Watchtower', because it meant tying down fleet carriers to the close defence of a land objective. This was not how Port

Moresby and Midway had been saved in May and June. To Fletcher it made no sense to saddle fleet carriers with a 'fixed address' for enemy attacks; and even less sense to commit fleet carrriers to an endless series of defensive battles in which the carriers' main defence — their fighters — would suffer such heavy losses that they would ultimately be unable to defend their own flight-decks.

In other words, the loss of too many fighters would inevitably be followed by the loss of more carriers. Neither Ghormley nor Nimitz could reject the logic of this, nor forget that carrier reserves in the Pacific now consisted only of *Hornet*. The Guadalcanal crisis could not have broken at a more untimely moment. Like Vandegrift's Marines, the Fleet would have greatly preferred to launch 'Watchtower' in 1943, when the new 'Essex' fleet carriers would be in service. However, *Essex*, first of the new class, was only launched the week before the landings on Guadalcanal, on 31 July, and *Lexington*, the second 'Essex', was not launched until 26 September, while the third, *Bunker Hill*, followed on 7 December. For the present, however, the demands of the Guadalcanal campaign re-stated the watchword of the English when faced with the Spanish Armada: 'what you have will have to do'. But the last four American fleet carriers were not expendable. If they went the way of *Lexington* and *Yorktown*, the Japanese would be immediately restored to the commanding position which they had held on the eve of Midway.

Ghormley and Nimitz therefore reluctantly endorsed Fletcher's decision to withdraw, hoping that Crutchley's cruisers and destroyers could protect Turner's transports until the Marine supplies had been landed. These hopes were immediately dashed by a savage encounter on the night of 8–9 August: the Battle of Savo Island. A powerful Japanese cruiser-destroyer force, after an undetected approach from Rabaul, fell on Crutchley's ships and sank four cruisers. Only the belief that daylight would reveal the Japanese warships to Fletcher's carrier aircraft stopped the Japanese commander, Rear-Admiral Mikawa, from carrying on to annihilate Turner's transports. Bereft now of surface protection as well as carrier air cover, Turner had no choice but to withdraw the landing force at sunset on 9 August — leaving Vandegrift's Marines on Guadalcanal with barely half their supplies unloaded.

The Battle of Savo Island introduced an entirely unforeseen factor into the Guadalcanal equation. This was the Japanese excellence in night gunnery and torpedo actions which, though desperately challenged by the Americans in repeated encounters, remained supreme until mid-November 1942. It put the American guarantee of seaborne supply to the Marines on Guadalcanal under threat by night as well as by day, enabling the Japanese to ship their own expeditionary force to Guadalcanal. If enough Japanese troops and supplies could have been landed they would have annihilated the Marines who, apart from their own courage, were saved by two pieces of pure luck. The first was the existing Japanese commitment to a parallel campaign in New Guinea. The Japanese 17th Army had begun its overland march on Moresby from Buna on 22 July, preventing it from throwing its full strength at Guadalcanal. The second was the ludicrous Japanese under-estimate of the Marine strength on Guadalcanal, which initially sent less than 2000 Japanese troops against 17,000 US Marines. These were wiped out in the first land action on Guadalcanal, which took place on 19 August — 48 hours after the first Japanese had landed.

Meanwhile, ordering his men to dig in to repel the Japanese when they came, Vandegrift had accepted that control of the sea approaches to Guadalcanal must be considered in dispute 24 hours a day. He told his Marines that their only chance was the new airfield, which they frantically prepared to receive aircraft. On 20 August, the day after the victory over the Japanese landing-force, the airstrip received its first aircraft, flown in from the escort carrier *Long Island*: nineteen Marine Wildcats and twelve Dauntlesses. The Marines named the airstrip 'Henderson Field' after Major Lofton Henderson, who had died on the morning of 4 June leading his Midway-based squadron of Dauntlesses against Nagumo's carriers.

From 20 August Henderson Field became the focal point of the Guadalcanal campaign. Though the Japanese would need time to land enough troops to destroy the US Marine garrison and capture Henderson, they could still destroy all the Henderson-based aircraft and render the airstrip unusable by bombing and shelling. This would deny the Americans daytime air cover for shipments of reinforcements and supplies. For their part, the Americans had to keep Henderson Field operational to keep their sealane open, at least by day. Meanwhile the cruiser-destroyer forces on the spot must try their best to stop the night runs of Japanese reinforcements and supplies covered by what was soon known as the 'Tokyo Express' — nightly Japanese cruiser/destroyer sorties from Rabaul. The

five murderous cruiser-destroyer night actions off Guadalcanal, from Savo Island in August to Tassafaronga at the end of November, fall outside this story. But both of the two major battles fought by day were carrier actions: the Eastern Solomons on 24 August and Santa Cruz on 26 October. Both saw the remnants of the Japanese and American carrier forces push themselves to the limit of endurance, in what might well be called the Verdun of the Pacific War.

Battle of the Eastern Solomons

The Japanese Plan

The operation ordered by Yamamoto which brought on the Battle of the Eastern Solomons retained the characteristic intricacy which had come to grief in the Coral Sea and Midway actions. It was the most ambitious operation by the Japanese Combined Fleet since Midway, and the objective was to cover the landing of 1500 troops on Guadalcanal. Their

In the Battle of the Eastern Solomons on 24 August 1942 a Japanese bomb bursts on the port side of *Enterprise*'s flight-deck. Though his camera and film remained intact to preserve this amazing image, photographer Robert F. Read was killed by the explosion. An hour later, with her flight-deck patched, *Enterprise* was steaming into wind at 24 knots, recovering her aircraft.

transports were escorted by Rear-Admiral Tanaka's cruiser/destroyer force, and given close support by Rear-Admiral Mikawa's four cruisers. Overall cover against intervention by American carriers was provided by *Shokaku* and *Zuikaku* under Nagumo's command. All the experience of Coral Sea and Midway notwithstanding, Yamamoto still hoped to force a decisive surface action with battleships, and had added a Vanguard Group of two battleships and three heavy cruisers. Commanded by Rear-Admiral Abe, this Vanguard Group was to precede Nagumo's two fleet carriers. Scouting ahead of the fleet was Vice-Admiral Kondo's Advance Force: six cruisers and the seaplane-carrier *Chitose*.

There were, however, two important innovations. Coral Sea and Midway had been notable for the negative role played by Japan's impressive submarine fleet, and this time Yamamoto planned a more active part for it. Six submarines were to spread out in a patrol line ahead of the fleet, while others were to lurk in the Coral Sea on the watch for the American carriers. Yamamoto also hoped to exploit the weakness displayed by the Americans on the first day of the Coral Sea fight: pouncing on the first likely Japanese carrier target and leaving the American carrier task force unprotected against a full-strength counter-blow. Rear-Admiral Goto, whose *Shoho* force had unwittingly acted as a decoy in the Coral Sea battle, was to play the same part again, this time deliberately, with a Diversionary Force: the light carrier *Ryujo*, a cruiser and two destroyers.

Yamamoto's planning contained much of the same dangerous reliance upon the enemy doing what Yamamoto hoped he would do. There was, for instance, no guarantee that the carefully-layered deployment of the Japanese Fleet would be sighted in the ideal sequence: first the submarines, then the Advance Force, then the Diversionary Force luring away the American carrier aircraft, then the Vanguard and carrier Striking Forces, and lastly — hopefully not sighted at all — the troop transports and their escorts. This time, however, the Americans made so many mistakes that the Japanese plan nearly succeeded. It was Frank Jack Fletcher's third and last carrier battle, and the one in which his judgement let him down the most.

21–23 August: The preliminaries

Even Yamamoto never counted on the Americans' failing to detect the Combined Fleet's move south from Truk to the Rabaul area, and by 21 August Fletcher had brought TF.61 forward to the eastern approaches of the Coral Sea. If the Japanese strength was still uncertain, Fletcher was commanding the most powerful task force which the US Pacific Fleet had ever sent out to tackle the Japanese: fleet carriers *Saratoga*, *Enterprise* and *Wasp* with the new battleship *North Carolina* in close support, nine cruisers and seventeen destroyers. For the first 48 hours after placing the northern approaches to Guadalcanal within range of his reconnaissance aircraft, Fletcher was content to wait for the Japanese to show their hand. On 23 August, however, events proved Yamamoto's planning to have been both right and wrong.

The first Japanese ships spotted on 23 August *were* submarines of the advance patrol line. Two were sighted in the forenoon and attacked by aircraft from *Enterprise*, but managed to dive and escape. The next ships sighted, a few hours later, were the transports and Tanaka's escort. They were not instantly recognisable as such — the troops had been embarked in four old destroyers and a converted light cruiser — but such a large cruiser/destroyer force heading south could only have one destination. Luckily for the Japanese, they were sighted by an island-based seaplane well out of range of TF.61: 300 miles to the north. As soon as the seaplane left, Tanaka reversed course to the north, together with the main Japanese fleet. Though Fletcher ordered *Saratoga* to attack, the 31 Dauntlesses and six Avengers which took off at 1445 therefore found nothing.

The Japanese course reversal was a tactic evolved from painful experience in the Coral Sea and Midway battles when many aircraft on both sides had been lost without firing a shot, 'splashed' with empty tanks after a fruitless search for the enemy. This time, however, the Americans had a refuge: Henderson Field, where *Saratoga*'s aircraft headed to refuel at dusk. Once replenished, they were able to rejoin *Saratoga* next morning without loss. However, Tanaka's ruse was not a total failure: it led Fletcher to make a fateful decision. Obsessed as ever by the need to keep his carriers topped up, he treated the elusive Japanese ships as a false contact, of which there had indeed been many in previous months, and detached *Wasp*'s task group to refuel 240 miles to the south. What he did not know was that the Japanese Fleet had reversed course again on the night of 23–24 August and was again heading straight for him, while he had reduced his carrier force by a third.

24 August: Fletcher snatches at the Japanese decoy

The Battle of the Eastern Solomons began on 24 August when a Guadalcanal-based aircraft sighted a Japanese carrier force 300 miles to the north, heading south. Unaware that this was only *Ryujo* and Goto's Diversionary Force, Fletcher promptly ordered TF.61 north to close the range and investigate, but this was easier said than done. The wind was blowing steadily from the south-east, forcing TF.61 to reverse course into it whenever aircraft had to be operated. Late in the forenoon Fletcher sent off a reconnaissance-in-force from *Enterprise*, consisting of 29 Dauntlesses and Avengers, and soon afterwards TF.61's radar detected what was obviously a Japanese air formation coming in from the west. These were actually a small strike group from *Ryujo*, launched to rendezvous with a 'Betty' formation out of Rabaul and attack Henderson Field early in the afternoon. This attack, however, was a failure. The Marine Wildcats on Guadalcanal were up and waiting; they shot down 21 of the attackers, for the loss of only three of their own.

Fletcher had meanwhile launched his first search-and-strike force at 1345: 30 Dauntlesses and eight torpedo-carrying Avengers, from *Saratoga*. They were unescorted, to keep back the maximum possible number of Wildcats, 53 in all, for the defence of TF.61; but while *Saratoga*'s strike force found *Ryujo* and the Diversionary Force, *Enterprise*'s search planes found the main Japanese carrier force. As at the Coral Sea, Fletcher had launched a major strike against a minor target.

In the morning, Fletcher's main natural enemy had been the wind; in the afternoon, it proved to be bad atmospheric interference, preventing him from diverting *Saratoga*'s aircraft to attack Nagumo. As with *Shoho* at the Coral Sea, *Ryujo* was overwhelmed by the strength of the American attack but though riven by repeated 1000 lb bomb hits, she took only one torpedo. *Ryujo* did not go down until 2000 on 24 August, by which time most of her surviving crew had been taken off. None of *Saratoga*'s aircraft were lost in the attack.

24 August: The Japanese counter-blow

As had happened before, the rival carrier forces had sighted each other roughly at the same time, and Nagumo launched his counterblow from *Shokaku* and *Zuikaku* as *Saratoga*'s aircraft hit *Ryujo*. The Japanese strike consisted of two waves: the first of 30 'Vals' and the second of eighteen 'Vals' and nine torpedo-carrying 'Kates', both waves having a strong Zero escort. The incoming first wave was detected on TF.61's radars at 1602, and no time was lost in preparing for action. All aircraft left in *Saratoga* and *Enterprise* were promptly launched, including thir-

Battle of Eastern Solomons, Aug. 24, 1942 & Battle of Santa Cruz, 26 October 1942

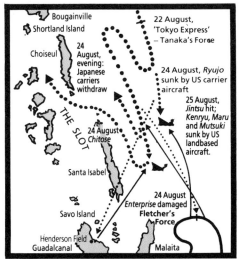

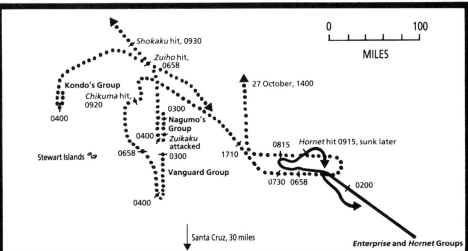

teen Dauntlesses and twelve torpedo-carrying Avengers ordered to find and attack the Japanese carriers. 'Buttoning up' continued with the now-routine draining of fuel lines, isolation of tanks and pumping CO_2 into empty lines and tanks to prevent explosions. The two carriers moved out ten miles apart, each at the centre of a defensive formation of escorts.

In the air battle which followed, the main American weakness again proved to be radio discipline and fighter direction. As at Midway, 'friendly' aircraft returning from the search-and-strike mission complicated the situation, but even so there were enough Wildcats in the air to have coped with the Japanese first wave — given taut radio discipline to enable the fighter control officers to do their job. The latter were not given the chance to detail a portion of Wildcats to handle the Zeros while the rest went for the 'Vals'. Instead, the fighter control frequency was flooded out with excited 'chatter' from the pilots, far too many of whom went for the Zeros. It is easy to be too censorious of this radio indiscipline, an important factor though it certainly was. The real culprit here was the fearsome reputation earned by the Zero in nine months of war. Any fighter pilot's first kill is an unforgettable moment, but in the Pacific War downing one's first Zero meant far more. (It may be worth remembering that the Zero's shadow had even reached into Tin Pan Alley. A particularly mawkish American popular song of this time moralised on the apotheosis of Johnny, whose schoolwork was so bad that folks were always saying 'Johnny's got a zero'. But Johnny grew up and became a US Navy pilot — 'and now folks cheer 'cause Johnny's got a Zero'.)

In any event, the Zeros attacking TF.61 on the afternoon of 24 August fulfilled their mission. At great cost to themselves, the Zeros and 'Kates' drew the Wildcats down towards sea level, allowing the 'Vals' to begin their dives. The attackers concentrated on *Enterprise*, to whose group *North Carolina* had been attached, doubtless in the belief that a carrier with a battle ship in company was a more warrantable target than one without. For most of the 'Val' pilots, this was the last mistake they ever made. No Japanese carrier men had ever attacked a battleship with fire-power like this one: twenty 5-inch DP, sixteen 1.1-inch in four quadruple mounts, 40 20 mm cannon and 26 .5-inch machine-guns. For all that, *Enterprise* suffered three heavy bomb hits in rapid succession, two of them exploding on lower decks, before the surviving attackers withdrew at 1648.

Though badly damaged internally and set on fire, *Enterprise* did not lose power, as had happened to *Yorktown* at Midway. The fires were fought, the flight-deck patched, and in little over an hour *Enterprise* was steaming into wind at a brisk 24 knots, recovering her aircraft. However, there was much sea water still aboard after the firefighting, and at 1821 some of it caused a major short-circuit in the steering-engine room, and the rudder jammed. There was no alternative but to stop ship until full steering could be restored. It took 38 minutes, an eternity with Japanese submarines known to be in the offing, and while *Enterprise* lay defenceless her radar detected what was clearly a second Japanese air strike searching for TF.61. Though the Japanese came within 50 miles of *Enterprise*, they never sighted TF.61, which withdrew south to refuel after *Enterprise* had got under way again and recovered her last aircraft.

Saratoga's group had meanwhile escaped unmolested from the afternoon's attacks. This was *Saratoga*'s first carrier battle and her later contribution was modest in comparison to that of *Enterprise*: a search-and-strike mission which found the battleships and cruisers of the Japanese Advance Force. Two Dauntlesses and five torpedo-carrying Avengers failed to make much of an impact on the Japanese warships which, faster than the carriers, evaded the American aircraft with ease; but the slower seaplane-carrier, *Chitose*, had a perilous voyage home to Truk with a flooded engine-room after her side was stoved in by near-misses from one of the Dauntlesses.

Eastern Solomons: The action assessed

The action ended with both sides withdrawing at dark on 24 August. It was one of the more unusual carrier battles of the Pacific War, with the customary tempering of aggression with caution far more pronounced than usual. Certainly, the hard results were more depressing for the Japanese than for the Americans. Though *Shokaku* and *Zuikaku* remained intact, Nagumo's air group had taken a terrible beating, with 90 Japanese aircraft lost, including those from the sunk *Ryujo*, to the Americans' twenty. As at Midway, however, Nagumo believed that his attacks had left at least one and maybe two American carriers crippled and burning. This hope was punctured by Kondo's Advance Force, which hurried south athirst for a night gunnery action, only to retire empty-handed at midnight with the news that the American carrier force must be presumed still intact.

Nagumo's caution in declining to renew the action on 25 August is understandable enough. After Midway, he was, after all, the only admiral ever to have lost a fleet of four carriers in a single day. It is interesting that Nagumo's opposite number at the Eastern Solomons was Fletcher. Though on opposite sides of the hill, each admiral believed in his heart that maintaining a strong carrier fleet in being was a lot more important than pushing through the Guadalcanal business. The junior admirals entrusted with the job of pushing through the Guadalcanal business naturally felt otherwise, and none more so than Rear-Admiral Tanaka. Dawn on 25 August found his transports left in the lurch without carrier cover, but Tanaka was determined to get the troops through to Guadalcanal. He was attacked, 120 miles north of Henderson, by Guadalcanal-based Dauntlesses hunting for Nagumo's vanished carriers. Fires were started aboard *Jintsu*, Tanaka's flagship, and one of the transports. The latter was dead in the water, her troops and crew being taken off by a destroyer alongside, when eight B-17s arrived on the scene from Espiritu Santo. Though the prodigious expenditure of bomb tonnage by the B-17s in earlier months had never been repaid by a commensurate proportion of hits, this time the B-17s not only had no fighter opposition but an immobile target, and both transport and destroyer were sunk. This marked the failure of the grand attempt at a daylight troop shipment to Guadalcanal under the wing of the Combined Fleet. Tanaka was ordered to withdraw with the surviving transports and resume troop shipments by the nightly 'Tokyo Express'.

Apart from his underlying determination to keep the American carrier fleet in being, Fletcher had wasted the chance of dealing a shattering blow at the dwindling stock of Japanese carriers by sinking or even crippling *Shokaku* and *Zuikaku*. His genuine achievement at the Eastern Solomons, the savaging of Nagumo's carrier air group, was largely invisible at the time; the visible fruits of victory, *Ryujo*'s sinking, were disappointingly small. The traumatic continuing success of the Japanese with their 'Tokyo Express' night runs also did much to discourage realization of the fact that Eastern Solomons represented the third successive defeat of a Japanese seaborne invasion.

August–September 1942: decimation of the American carriers

In the short term, Japanese discomfiture in the Eastern Solomons fight enabled Fletcher's task force — like a Saxon English army winning a fleeting victory over the Danes — to 'hold the place of slaughter' and cover the

reinforcement of the Marine air strength operating from Henderson Field. By the end of August 1942, 64 Marine aircraft were operating from Henderson, extending yet another brief respite to Vandegrift's hard-pressed troops. This was only achieved by keeping the American carriers on a fatally predictable beat, the 400-mile stretch of the Santa Cruz basin between San Cristobal and Espiritu Santo. And the result, due very largely to the US Navy's delinquency with anti-submarine precautions, led to the frightening decimation of the carrier task force in less than a month from the Eastern Solomons battle.

With *Enterprise* recalled to Pearl Harbor to repair her Eastern Solomons damage, this left *Saratoga* and *Wasp* to keep the precarious carrier umbrella extended over Guadalcanal, reinforced by *Hornet*. The first to fall victim in the waters of 'Torpedo Junction' was *Saratoga*, crippled by the submarine *I-26* on 31 August; her damage put her out of service for the next three months. Six days later *I-11* came within feet of scoring a deadly 'left and right', when her torpedoes narrowly missed not only *Hornet* but *North Carolina* as well. Even this narrow escape did not induce the task force to change its patrol beat or dangerously low-speed manoeuvering, and on 15 September it paid the penalty. A combined submarine attack by *I-15* and *I-19* blew the destroyer *O'Brien* out of the water, set *Wasp* blazing to destruction with three torpedo hits, and damaged *North Carolina* with a single hit forward.

Thirty-five years later the devastating effect of the attack on *Wasp* was vividly recalled by Raymond J. Reyes, one of the stricken carrier's survivors:

I was a rear-seat gunner in VS-72, Air Group 7, permanently assigned to Ensign Paritsky, USN — one of the best. On the afternoon of Sept. 15th we had just landed at approx. 1457 from a support patrol mission, covering transports out of Espiritu Santo. The *Wasp* had turned into the wind and planes were landing as they approached the carrier. Normally all planes would rendezvous before landing and wait for the carrier to head into the wind before proceeding to land, but being in a combat zone things weren't exactly done according to Hoyle.

As I recall, the afternoon of the 15th was a bright sunny afternoon, the kind of day one likes at sea — wind 15 to 20 knots, the sea not necessarily rough, just right for a sunny cruise, blue skies with a white cloud here and there.

Like I said, we had just landed, and I was anxious to get to our Ready Room. It was my turn to read a diary which had been written by one of our rear-seat gunners who was in the Battle of Midway. It would have made a wonderful book.

I remember getting the book in the Ready Room. Planes were still landing as I stepped out on the port catwalk to read it outside, since it was such a nice day. But I never got to sit down. As I bent over to sit all hell broke loose. The ship rocked from an

explosion and the diary went flying out of my hand into the Deep Six. My first reaction was to try and save the diary, but this was impossible. I remember looking up and seeing what looked like bombs coming down on us. But it was debris coming back down from the original explosion. Depth-charges had blown up on Number Two Elevator and had sent most of the elevator hundreds of feet into the air.

I thought we were being attacked by dive-bombers. I heard at least three explosions before the word was passed that torpedoes had hit us.

Then the destroyer *O'Brien* was sunk — and that is the understatement of the year. I had moved aft with others to the fantail of the flight-deck by this time. I remember the *O'Brien* getting hit and enveloped in water. When the water settled, there was no ship there.

Looking over to the horizon I could see the carrier *Hornet* going balls-out in a 180° turn, getting the hell out of there, with the *North Carolina* protecting her. Then we saw her take a torpedo in her bow. It didn't even faze her — she stayed right there protecting the *Hornet*.

By now I was in the water, and was later picked up by the destroyer *Duncan*. I was still on board with other survivors when she was ordered with other destroyers to sink the *Wasp*, at about 2215 that night, because she was still afloat. But the next morning PBYs out of Espiritu Santo reported the *Wasp* still afloat, though capsized, with what appeared to be at least 12 persons still alive on her hull. It wasn't till noon on the 16th that B-17s out of Espiritu Santo went out and finally sank her. At least B-17s, not the Imperial Navy, sank the *Wasp*. I know. I was there.

Unlike *Lexington* at Coral Sea and *Yorktown* at Midway, *Wasp*'s fate struck so quickly that there was no time for an orderly 'Abandon Ship'. In the shattering explosions tearing the ship from stem to stern 193 men died, with Reyes and his fellow survivors taking to the water in a *sauve qui peut*. Yet if ever a warship went to her doom with her last mission fulfilled it was *Wasp*. The transports she had been covering landed 4000 men of the 7th Marines to join Vandegrift's weary, fever-ridden garrison on Guadalcanal. They were badly needed. By the beginning of September, the night runs of the 'Tokyo Express' had already raised the Japanese strength on Guadalcanal to over 5000 men. With the unremitting daylight air attacks from Rabaul, these were more than enough to keep Vandegrift firmly on the defensive.

After the disastrous events of 15 September it was clear that the crisis not only of the

Wasp, burning and riven by repeated fuel explosions after taking three torpedoes from the submarine *I-19* on 15 September 1942. On that day, 'Torpedo Junction', TF.61's patrol area between Espiritu Santo and San Cristobal, really earned its name; as well as inflicting mortal damage on *Wasp*, Japanese submarines also sank the destroyer *O'Brien* and damaged the battleship *North Carolina*. The attack on *Wasp* was all the more devastating because one of the torpedoes detonated depth-charges on No. 2 Elevator, blowing it clean out of the ship. Though *Wasp* later capsized she remained afloat until noon on 16 September, when she was finished off by B-17s from Espiritu Santo.

Guadalcanal campaign but of the whole Pacific War had arrived. On New Guinea, Japanese forces had battled their way across the Owen Stanleys to within 30 miles of Port Moresby. Never dreaming that his troops on New Guinea would not reach their objective, General Hyakutake of 17th Army now turned his full attention to Guadalcanal. In the three weeks after 15 September the flow of Japanese reinforcements to the island continued unabated, with Hyakutake and his staff landing on the night of 9–10 October. With *Hornet* as the only operational American carrier left in the Pacific, Ghormley was powerless to prevent the Japanese from running in troops by day as well as by night. By the middle of October, the Japanese strength on Guadalcanal had virtually reached parity with that of Vandergrift's Marines — about 22,000 men — and the Japanese Navy was preparing to join the bombers in battering Henderson Field into uselessness. This would be the immediate prelude to Hyakutake's grand offensive, which would annihilate the Marine beach-head. The knife-edge on which the campaign was now balanced may be judged by the desperate events of 11–26 October which culminated in the carrier Battle of Santa Cruz — the last victory of the Japanese carrier arm in the Pacific War, yet the immediate prelude to American victory on Guadalcanal.

Battle of Santa Cruz

Prelude: The ordeal of Henderson Field

Two nights after Hyakutake and his staff were landed on Guadalcanal, another 'Tokyo Express' came down 'The Slot' — the wide sound running down the middle of the Solomon Islands chain from Bougainville to Tulagi. This was no mere supply-and-reinforcement run. It included Rear-Admiral Goto's cruiser/destroyer squadron, whose mission was to carry out the first of a decisive series of bombardments of Henderson Field.

For the first time, however, an intercepting American squadron used its radar technology to good advantage. Off Cape Esperance, Rear-Admiral Scott's force drove off the Japanese, sinking a cruiser and a destroyer and inflicting heavy damage on the others; Goto himself was mortally wounded. The day after the battle, 13 October, an American troop convoy from Nouméa landed 3000 US Army troops on Guadalcanal, while the air group on Henderson was brought up to 90 aircraft. However, the pilots operating out of Henderson still lacked radar direction, which alone could convert them from a tactical to a strategic air force, and the true weakness of their position was soon made clear.

On the afternoon of 13 August two heavy

A search-and-strike mission of two 'buddy system' Dauntlesses heads out from *Enterprise*. Their role was not necessarily limited to reconnaissance: one such pair of Dauntlesses knocked the Japanese light carrier *Zuiho* clean out of the Santa Cruz fight on 26 October before battle had been fairly joined, in a brilliant intruder attack.

raids came in: level bombers making high-altitude runs to churn up the airstrip, which the Marine fighters failed to prevent. This was only the prelude to a far more terrifying ordeal on the night of 13–14 October: a 90-minute bombardment from the battleships *Kongo* and *Haruna*, with a combined broadside of sixteen 14-inch guns. Their huge shells knocked out half the aircraft and, having set the fuel dump ablaze, reduced the ground crews to the painfully slow expedient of 'bucket brigade' refuelling. There were two more air raids on the 14th, followed by another savage bombardment on the night of 14–15 October: 752 8-inch shells from the cruisers *Chokai* and *Kinugasa*. Early on the morning of 15 October, 4500 Japanese troops were landed at Tassafaronga Point from five transports. The handful of Marine aircraft able to get airborne attacked and wrecked three of the transports, but only after the troops had landed. Japanese troop strength on Guadalcanal had now reached zenith and on the night of 15–16 October the cruiser *Myoko* and *Maya* treated Henderson Field to the heaviest bombardment yet: no less than 1500 8-inch shells. Hyakutake now prepared to launch his offensive, backed by the full weight of the Combined Fleet, which the American Fleet seemed unable or unwilling to contest.

At Pearl Harbor, Nimitz bleakly spelled out the worst admission he had ever had to make: 'It now appears that we are unable to control the sea in the Guadalcanal area. Thus our supply of the positions will only be done at great expense to us.' It took a big man to use the future tense — '*will* only be done' —

instead of the conditional — '*could* only be done'. But this was as nothing to his next sentence: 'The situation is not hopeless, but it is certainly critical.' Nimitz now decided that the time had come for a change of command at COMSOPAC; Ghormley was clearly not the vital leader demanded by the situation, a man who would make it crystal clear that the Navy would not let the troops down, no matter at what cost. On 18 October Ghormley was relieved as COMSOPAC by Halsey, who flew into Nouméa with the inspiring battle cry of 'Kill Japs, kill Japs, kill more Japs!'

No American serviceman in the South Pacific, sailor, soldier or Marine, doubted that the aggressive Halsey was the man to give the Japanese a hiding at sea. For the moment, however, it was equally clear that it would be folly to expose the lone *Hornet* until warship reinforcements arrived. Two vital ships were already making for the South Pacific at their best speed, the hastily-repaired *Enterprise* and the new battleship *South Dakota*, but for the crisis-ridden opening week of Halsey's command — 18–24 October 1942 — it was the land battle for Guadalcanal which predominated. Though Vandegrift's hemmed-in garrison continued to fight superbly, away to the north the Japanese Combined Fleet was poised to exploit what seemed to be the inevitable capture of Henderson Field by Hyakutake's soldiers.

The Japanese plan

The moment that Henderson Field was occupied, it was to be turned against its former

Hornet bears the brunt of the first Japanese carrier attack in the Battle of Santa Cruz on 26 October 1942. Here she is seen under simultaneous torpedo and dive-bombing attacks. The smoke pouring from her bow is the fire started by the crashing 'Kate' torpedo-bomber.

owners by flying-in aircraft from no less than four Japanese carriers: *Shokaku* and *Zuikaku*; *Zuiho*, sister-ship of the sunk *Shoho*; and *Junyo*, a recently-completed conversion from a luxury liner design. Never before — or, for that matter, since — has a carrier fleet sortied with its operations dictated by the outcome of a land battle, and with the express intention of transferring the bulk of its aircraft from ship to shore at the earliest opportunity. Because of this, the Combined Fleet's deployment was even more convoluted than usual and the names of its task forces were particularly misleading.

In overall command was Admiral Kondo, flying his flag in the cruiser *Atago*. Kondo wore a 'second hat' as commander of the 'Advance Force' which comprised two battleships, four heavy cruisers, a light cruiser, twelve destroyers and one of the four carriers, *Junyo*. But in fact this 'Advance Force' was the rearmost of the Combined Fleet's three task forces, cruising some 120 miles north-west of Nagumo's Carrier Force. Nagumo had *Shokaku*, *Zuikaku*, *Zuiho*, one cruiser and eight destroyers. The last time his operations had been dictated by the prior suppression of an American island garrison had been that of the Midway fiasco. On the eve of Midway Nagumo had not been under orders to transfer the bulk of his aircraft ashore as soon as the place fell — but then at Midway the American garrison had not been fighting for its life against an equally powerful Japanese force already lodged ashore. Steaming about 60 miles ahead of Nagumo's carriers was the third element of the Combined Fleet: Rear Admiral Abe's Vanguard Force, two battleships, three heavy cruisers, a light cruiser and seven destroyers. It all added up to four battleships, four carriers, fourteen cruisers and 30 plus destroyers.

Once again, Yamamoto's planning reflected the old weakness of expecting the enemy to do what was required of him: in this case, to get beaten according to schedule. The Combined Fleet was in position by 22 October, the day appointed for the capture of Henderson Field, but four days later the Marines were still holding out. Yamamoto had to advise Hyakutake that the fleet's fuel was running low and that at all costs Henderson Field must be taken on 22 October. Yamamoto was also again hoping for a decisive gunnery action to be clinched by his battleships. The Combined Fleet's battleships were pushed well forward to cope with any American carrier-based intervention, in the face of all experience to the contrary over the past ten months.

Halsey's order — 'Attack Repeat Attack!'

Halsey had always known that SoPac's naval forces were faced with an all-or-nothing engagement every bit as vital as the Midway ambush, and by 24 October he had the force with which to mount a credible challenge to the Combined Fleet.

The SoPac fleet as commanded by Rear-Admiral Thomas C. Kinkaid, a veteran of Coral Sea and Midway and a worthy successor to Fletcher. Like his opposite number, Kondo, Kinkaid wore a 'second hat': commander of TF.61, comprised of *Enterprise*, *South Dakota*, two cruisers and eight destroyers. On 24 October, TF.61, coming down from Pearl Harbor, made rendezvous with the other SoPac carrier group, TF.17, with *Hornet*, four cruisers and six destroyers. The commander of TF.17, Rear-Admiral George D. Murray, was an old carrier hand. He had been Captain of *Enterprise* from Pearl Harbor to Midway, and this was to be his first action since promotion to flag rank. In the event of a conventional surface fleet action the American carrier force had the backing of a battle squadron: Rear-Admiral Willis A. Lee's TF.64, with the battleship *Washington*, three cruisers and six destroyers. TF.64 had been formed only the week before as a hopeful antidote to the night supremacy of the 'Tokyo Express'.

Halsey left Kinkaid in no doubt that the Fabian tactics previously favoured by Fletcher were out: his job was to upset the Combined Fleet's apple-cart by offensive action. Kinkaid was to enter the Coral Sea by a northerly sweep round the Santa Cruz Islands, the eastern outliers of the Solomons group. His mission would then be 'to intercept enemy forces approaching the Guadalcanal-Tulagi area'.

Though the American warships were outnumbered by nearly two to one, the Americans held many of the favourable cards which they had played with such effect at Midway. The return of the *Enterprise* gave them more carrier strength than the Japanese had believed possible. The SoPac fleet was also well served with long-range, land-based search and strike aircraft, and the Americans also held the only operational airfield, Henderson, in the combat area. First touch with the Japanese (also as at Midway) was made by PBYs at noon on 25 October. Kondo's northerly withdrawal for the night of 25–26 October meant that a search-and-strike mission sent out by Kinkaid returned empty-handed, though unsuccessful attacks on the Japanese fleet were made by B-17s and torpedo-carrying PBYs.

While Kinkaid continued to advance northwestwards towards the Coral Sea, Kondo reversed course to be in position, ready for the fall of Henderson Field, by first light on 26 August. The Japanese fleet was sighted again, now heading south and 300 miles north-west of Kinkaid, shortly after midnight. Two torpedo-carrying PBYs launched a surprise attack three hours later, narrowly missing *Zuikaku*. The distance between the two fleets was now down to 200 miles. This narrow escape caused Kondo to turn back to the north, but Kinkaid's steady northwesterly advance prevented the distance from widening. Kinkaid's first mission of the day, sixteen Dauntless scout-bombers from *Enterprise*, was launched at 0512. By this time Halsey, all his aggressive instincts roused by the night attack of the Catalinas, had flashed an imperative signal to Kinkaid: 'ATTACK — REPEAT — ATTACK!'

The first strikes are launched

Though Kinkaid needed no such urging, he could still not forget the odds against him and was determined to follow the precedent set by Fletcher and Spruance at Midway: hold back the first strike until the position of the Japanese carriers had been accurately fixed by his own scout aircraft. His only mistake — prompted by fears of a surprise attack such as had savaged Nagumo's fleet at Midway — was

not to have his first strike force armed and fuelled ready for instant launch. Nagumo's carriers were sighted less than 200 miles away at 0650, but it took until 0730 before the American first wave took-off, and piecemeal at that: eight Wildcats, six torpedo-carrying Avengers and fifteen Dauntlesses from *Hornet*. Another half-hour passed before *Enterprise*'s contribution was airborne: eight Wildcats, nine torpedo-carrying Avengers, and nine Dauntlesses, the dive-bomber element necessarily restricted because of the sixteen Dauntlesses launched at 0512.

Nagumo — aided, it must be said, by the greater expertise of his hangar and flight-deck crews — had been quicker off the mark. The first reconnaissance report of an American carrier reached him in *Shokaku* at 0658. It took *Shokaku*, *Zuikaku* and *Zuiho* just 20 minutes to launch the Japanese first wave of 65 aircraft. To maximise chances of the 'Kates' and 'Vals' winning through, an unusually high proportion of escorting Zeros was added: about half the total force.

Thus, by 0730, both carrier fleets had launched their first strikes at each other, the Japanese with a 20-minute lead and in much greater strength. For all that, it was the American carrier aircraft, not the Japanese, which drew first blood.

Enterprise's scout bombers knock out *Zuiho*

The first attack in the Battle of Santa Cruz was delivered at 0740 by two of the search-and-strike Dauntlesses from *Enterprise* which had taken off at 0512. The search had been conducted on the 'buddy system' — a leader with his back covered by a wingman — and the first pair to sight Nagumo's carriers, Lieutenant-Commander Lee and Ensign Johnson, had been jumped by Zeros of Nagumo's combat air patrol. Lee and Johnson not only shot down three Zeros and escaped but their sighting report was picked up by another pair of Dauntless pilots, Lieutenant-Commander Strong and Ensign Irvine. With a professionalism which the wiliest Japanese veterans would have envied, Strong and Irvine used the same cloud cover into which Lee and Johnson had escaped to stalk the Japanese carriers. They reached a perfect attacking position and at 0740 both dived on *Zuiho* without a gun being fired at them, either from AA or Zero. Their two single 500 lb bombs ripped open *Zuiho*'s after flight-deck, making it impossible for her to operate aircraft.

This brilliant intruder attack reduced the Japanese carriers by 25 per cent before battle was fairly joined. But the all-important Japanese first strike was already on its way; and

Shokaku and *Zuikaku* were still able to launch a second strike force of 44 aircraft at 0822.

The first strikes — *Hornet* and *Shokaku* damaged

This was the first carrier battle in which simultaneous Japanese and American air strikes fell in with each other on the way to their targets. The American strike force was disjointed; the Japanese force was not only compact but had a comfortable numerical advantage in escorting fighters. In a brief aerial *mêlée* halfway between the enemy carrier forces, twelve Zeros fell on *Enterprise*'s strike force. Four Wildcats and four Avengers went down, in exchange for three Zeros. The net result was a 50 per cent weakening of *Enterprise*'s torpedo aircraft contribution, while the Japanese strike force remained intact — and the Japanese second wave was already airborne.

With its 20-minute lead, the Japanese first wave was the first to attack. *Enterprise*, with the best radars in TF.61, had been entrusted with fighter control and located the incoming Japanese aircraft at 0840, but American fighter co-ordination on this occasion was as poor as at the Eastern Solomons. *Hornet*'s Wildcat pilots were not deployed far enough out and were mostly left to rely on 'eyeball' sightings rather than direction by radio. The result was American confusion all round — visual 'clutter' on the radar screens and undisciplined babble in the earphones — and far too many Japanese strike aircraft getting through to launch their attacks. Against 20 'Kates' and about fifteen plunging 'Vals', the massed gunfire of the American defensive formations was left as the last defence for the vulnerable American carriers.

The two American carriers, each protected by its own screen, had moved apart as usual to split the Japanese attack — but a meteoro-

In the lull between the Japanese attacks, Wildcats just recovered aboard Enterprise *(note the still-raised arrester-wire in the foreground) have their wings folded before being struck below. A flight of Wildcats sent up to maintain the standing combat air patrol can be seen in loose formation above, at centre left of the picture.*

logical freak, born of typical Coral Sea weather, left *Hornet* to bear the brunt. At 0900 *Enterprise* and her task group, ten miles north-west of *Hornet*, took cover in a timely rain squall. *Hornet* was not so lucky and was left out in the clear. The AA gunners of *Hornet*'s group achieved wonders, shooting down twelve of the fifteen 'Vals', and over half the 'Kates', but it was not enough to save *Hornet* from murderous punishment between 0905 and 0915. The 'Val' squadron commander, hit before he had dropped his bombs, deliberately crashed his aircraft on target. The 'Val' wiped out the signal bridge, penetrated the flight-deck and caused an enormous fire below. *Hornet* would probably have

survived this blow, but not the two torpedoes which ripped open the starboard side just two minutes later. Flooding two boiler-rooms as well as the forward engine-room, the torpedoes left *Hornet* virtually powerless and dead in the water, listing heavily to port. Three more 500 lb bomb hits followed, two bursting deep below; and finally a 'Kate', set ablaze during its attack, was deliberately flown into *Hornet*'s bow, blowing up near the forward elevator. Though *Hornet*'s crew gallantly set about trying to bring her fires under contol with the aid of destroyers moving in close alongside, the shattered carrier's ordeal was not yet over.

Twenty minutes after *Hornet*'s ordeal by fire began, her air group closed on Nagumo's carriers 200 miles to the north-west. There were only eight Wildcats to protect fifteen Dauntlesses and six Avengers, and their task was rendered impossible by the group straggling into two sections during the flight out.

The four Wildcats which managed to stick with the Dauntlesses were drawn off by combat air patrol Zeros from *Junyo*, and two were shot down. Yet, though harried by Zeros before and during their attacks, eleven of *Hornet*'s Dauntlesses pushed over to attack *Shokaku* at 0930. They were rewarded with four shattering 1,000 lb bomb hits which wrecked both the flight-deck and hangar-deck and cut *Shokaku*'s speed to 21 knots. However, *Hornet*'s avengers were not poised to give the *coup de grace* with torpedoes. They only managed to find Abe's Vanguard Force, but the torpedoes they dropped at the cruiser *Suzuya* missed.

The Vanguard Force also attracted the attention of the survivors of the *Enterprise* striking force, pressing on with their mission after the mauling which they had suffered from the Zeros. Their persistence was rewarded by a Dauntless scoring a damaging direct hit on the heavy cruiser *Chikuma*.

The second Japanese attack at Santa Cruz concentrated on *Enterprise*, whose 5-inch battery is here seen throwing up a dense umbrella of flak as the dive-bombers head in to attack. The wake in the foreground is that of the light cruiser *San Juan*, taking evasive action at high speed. *San Juan* had the luck to be hit by a bomb which sliced clean through her light hull plates before bursting.

Opposite
A bomb bursts astern of *Enterprise* as she continues to hit back at the dive-bombers at Santa Cruz. Though eighteen of the 23 'Vals' which attacked her were shot down, *Enterprise* still took two bomb hits on her flight-deck. On the horizon to the right, the battleship *South Dakota* adds her impressive modern fire-power to the AA barrage.

By 1000, therefore, both the American and Japanese carrier forces had had their strike capacity reduced by half; but the balance was about to be tilted in favour of the Japanese by the second wave from *Shokaku* and *Zuikaku*, followed by a third attack, from *Junyo*.

The second and third Japanese attacks

The second Japanese attack did not repeat *Hiryu*'s mistake at Midway, and resume the assault on the battered *Hornet*. This time the Japanese objective was *Enterprise*, whose presence in the area had been detected from intercepted messages over the ship-to-ship radio telephone. The Japanese airmen were also favoured by a coincidental attack on Kinkaid's force by the submarine *I-21* which had approached without being detected by the screen of American destroyers. The attack could not have been delivered at a more crucial moment, just after *South Dakota*'s

radar had detected the approaching Japanese aircraft at 55 miles' range. Fortunately for the main targets of the task force, all of *I-21*'s salvo of torpedoes missed except for one. This hit the destroyer *Porter* which, wandering into the line of fire to pick up a downed air crew, was hit fair and square in the engine-room. The distraction caused by *I-21*'s attack effectively prevented any Wildcats from being directed against the Japanese aircraft, which attacked from 1005.

For the second time in the Pacific War, Japanese carrier crews experienced the terrifying fire-power mounted by modern battleships. *South Dakota* carried four less 5-inch DP guns than *North Carolina*, her main AA punch being delivered by 56 rapid-fire 40 mm guns (later in the war increased to 68). Less than five of the 23 'Vals' which braving this torrent of fire to attack *Enterprise* lived to tell the tale. Only two bombs hit, both of them on the flight-deck. Though major repairs were

needed after the action to get the forward elevator working again, *Enterprise* retained full power and manoeuvrability. Though subjected to a two-sided 'anvil' attack by the nine out of 24 'Kates' which were not hacked down by the Wildcats and AA fire, *Enterprise* evaded all torpedoes launched at her but, with *Hornet* still burning furiously to the west, *Enterprise* could not take on the orbiting aircraft until her flight-deck had been patched, and this work was still being rushed forward when, at 1121, TF.61 was subjected to a third attack from *Junyo*'s 29 aircraft.

Kinkaid's force was now steaming under overcast of the same type which had favoured the first American attack on the Japanese carriers, and the *Junyo* strike took full advantage of the fact. Luckily, the AA gunners and the Wildcat pilots overhead were fully alert and shot down eight of the twenty bombers which suddenly attacked through the cloud at 1121. The others went for *South Dakota* and the escorting light cruiser *San Juan*, scoring single bomb hits on each ship. Both hits were rendered innocuous by totally different causes, that on *South Dakota* being shrugged off by the battleship's 18-inch turret armour, that on *San Juan* slicing clean through the ship's wafer-thin plates to explode in the sea.

Kinkaid's decision to withdraw

By noon on 26 August the active phase of the battle was virtually over, and all the signs pointed to a Japanese victory. Kondo still had two intact carriers, *Zuikaku* and *Junyo*, while the damaged *Enterprise* was crammed with aircraft from her own group and that of *Hornet*. With four Japanese battleships ready and eager to engage *South Dakota*, Kondo had every chance of inflicting a shattering defeat on the SoPac fleet in a night gunnery action — unless Kinkaid did what Spruance had done on the night of 4 June, and ordered a withdrawal. He did so with a heavy heart, accepting that this meant abandoning *Hornet*, which the cruiser *Northampton* was attempting to take in tow. Kinkaid's overriding duty, having foiled the Japanese attempt to tip the Guadalcanal battle in their favour with the large-scale intervention of carrier aircraft, was now to keep in being the fleet which Kondo had failed to destroy with a strength advantage of two to one; and this he accordingly did.

Last phase: Death of the *Hornet*

As Kinkaid withdrew to the south-east, evading the heavy sweep of Kondo's battle squadrons, the afternoon of 26 October saw the last handfuls of Japanese carrier aircraft make repeated attempts to finish off *Hornet*. There were four such attacks, at 1515, 1540, 1550 and 1702, none of which sank *Hornet* but served to increase her list and render her damage clearly irreparable. After the last attack two of the American destroyers in company tried to sink her with torpedoes, but this only demonstrated the gross inadequacies of American torpedoes in this, the eleventh month of the Pacific War. Eight of the sixteen torpedoes fired in this sad piece of target practice ran wild, and those that hit failed to sink *Hornet*. The destroyers then turned to 5-inch gunfire, raking *Hornet* with over 400 rounds, but this only raised the fires aboard *Hornet* to incandescent levels, a beacon for the advancing Japanese. The American destroyers hastily withdrew, in the knowledge that at least *Hornet* would not now fall as a trophy to the Japanese. And so it proved. When Abe finally arrived on the scene later that night, he took one look and ordered the

blazing carrier to be sunk with torpedoes. No American carrier ever died harder than *Hornet*, which had remained afloat after being hit by three Japanese and eight American torpedoes, five bombs, two crashing aircraft and over 400 5-inch shells.

Santa Cruz: The action assessed

The aftermath of Santa Cruz saw the Combined Fleet patrolling the battle area from which it had driven the Americans, only to retire empty-handed and frustrated on the afternoon of 27 August. Kondo and Nagumo had won an empty victory because, even if both of Kinkaid's carriers had been wiped out with minimal loss to the Japanese, Henderson Field had still not been taken. Indeed, by the afternoon of 26 August, the Japanese 17th Army had suffered a shattering defeat in its reckless attacks on Guadalcanal. Over 2500 Japanese dead lay before the intact American lines, while American casualties had been light.

Santa Cruz was therefore not only an empty victory, it was also a Pyrrhic one. If Hyakutake's troops had wiped out the American garrison and taken Henderson, the Combined Fleet could only have flown in an instant air group by stripping every single carrier in the area, thus leaving the Combined Fleet entirely bereft of seaborne air cover. The reckless expenditure of Japanese aircraft and crews in the attacks at Santa Cruz had left the last Japanese carriers virtually without offensive or defensive capability, for, by the evening of 26 October, the entire Combined Fleet was down to its last 100 aircraft of all types, while the American flow of replacement aircraft and crews to the SoPac area continued to increase. Moreover, Santa Cruz had rendered non-operational the last two Japanese fleet carriers, *Shokaku* for extensive repairs, *Zuikaku* for the provision and training of a replacement air group. The remaining Japanese carrier aircraft were distributed between the only operational carriers in the south-west Pacific: the lightweight *Junyo* and *Hiyo*, both converted liners unable to make more than 26 knots. With Henderson Field not only still operational but being expanded, this was barely enough to provide the Combined Fleet with air cover by day, let alone take decisive offensive action in the Guadalcanal area. There was no alternative but to resume the night runs by cruiser/destroyer forces, with battleship fire-power added with the intention of neutralising Henderson Field. On the other hand, until *Enterprise* could complete temporary repairs at Nouméa, Halsey was obliged to make daytime supply runs under cover from Henderson Field and commit his own

battleships to frustrate the Japanese by night.

The result was the protracted encounter usually known as the 'Naval Battle of Guadalcanal' (12–15 November 1942) which began disastrously but ended with outright victory for the Americans, severing the nightly Japanese sealane to Guadalcanal and making it certain that Japan would never succeed in reconquering the island by night or day.

Battle of Guadalcanal

'First Guadalcanal', 12–13 November

The Naval Battle of Guadalcanal was concentrated in two major night actions, the first occurring on the night of 12–13 November. It was the climax of ten nights of supply-runs by Japanese cruisers and destroyers, totalling 65 warships, between 2 and 9 November, and the sailing of a major American supply convoy from Nouméa and Espiritu Santo which arrived off Guadalcanal on 11 and 12 November. Air reconnaissance on 12 November detected the massing of a powerful Japanese fleet, including two battleships, which would arrive off Guadalcanal that night. Admiral Turner's transports thereupon withdrew, leaving Rear-Admiral Callaghan to defend Henderson Field with five cruisers and eight destroyers.

In the ensuing night battle Callaghan and his staff were killed on the bridge of the flagship *San Francisco* by 14-inch shells from the battleship *Kirishima*, three American destroyers were sunk and a fourth crippled and three cruisers were battered into wrecks — one of them, *Juneau*, being blown out of the water on the morning of 13 November by a torpedo from the Japanese submarine *I-26*. Even so, the Americans were let off lightly: *Kirishima* and her consort *Hiei* had to fight with thin-walled shells intended for the bombardment of Henderson Field, not armour-piercing shell, nor did the two battleships escape unscathed. *Hiei* suffered considerable superficial damage from the armour-piercing shells fired by the American cruisers and was unable to disengage with *Kirishima* under cover of darkness. First light on 13 November revealed *Hiei* making a painful retreat 10 miles north of Savo Island, well within the reach of the strike aircraft based on Henderson Field, and of *Enterprise*, which had sailed from Nouméa on the previous day with repair crews still working on her damaged elevator.

Coming up from the south, Kinkaid launched a search-and-strike mission at dawn to harry the Japanese withdrawal up 'The Slot', but the ten aircraft launched found no targets. Kinkaid then launched nine torpedo-carrying Avengers, escorted by six Wildcats, on another search-and-strike mission. These aircraft were under orders to land at Henderson Field and operate from there after completing their mission, in the course of which they sighted *Hiei*. The first attack by *Enterprise*'s aircraft, at 1020, made certain that *Hiei* would not escape. Two torpedo hits were scored, one right aft jamming the rudder hard over and leaving the battleship steaming in circles. After landing at Henderson to refuel and rearm, the *Enterprise* force returned to *Hiei* three hours later with eight Marine Dauntlesses. Though *Hiei* survived the dive-bombing attacks, she was left dead in the water by two more torpedoes from the Avengers. As evening approached on 13 November her crew was taken off and she was scuttled, the

first Japanese battleship lost in the Pacific War.

Despite this heartening success, Kinkaid and his battle group, Lee's TF.64, were too far south of Guadalcanal to prevent another night bombardment of Henderson Field on the night of 13–14 November. This was carried out by three of Mikawa's cruisers, which destroyed eighteen aircraft and damaged 32 others, but the half-hour bombardment did not make the field unusable. As Mikawa's cruisers retired on the morning of the 14th they were furiously attacked. First to strike were six Avengers, seven Dauntlesses and seven Wildcats from Henderson, crippling one of the cruisers and damaging a second without loss. One of these, *Kinugasa*, was further damaged by two scout-bombers from *Enterprise* — heralds of the seventeen Dauntlesses from *Enterprise* which sank *Kinugasa* in short order and damaged the cruisers *Chokai* and *Maya*.

Almost at once, however, Mikawa's battered cruiser force became of secondary importance. The night bombardment of Henderson had been carried out to give temporary relief to a powerful daylight supply run on 14 November: eleven transports escorted by eleven destroyers, covered by Zeros from *Hiyo* and *Junyo*, with Rear-Admiral Tanaka ('Tenacious Tanaka', as he was nicknamed in reluctant admiration by his enemies) in command. If Mikawa's bombardment had been more effective, and if *Enterprise*'s return had

Hornet, swathed in the smoke of her fires, with destroyers taking off her crew. Repeated Japanese air attacks throughout the afternoon of 26 September frustrated all attempts to save her. Though set ablaze by eight torpedoes and over 400 rounds of 5-inch shell in attempts to sink her, *Hornet* obstinately stayed afloat and had to be abandoned. It fell to the Japanese to give her the *coup de grace* when they arrived on the scene after nightfall.

not been so timely, the gamble might just have succeeded. As it was, Tanaka's convoy was discovered and attacked by scout-bombers from *Enterprise* as early as 0830, a prelude to a murderous sequence of air attacks which continued throughout the day by strike aircraft from Henderson Field, *Enterprise* and even B-17s flying up from Nouméa. Against these attacks the Zeros from *Hiyo* and *Junyo* failed completely, another encouraging sign of how far downhill the Japanese fleet air arm had gone since its displays of prowess in the spring and early summer. By the time nightfall gave way to night, ending the American air attacks seven of Tanaka's eleven transports had been knocked out, with the wretched troops hastily transferred to the escorting destroyers. Determined to deliver what he knew to be vital reinforcements, Tanaka pressed on through the night with his last four transports.

Meanwhile, Kinkaid and Lee were preparing to counter another massive blow at Henderson Field in what developed into the second night action in the Naval Battle of Guadalcanal. For the first time in the Pacific War, battleship was to fight battleship.

'Second Guadalcanal', 14–15 November

By nightfall on 14 November Admiral Kondo was approaching Guadalcanal again, bent on carrying out the battleship bombardment of Henderson which had been foiled by Callaghan's cruisers and destroyers two nights previously. The Japanese force consisted of the battleship *Kirishima*, three cruisers and six destroyers, with an advance screen consisting of a light cruiser and three destroyers. It was sighted on the afternoon of 14 November by the American submarine *Trout* and Lee's TF.64, the battleships *South Dakota* and *Washington*, screened by four destroyers, was promptly detached to intercept.

For the coming encounter Lee held two important cards: the advantage of radar and an overwhelming advantage in heavy-calibre fire-power — eighteen 16-inch guns against eight 14-inch — but the ensuing battle was a desperate affair. *South Dakota* suffered a power failure which not only 'blinded' her search radar but silenced her gunnery control as well: she suffered heavy superstructural damage and was incredibly lucky to be hit by none of the 34 torpedoes fired at her. Two of the American destroyers were sunk and the other two damaged. It was *Washington*'s fire-power that turned the tide, smashing *Kirishima* to a wreck with nine 16-inch direct

hits and over 35 5-inch hits. The burning battleship was scuttled before daylight, along with the destroyer *Ayanami*, the only other Japanese warship lost in the action. A third American destroyer, *Benham*, had to be abandoned and sunk. The tailpiece to 'Second Guadalcanal' was the arrival of Tanaka's last four transports off Tassafaronga Point at first light on 15 November. To make sure of getting the troops ashore, Tanaka ordered the transports to beach themselves. All four were destroyed that day under unremitting air attacks from Henderson Field and *Enterprise*. The net gain to Hyakutake's army was about 2000 troops and a handful of supplies, in return for the annihilation of an entire transport fleet eleven strong.

Guadalcanal: The turning-point

The tremendous events of 12–15 November marked the turning-point not only of the Guadalcanal campaign, but of the entire Pacific War. The loss of two Japanese battleships in 48 hours, in waters hitherto dominated by the Japanese Navy at night, was shocking enough, even without the massacre of the transports by which alone the Japanese troops on Guadalcanal could be supplied and reinforced. The cumulative losses in the naval Battle of Guadalcanal meant that Halsey's SoPac forces now dominated the approaches to Guadalcanal by night as well as by day. Yamamoto therefore made the momentous decision to withdraw all his heavy warships to Truk. After 15 November the last tenuous links with Hyakutake's weary, starving, fever-ridden army were maintained by sporadic high-speed runs at night by Japanese destroyers. No more could be done but stave off the inevitable end.

The Americans wasted no time in gathering the fruits of their victory. In the ten days after Second Guadalcanal', Vandegrift's 1st Marines were relieved by an entire infantry division and two new Marine regiments but this time not so much as an extra round of ammunition or bag of rice reached Hyakutake's men. Vastly expanded and increased in length Henderson Field was built up into a formidable air base operating 127 aircraft, including eight B-17s transferred from Espiritu Santo. This transfer of SoPac's forward land air base from the New Hebrides, a strategic advance of some 570 miles, was the final guarantee that the American grasp on the eastern Solomons was secure.

None of this prevented the SoPac naval forces from having to endure a final humiliat-

ing defeat off Guadalcanal on the night of 30 December. This occurred off Tassafaronga when Tanaka led eight destroyers to unload supplies for the troops. These supplies were not to be landed directly but ditched in buoyant containers and left to float ashore. Tanaka's force was intercepted by Rear-Admiral Wright with five cruisers and six destroyers. In a brilliantly-fought torpedo and gun action, Tanaka sank one cruiser and crippled three others for the loss of only one of his own destroyers, the other seven escaping untouched. Three attempts at similar supply-runs in December, however, failed to deliver more than a trickle of supplies; and on 4 January 1943 the Japanese Imperial General Staff ordered the evacuation of the surviving troops from Guadalcanal. At the cost of three more Japanese destroyers, the evacuation was successfully accomplished in sucessive night runs during the first week of February 1943.

By the time that the Japanese order to evacuate Guadalcanal had been given, the American carrier arm had at last reached the end of eight months' of unremitting losses: *Lexington* at Coral Sea, *Yorktown* at Midway, *Wasp* and *Hornet* off Guadalcanal. Twice during the battle for Guadalcanal — after the Eastern Solomons and Santa Cruz — the battered but unsinkable *Enterprise* had returned to the fray in the nick of time. By the New Year of 1943, *Enterprise* was alone no more: *Saratoga* had returned to the South Pacific to join Halsey's command, together with four of the older battleships repaired since the Pearl Harbor raid. If Guadalcanal was the campaign which turned the course of the Pacific War, the fleet carriers were the ships without which the Americans would certainly have lost Guadalcanal. The fleet carriers were, in every sense, the saviours of the Pacific War.

Moreover, the days when an American carrier fleet consisted of only two carriers were now numbered. As 1943 opened, massive carrier reinforcements were preparing to join the Pacific Fleet — reinforcements which, as Yamamoto had gloomily predicted on the eve of the war, Japan could never hope to match. These new American carriers would be operating ever faster, harder-hitting combat aircraft, manned by aircrew with an aggressive confidence in themselves and in their weapons. After Guadalcanal, the days when the American carriers had been the last bulwark against total defeat were over. From the New Year of 1943, they became the guarantors of total victory in the Pacific.

5
Third Generation:
'Essex' and 'Independence'

On 26 October 1942, the loss of *Hornet* at Santa Cruz reduced the US Pacific Fleet to an operational carrier strength of one: *Enterprise*. Thirteen months later, when the newly-formed US 5th Fleet began the advance on Tokyo across the Central Pacific by attacking the Gilbert Islands, the assault was both spearheaded and safeguarded by six large and five light carriers, with, in addition, six light-weight escort carriers giving tactical air cover to the two groups of the amphibious invasion force. There are few more convincing examples of the immense resources of the American war machine, which, in less than a year, had raised the US Navy's carrier fleet from the verge of extinction to become the most powerful naval force in the world.

The groundwork for this enormous carrier-

The Grumman TBF Avenger began to replace the death-trap TBD Devastator as the principal carrier strike aircraft in the summer of 1942. The Avenger had twice the bomb-load and double the horsepower of the Devastator. Its fully-retracting undercarriage enhanced streamlining and performance. The biggest boon, however, was the twin .30 machine-gun turret for the rear gunner, at last giving him some genuine fire-power to hose back at the Zeros.

Avengers on deck. The aircraft in the foreground shows the open doors of the capacious bomb bay, which could also carry a torpedo internally — an immense advantage on long flights to the target, because of the elimination of the drag penalty of an externally-slung torpedo.

This view of an Avenger at launch shows a marked outline similarity to the doughty Grumman F4F Wildcat fighter. When the first Avengers were rushed out to Midway in May 1942, the type was still not included on any American aircraft recognition chart. The incoming Avengers were saved from being shot down by Midway's trigger-happy gunners by a neatly coined recognition tag: 'The TBF's like a pregnant F4F'. The Avenger's good streamlining often made its rear turret hard to spot from a distance. In August 1942, over Guadalcanal, Zero ace Saburo Sakai narrowly escaped death when he dived on a flight of Avengers which he had falsely identified as Wildcats. Flying straight into a deadly cone of .30 fire from four rear turrets, Sakai suffered terrible cranial wounds and the loss of his right eye. He still managed to nurse his aircraft 550 miles back to base at Rabaul, and kept flying Zeros to the end of the war.

building programme had been laid years before. It had started two months before the European war broke out in September 1939, and by the late summer of 1940, with the signing of Roosevelt's Two-Ocean Navy Bill, no less than eleven carriers of the new 'Essex' class had been ordered. The new class represented a deliberate attempt to incorporate all the best features of the 'second generation' carriers, and the first seven ships of the 'Essex' class (CVs. 9–15) were all built in the Newport News yards which had produced *Ranger*, *Yorktown*, *Enterprise* and *Hornet*. The other yards subsequently used for later ships of the class were Bethlehem, which had built *Lexington* and *Wasp*, and New York.

The trouble with the 'Essex' class carriers was that so much painstaking planning had gone into them that none had even been launched by the time of Pearl Harbor in December 1941. The war crisis of 1941–42 forced the United States to learn one of the most obvious yet most easily-forgotten lessons of sea power, as Britain had had to do in 1939–40: that when a peace-loving naval power suddenly goes to war it has to fight with what it has, not with what it will have in a couple of years if the enemy is kind enough to wait. The planning of the 'Essex' class had certainly not been wasted — they were the best 'massed-produced' fleet carriers ever built — but there seemed every chance of the Japanese Navy winning a runaway victory in the Pacific before any of the new carriers could join the American Fleet. In 1942, when four peacetime fleet carriers were lost in action (*Lexington*, *Yorktown*, *Wasp* and *Hornet*), only three 'Essex' class hulls were launched to replace them (CVs.9, 16 and 17). As none of these would be ready to join the Fleet until the second half of 1943, a stopgap was desperately needed.

The urgency of the crisis produced a rapid solution: the conversion of the first hulls of the 'Cleveland' class light cruisers — ordered, like the 'Essex' class carriers, in the 1940 Program — as light fleet carriers or CVLs. The 'Clevelands' were chosen because their hulls were already taking shape but had not yet passed the 'point of no return' in construction; and the chosen prototype was the cruiser *Amsterdam* (CL.59) on which work as a cruiser was halted in January 1942. This was a conversion with no time or room for frills — 'utility', in wartime jargon. The biggest problem was how to build a hangardeck, flight-deck and small island on to the slim foundation of a cruiser hull without making the end product dangerously top-heavy. This was tackled by giving the hull additional underwater beam with bulges, or 'blisters', the portside blister being weighted

with concrete to offset the weight of the island structure. The fear of top-heaviness also ruled out the combined trunking of the boiler uptakes into a single funnel; venting was confined to four small funnels angled outboard on the starboard side. The old conflict, familiar since the time of the conversion of *Lexington* and *Saratoga* nearly 20 years earlier, between internal capacity and gun armament again arose. Four 5-inch guns were originally stipulated, but these had to be abandoned to prevent their mountings and magazines eating into aircraft accommodation. The final compromise was an AA battery restricted to 26 40 mm guns, and accommodation for 45 aircraft.

By April 1942 so many problems had already been solved with the former *Amsterdam* that eight further conversions were ordered and the 'Independence' class light fleet carriers were in business, four of them having been launched by the time that the Japanese evacuated Guadalcanal in February 1943. Table 3 indicates the full extent of the 'Independence' programme, not the least of the many miracles achieved by American production in World War II.

The sheer numbers of new American heavy and light fleet carriers, fifteen in all, which

joined the Fleet down to the end of 1943 meant that an entirely new phase of the Pacific War had begun. Never again would carrier battles in the Pacific be fought between small task groups of two or three carriers on each side, as had been the case in 1942 from Coral Sea to Santa Cruz. It is interesting to compare the 'Essex' and 'Independence' classes with their Japanese opposite numbers, or nearest equivalents, *Essex* with *Shokaku* and *Independence* with *Ryuho*, the latter being an emergency carrier conversion from a submarine tender completed in November 1942 (Table 4). It is also of interest to compare this table with that for the Washington Treaty-limited carriers earlier in the book (Table 2, page 31).

From these figures it will be seen that the third generation of American fleet carriers not only enjoyed the advantage of bigger air groups, but their powerful 4-shaft propulsion was married to handier proportions — a far less elongated ratio of length to beam. This produced much greater manoeuvrability and, hence, under Japanese air attack, greater survivability. This manoeuvrability was allied with great strength of construction. Battle experience soon showed that, ship for ship, the American third-generation fleet carriers

---

TABLE 3

THE 'INDEPENDENCE' CLASS LIGHT FLEET CARRIERS

Cruiser	Hull Number	CVL	Hull Number	Launched
Amsterdam	CL.59	*Independence*	CVL.22	22 August 1942
Tallahassee	CL.61	*Princeton*	CVL.23	18 October 1942
New Haven	CL.76	*Belleau Wood*	CVL.24	6 December 1942
Huntingdon	CL.77	*Cowpens*	CVL.25	17 January 1943
Dayton	CL.78	*Monterey*	CVL.26	28 February 1943
Crown Point	CL.85	*Langley*	CVL.27	22 May 1943
Wilmington	CL.79	*Cabot*	CVL.28	4 April 1943
Buffalo	CL.99	*Bataan*	CVL.29	1 August 1943
Reprisal	CL.100	*San Jacinto*	CVL.30	26 September 1943

TABLE 4

COMPARATIVE DATA TABLE OF AMERICAN AND JAPANESE CARRIERS, 1943

	Essex	*Shokaku*	*Independence*	*Ryuho*
Displacement (tons)	27,100	25,675	11,000	13,360
Length Overall (ft)	872.00	844.75	622.50	707.40
Max. Beam (ft)	147.50	85.40	109.25	64.25
Draught (ft)	28.50	29.00	26.00	21.75
Machinery	4-shaft turbines	4-shaft turbines	4-shaft turbines	2-shaft turbines
S.H.P.	150,000	160,000	100,000	52,000
Max. Speed (kts)	33	34	31.60	26.50
Armament	12 × 5-inch 44 (later 68) × 40 mm	16 × 5-inch 70 × 25 mm	26 × 40 mm	8 × 5-inch 38 × 25 mm
Max. Aircraft	100	84	45	31
Complement	3500	1660	1560	—

Curtiss SB2C Helldiver aboard *Bunker Hill* (CV.17) in the summer of 1944. The Helldiver was a potent successor to the ageing SBD Dauntless in the dive-bombing role. It had 800 miles more range than the Dauntless, was armed with two 20 mm cannon for strafing attacks, and could also carry a torpedo internally, like the Avenger.

could stand heavier punishment than the scatter of Japanese carrier conversions frantically completed after the Midway fiasco. Four American fleet carriers had been sunk in the six months between April and November 1942, but from November 1942 to the end of the war — 34 months in all, with far greater numbers of American carriers exposed to attack — only one American fleet carrier was lost, the 'Independence' class *Princeton*.

For sheer numbers of ships completed in less than three years, the third-generation American carrier fleet has never been surpassed. By the end of the war in mid-August 1945, twenty 'Essex' class carriers had been launched, with another four following by the end of the year and being retained for postwar service; the last batch of six 'Essex' class carriers had been confidently cancelled in late March 1945. In comparison to this prodigious output, the Japanese, who had held a decisive advantage in carrier numbers until Midway in June 1942, laid down only one class of six fleet carriers in 1942–43. This was the 'Unryu' class, of which two, *Unryu* and *Amagi*, had been launched by the end of 1943. By the end of the war, however, both *Unryu* and *Amagi* had been sunk, in Japanese waters, and only one other ship of the class, *Katsuragi*, had been completed.

One basic reason for this lamentable comparison was Japan's limited industrial capacity. In 1943 alone, the United States produced 90 million tons of steel while Japan's steel production for the year was a mere 7.8 million tons, and that was 2 million tons short of target. However, the fundamental reason was the failure to assign top priority to heavy carrier construction in the prewar years. The leading obsession in Japanese prewar construction was that of the 'unsinkable' super-battleship, not the heavy fleet carrier. Where the Americans mass-produced the 'Essex' class carriers, the Japanese concentrated on the 'Yamato' class super-battleships. Of these, only two, *Yamato* and *Musashi*, were completed *as* battleships. The third 'Yamato' hull, *Shinano*, was converted with immense effort into a giant maintenance carrier, and was not ready for sea until November 1944.

A flight of Chance Vought F4U Corsairs wings its way back to the new 'Essex' class *Yorktown* (CV.10) after a pre-invasion strike at the Gilberts in October 1943. An immensely powerful fighter, the Corsair could also carry two 1000 lb bombs and had a range of 1560 miles. Its gun armament was six .50 machine-guns, two more than the Wildcat.

A Marine Corps Corsair pilot gets the 'go' for take-off. Ferrying Marine Corps aircraft to operate from newly-won and usually newly-created airfields ashore was a frequent task for the carriers, one of immense importance in speeding the American advance across the Central Pacific.

A flight of Chance Vought F4U Corsairs wings its way back to the new 'Essex' class *Yorktown* (CV.10) after a pre-invasion strike at the Gilberts in October 1943. An immensely powerful fighter, the Corsair could also carry two 1000 lb bombs and had a range of 1560 miles. Its gun armament was six .50 machine-guns, two more than the Wildcat.

knots, and carried 53 aircraft, but *Ryuho*, with $26\frac{1}{2}$ knots and 31 aircraft, *Kaiyo*, with 24 knots and 24 aircraft, and *Shinyo*, with 22 knots and 33 aircraft, were inadequate.

In every way, therefore, the flood tide of new American carriers joining the Pacific Fleet from the second half of 1943 surpassed the opposition both in quantity and quality, but this was not the only American advantage. The new carriers were not only accompanied but were actually preceded by a new generation of faster, harder-hitting, better-protected carrier aircraft. The first of the new breed, replacing the inadequate TBD Devastator strike aircraft, had been the excellent Grumman TBF/TBM Avenger torpedo-bomber. Though production of the worthy SBD Dauntless continued until July 1944 it was supplemented by the Curtiss SB2C Helldiver, which at 294 mph was not only 42 mph faster than the Dauntless but could carry a torpedo as an alternative weapon to bombs. It also had two 20 mm cannon to strengthen its punch when engaged in air combat and above all when making strafing attacks.

The most important American carrier aircraft to join the Fleet in 1943 were the new fighters. The carrier actions of 1942 had shown that fighters were not only the most vital element in any carrier's defence arsenal, but that they could, by inflicting enough losses, actually win the battle by mauling enemy air groups to the point of impotence. The two new American naval fighters which entered service in 1943 were excellently suited to the tasks of strike force escort, surface attack and carrier defence. The first of them, the Chance Vought F4U Corsair saw action over the Solomons in March 1942, operated by Marine Corps squadrons from ground bases. This was a fighting machine of such enduring excellence that it served long after the war, and was the last piston-engined fighter built in the United States. By existing fighter standards the Corsair was a hulking, crank-winged brute, with a loaded weight of 12,399 lbs, 5397 lbs more than the F4F Wildcat, and 6352 lbs more than the A6M5b Zero, but it had a top speed of 446 mph, a maximum range of 1562 miles, and could also carry two 1000 lb bombs, or, later, eight rocket projectiles or RPs. Entering operational service some six months later than the Corsair, Grumman's admirable successor to

Like *Unryu* and *Amagi*, *Shinano* was sunk in Japanese waters — on her first voyage, before her fitting-out was even complete.

Apart from the three 'Unryus', none of which saw action, Japan after Midway produced only *one* heavy fleet carrier built as such from the keel up. This was the 29,300-ton *Taiho*, laid down in July 1941 but not completed until March 1944. Designed for 33 knots, *Taiho* was completed, after the bitter experience of Midway, with an armoured flight-deck. Apart from the white elephant *Shinano*, *Taiho* was the only carrier in either

the Japanese or American Pacific fleets to be equipped with this vital aid to survival against dive-bombing attacks. Ironically, the instrument of *Taiho*'s early destruction was the submarine torpedo.

Apart from *Taiho* and the 'Unryus', Japan's last generation of aircraft-carriers was provided by a welter of improvised conversions, all but *Ryuho* from liner hulls. The seaplane-carriers *Chitose* and *Chiyoda* were also converted into light carriers of the 'Shoho' type, and were the only carriers in this ill-assorted group with 4-shaft propulsion; they could make 29 knots, but could only carry 30 aircraft apiece. None of the others was at all suitable for fleet work at speeds of 30 knots and over: *Chuyo*, *Taiyo* and *Unyo* could make only 21 knots, and carried just 27 aircraft although *Hiyo* and *Junyo* could make $25\frac{1}{2}$

Corsair strike, *Bunker Hill*, 1944. The aircraft are fitted with long-range fuel tanks and armed with the new weapon: underwing rocket projectiles, salvos of which gave each carrier strike aircraft the same hitting-power as a cruiser's gunnery broadside. Ace rocketers attacking ships would go in with guns blazing, 'walking' their bullet splashes on to the target and firing their rockets the moment the bullets struck home.

Opposite
Hellcat maintenance, July 1944, with the coast of Saipan visible in the background. This aircraft is *Minsi II*, flown by Commander David McCampbell, the Air Group Commander of *Essex* (CV.9). Note the safety lock across the cowling to prevent an accidental engine start during servicing, and the parachute pack dumped out of the way on the nose.

Fine shot of a Navy Corsair taking off on a strike mission in 1944, armed with a four-missile salvo of rockets. This is the F4U-4 variant, with a maximum speed of 446 mph at 26,000 feet.

the F4F Wildcat was the F6F Hellcat. Here was another fast-moving heavyweight, with a maximum speed of 376 mph, at a loaded weight of 11,381 lbs, and a six-gun battery of .50-inch machine-guns instead of the four guns of the Wildcat. Like the Corsair, the Hellcat was powerful enough to carry a pair of 1000 lb bombs, but the Hellcat had always been designed and produced to put an end to the Zero's supremacy, and this indeed it speedily accomplished.

Although the Avenger, Helldiver, Corsair and Hellcat all entered service in 1942–43, the Japanese were at least two years behind in introducing comparable improvements. When their new types did appear it was in depressingly low numbers, due to Japan's hopelessly outstripped industrial capacity. The latest and best Japanese aircraft did not entered service at all, the producing factories being destroyed in the American bombing of Japan in 1944–45. To take just two examples, the Japanese equivalent of the Avenger was the Nakajima B6N2 'Jill', successor to the 'Kate'. The 'Jill' did not enter service until summer 1944 and only 1268 were produced, in comparison to 9756 Avengers turned out by Grumman and Eastern Aircraft for US Navy service, and nearly a thousand more produced for the British Fleet Air Arm. Then there was the excellent Kawanishi N1K1-J *Shiden* (Lightning), given the Allied code name 'George', and its even better successor the *Shiden-Kai* ('George 21'). This fine fighter,

with four 20 mm cannon to the Hellcat's six machine-guns, had a flashing performance, but did not enter production until the end of 1943, and production of both variants did not exceed 1435; in comparison, Hellcat production, excluding aircraft for the British Fleet Air Arm, totalled 10,919. The plight of Japan's air forces was perhaps best typified by the Zero's successor, the Mitsubishi A7M2 *Reppu*, which did not fly until May 1945. In the opinion of both Japanese fighter pilots and of Americans who test-flew it after the war, the *Reppu* outclassed every American fighter in service — but only *eight* of the type had been completed by the end of the war, full-scale production being rendered impossible by the wrecking of the Mitsubishi factories under American bombing.

Another American advantage was the superior use of superior manpower. At its zenith in 1941, the Japanese navy had about 3500 naval pilots, most with between 500 and 800 hours experience and many with combat experience from the Chinese war. By the end of 1942 the US Navy had over 31,000 naval pilots in training, none of whom was assigned to an operational squadron without at least 600 hours' air time in training. In 1943, the Japanese equivalent, after the heavy aircrew losses in the 1942 carrier battles and the introduction of emergency training programmes to produce 'instant aircrew', was assigned to an operational squadron with only 50 to 100 hours' training air time. It was small

wonder that only 40 per cent of Japanese aircrew losses from 1943 resulted from combat; a staggering 60 per cent was due to accidents and crashes in training or in ferrying aircraft. Here again, the American big battalions had the edge in both quality and quantity.

Even with all the new carriers, the new carrier aircraft and the ever-growing stream of well-trained and experienced aircrew on which to draw, the American fleet carrier arm still had one overwhelming advantage which its Japanese counterpart had never enjoyed, even at the height of its strength and its success in 1941–42. This was the creation of a 'parallel fleet' of light escort carriers to give separate air cover to the transports and freighters of the amphibious fleets from autumn 1943. This gave the task groups of the American fleet carrier arm an operational freedom unknown in any navy before or since 1943–45.

For the first half of 1943, however, the new era of carrier warfare had yet to dawn, as the first carriers of the 'Essex' and 'Independence' classes completed fitting-out and their air groups continued training on the new aircraft types. The American carrier strength in the South Pacific remained at the low level to which it had been reduced in September–October 1942 and there was no chance of recalling *Enterprise* and *Saratoga* for the prolonged spell in dockyard hands which both ships badly needed. The first carrier reinforcement came not from the United States but all the way from Britain: the protected fleet carrier HMS *Victorious*.

After the loss of *Hornet* at Santa Cruz, even the anglophobic Admiral King had had no option but to ask the British to lend a fleet carrier for Pacific service. Willing enough though they were to respond in kind to the despatch of an American squadron to serve with the British Home Fleet in the summer of 1942, the British had been unable to respond at once. Every available British carrier, as well as the American *Ranger*, was earmarked to cover the first Allied seaborne invasion in the European Theatre of Operations: 'Torch', the Anglo-American invasion of French North Africa. 'Torch' was finally launched on 8 November 1942 but the British Admiralty could spare no carriers until the success of the venture was assured, and *Victorious* did not sail for the Pacific until 19 December. She reached Pearl Harbor on 4 March 1943, but two months, by no means an excessive period, were needed for training in American signalling techniques and the operating of American aircraft. Finally, on 8 May, *Victorious* sailed for Nouméa to join Halsey's command, releasing *Enterprise* for repair and refit.

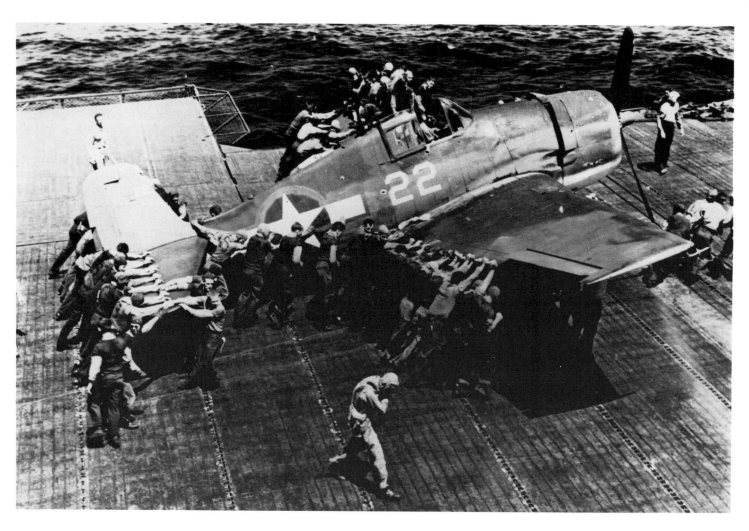

How the 'Essex' class carriers looked two years later: *Bunker Hill* at Puget Sound in January 1945. Note the additional sponsons for rapid-fire 40 mm weapons, raising the allocation of 40 mm guns from 44 to 68.

Opposite above
Not even the Hellcat was immune from the occasional engine failure, when there was no alternative to plenty of manpower to wheel the aircraft out of the way. The outboard flight-deck elevator can be seen behind the tailplane as the disgusted pilot walks away from his aircraft. The carrier is the second *Lexington* (CV.16), in 1944.

Opposite left
First of the new breed: *Essex* at Hampton Roads in January 1943, with a 'factory finish' paint job including the flight-deck planking, and outboard elevator vertically raised before being lowered flush with the ship's side. The most obvious feature is the dramatic increase in AA armament: four twin and four single 5-inch mounts, and 44 40 mm.

By the time that *Victorious* arrived in the South Pacific, it was already clear that the Japanese had done Halsey an enormous favour by adopting what soon proved to be a disastrous new strategy. Instead of hoarding his naval aircraft to build up new air groups for *Shokaku*, *Zuikaku*, *Hiyo* and *Junyo*, then forcing a carrier action with *Enterprise* and *Saratoga*, Yamamoto had squandered his available naval aircraft in a land-based air offensive against the Americans in New Guinea and the Solomons. This was Operation 'I', to which were committed 96 naval Zeros and some 70 strike aircraft, 65 of them 'Vals', from the carrier arm. Operation 'I' was launched on 1 April 1943 with the objective of regaining Japanese air supremacy over the entire South-West Pacific area, but, as so often happens with attrition strategies, the attrition was suffered by the wrong side. By 13 April, four major Japanese air sweeps over the Solomons and New Guinea had resulted in the biggest air battles yet seen in the Pacific War; and Yamamoto was well pleased. From the reports served up to him, he believed that 'I' had already accounted for 175 American aircraft, a cruiser and two destroyers. In fact,

less than twenty American aircraft had been destroyed, plus one destroyer, an anti-submarine trawler, a tanker and a merchantman sunk, a minesweeper damaged and a merchantman beached in exchange for over 36 Japanese aircraft destroyed. This was no vengeance for the 'Battle of the Bismarck Sea' of 2–3 March, when American land-based aircraft had sunk seven transports and four destroyers carrying troops from Rabaul to New Guinea.

Yamamoto did not live long enough to realise what a failure 'I' had been. On 18 April, with his movements forecast by American intelligence, Japan's leading naval strategist was shot down and killed on a flight from Rabaul to Bougainville by US Army Air Forces P-38 Lightning fighters which had flown up from Guadalcanal to ambush him. The circumstances of Yamamoto's death were the most convincing demonstration possible of the failure of 'I' and the retention of air supremacy by the Americans in the South Pacific Area.

By the time Yamamoto died, American strategy for the Pacific theatre after the Guadalcanal triumph was rapidly falling into

Launch of the new *Lexington* (CV.16) on 26 September 1942. The retention of the open bow, as featured in every American carrier since *Ranger*, permitted location of a 40 mm sponson in the eyes of the ship, below the forward edge of the flight-deck.

Opposite
'Hull 397' becomes USS *Ticonderoga* (CV.14) as she takes the water on 7 February 1944, also at Newport News.

Launch day for *Franklin* (CV.13) at Newport News on 14 October 1943. From this angle the superimposition of flight-deck and hangar deck above the main hull is particularly striking.

place. This was signified in March 1943 by the creation of two new American fleets, the 3rd and 7th Fleets. The 3rd Fleet, based on Nouméa and Espiritu Santo, was commanded by Halsey, who also retained his 'second hat' as ComSoPac. Its task was to support the forthcoming advance up the Solomons to Bougainville which had begun on 21 February with unopposed landings on the Russell Islands and which was scheduled to assault New Georgia (central Solomons) in midsummer. The 7th Fleet was created to support MacArthur's SoWesPac's forces off New Guinea and New Britain during the clearance of northern New Guinea and the isolation of Rabaul. The first commander of the Australian-based 7th Fleet was Vice-Admiral Arthur S. Carpender, but on 26 November 1943 he was succeeded by Vice-Admiral Thomas C. Kinkaid of Santa Cruz fame.

From the start it was obvious that neither 3rd Fleet nor 7th Fleet, in their immediate operational tasks, need depend on fleet carrier support for their all-important air cover. The latter could now be provided by the ever-growing US Marine and Army air forces attached to both SoPac and SoWesPac commands: SoPac from the enormous air base being built up around the former airstrip of Henderson Field on Guadalcanal, and SoWesPac from its airfields in New Guinea and Australia. The desperate days of August–November 1942, when there had been no option but to expose fleet carriers and new battleships off Guadalcanal, were over. There was no longer any need for heavy fleet units to be put at risk as the Solomons campaign continued; and the New Guinea campaign was a land battle, fought on the greatest landmass in the Pacific apart from the Australian continent.

Thus, for the first half of 1943, Halsey's two fleet carriers had only to keep clear of Operation 'I', which petered out at the end of April, then resume a watching brief, alert for any unforeseen sorties by Japanese carriers. No such sortie was ordered by Yamamoto's successor, Admiral Mineichi Koga, whose main concern was strengthening the perimeter defences of the Japanese Empire. As a result, SoPac and SoWesPac assumed the supportive role with which the fleet carriers had hitherto been tasked. This had profound results on American strategic planning.

The effective release of the fleet carriers from the South-West Pacific theatre gave new weight to the US Navy's foremost strategic argument in 1943: that the direct road to Tokyo lay across the Central Pacific, not obliquely angled northwards through the Philippines via the Solomons and New Guinea. King and Nimitz were in broad agreement that the Navy's task was to bring about the defeat of Japan by the speediest possible means: neither was, like MacArthur, personally pledged to 'return' to the Philippines. This led to a struggle between MacArthur on the one hand and King and Nimitz on the other over whether the liberation of the Philippines should or should not be the prime naval objective of the Pacific War.

The solution, established at the 'Trident' Conference between Roosevelt, Churchill and the Joint Chiefs between 12 and 25 May 1943, was a compromise. MacArthur's 'Elkton' plan — to use the Solomons and eastern New Guinea as bases for the neutralisation of Rabaul, before reconquering the rest of New Guinea as a springboard for the invasion of the Philippines — was to go ahead. However, so was the Central Pacific offensive, entrusted to Nimitz, which had the conquest of Kwajalein Atoll in the Marshall Islands as its first major objective. Unlike the task confronting MacArthur in SoWesPac, however, the Central Pacific offensive demanded solutions to problems which had never been posed before in the history of naval warfare.

All these problems stemmed from one root: distance from base. The first Pacific invasion, of Guadalcanal, had only to traverse some 750 miles of sea from New Caledonia, covered the whole way by land-based air cover in the form of B-17s and PBY reconnaissance. Kwajalein was 2500 miles from Pearl Harbor, the main base of the Central Pacific Force in 1943. Both the invasion fleet and its covering task groups of carriers and fast battleships would have to be maintained at sea; new carriers for the fleet were only the start of the logistics problems. Also required were much greater fleets of supply vessels: scores of fast oilers, storeships, repair and replenishment ships, and transports to maintain the warships of the Fleet and the troops whose passage they secured. Once taken, Kwajalein would have to be converted into a proper base for the next bound: a mere 1400 miles north-westward to the Mariana Islands. That the Central Pacific offensive got under way as early as November 1943, only five months after the decisions taken at the 'Trident' Conference, was an incredible achievement.

To sum up, even the British, in their ceaseless blockade of Napoleon's continental Empire some 140 years before, had never

Portside profile of *Lexington*

Bow quarter view of *Bunker Hill* as completed, showing forward portside AA mountings.

Hancock (CV.19) sporting a striking dazzle camouflage scheme, intended to break up the ship's silhouette and make snapshooting by enemy submarines — a hazard to carriers from start to finish of the Pacific War — as difficult as possible.

In business: *Ticonderoga* leaves Hampton Roads on 26 June 1944, with the Hellcats and Avengers of her newly-embarked air group ranged on deck.

The new *Wasp* (CV.18) as completed in autumn 1943. Her original name, *Oriskany*, was reassigned to CV.34, one of the last 'Essex' class carriers to be completed after the war.

Ticonderoga landing-on aircraft in June 1944. The aircraft ranged right forward are already being struck down to the hangar deck via the forward elevator. The last aircraft down are being moved to the outboard elevator to clear the deck for the next arrival, already 'in the groove' for landing.

attempted what Nimitz was required to do in late 1943. So great were the distances involved that it would only be possible to rest and repair the fighting ships and logistic fleet in rotation. When Nimitz opened the Central Pacific offensive, he did so in the knowledge that he was sending his country's strongest fleet to sea — and that it could never return *as* a fleet until Japan had been beaten and the war was over.

Birth of the 5th Fleet

The commander chosen by Nimitz for the ships of the Central Pacific Force — designated 5th Fleet from 15 March 1943 — was Vice-Admiral Spruance, returning to sea for the first time since his triumph at Midway. His first task was to plan the conquest of the Gilbert Islands, which Nimitz had insisted must precede the attack on Kwajalein in the Marshalls. By taking the Gilberts first, the Marshalls attack would be relieved from the threat of any flanking land-based air attacks from the atolls of Tarawa, Betio and Makin in the Gilberts. The Gilberts also had the advantage of lying within range of the land-based US 7th Air Force at Funafuti in the Ellice Islands.

The landings on the Gilberts were entrusted to the Assault Force under Rear-Admiral Richmond K. Turner, who had had the same job at Guadalcanal and the central Solomons. The Assault Force comprised two

task forces, the Northern Attack Force (TF.52) sailing from Pearl Harbor, and the Southern Attack Force (TF.53) from New Zealand and Efate in the New Hebrides. Each sailed with a force of three escort carriers, a battle squadron and a powerful cruiser/destroyer force, a combination which provided tactical air cover and ample fire-

power for pre-landing bombardments.

The cutting edge of 5th Fleet, however, was the Fast Carrier Force, designated Task Force 50, commanded by Rear-Admiral Charles A. Pownall. TF.50 blended the speed, range, and hitting-power of six large and five light fleet carriers: *Saratoga*, *Enterprise* and the first four 'Essex' class to enter service,

The new *Yorktown* (CV.10) in May 1943, taking on her air group shortly after commissioning. By the end of the war her nickname in the Fleet was 'The Fighting Lady'.

Independence (CVL.22) with her air group aboard, underway at San Francisco on 15 July 1943. From this angle the distinctive 'cruiser' hull lines of the 'Independence' class carriers (conversions from 'Cleveland' class cruisers) stand out clearly.

Essex, Yorktown, Lexington and *Bunker Hill*, with the first five 'Independence' class CVLs, *Independence, Princeton, Belleau Wood, Cowpens* and *Monterey*. TF.50's role was at once grandiose and simple: to guarantee total security to the Assault Force against attempted Japanese molestation by sea or air, considerably assisted in the latter part of the role by bombardments of all Japanese airfields in the area. Nimitz's carrier armada was not restricted to the Central Pacific theatre only, and, from November 1943, it was repeatedly required to give assistance to SoPac and SoWesPac operations. To this end, the marvellous flexibility imparted by the organisation of the carrier fleet into separate task groups proved invaluable. The operations of November 1943 were a case in point. To keep the Japanese guessing and their defences at full strength, the attack on the Gilberts was timed to follow closely upon Halsey's SoPac landings on Bougainville in the northern Solomons. Task groups from the Fast Carrier Force would find themselves giving support

Top
December 1944: the 'Independence' class *Langley* (CVL.27) returning to Ulithi with TF.37 after air strikes on the Philippines. The 'Essex' class carrier immediately astern in *Ticonderoga*, with the upperworks of the battleship *Washington* beyond.

Above
The modest dimensions of the 'Independence' class carriers are particularly obvious in this view of *Cabot* (CVL.28). The aircraft are Hellcats.

to both operations, switching from one theatre to the other with the ease imparted by the fleet carrier's matchless speed and range.

Task group composition varied constantly, but a typical allocation would be one heavy and two light carriers, one or two fast battleships, one or two heavy cruisers, and an outer circular screen of eight to ten destroyers. The close support of battleships and

heavy cruisers not only rendered the carriers safe from enemy surface attack, but gave the carriers the benefit of their formidable AA batteries. If circumstances required, the battleships and heavy cruisers could be concentrated in a separate task force: the 'Battle Line'.

The third element under Spruance's command was designated Task Force 57 in

November 1943. This was the land-based air force which not only saw the invasion force on its way but moved in to operate from each new land base, as soon as it had been made secure by the invasion forces and rendered operational by the famed Construction Battalions (CBs, or 'Seabees'). TF.57 was commanded by Rear-Admiral John H. Hoover. Its complement of flying-boats and bombers included over 100 four-engined B-24 Liberator bombers which had helped tip the scale against the U-boats in the North Atlantic earlier in the year.

5th Fleet Carrier Operations

1: Bougainville and Rabaul, 1–6 November 1943

The first demonstration of 5th Fleet's tremendous flexibility and hitting-power came in November 1943, with task groups of the Fast Carrier Force hitting targets from the Marshalls to Bougainville, a 1600-mile arc of

operations. Expressed in its simplest terms, the idea was to make the Japanese expect American invasions in the Marshalls, the Gilberts, at Rabaul and at Bougainville, then actually invade not one but two of them — Bougainville and the Gilberts. To achieve this, Pownall's eleven carriers were deployed in three big task groups: Northern, Southern and Reserve. Northern Task Group hit the Marshalls, Southern Task Group hit the Gilberts and Rabaul, and the Reserve Task Group — *Saratoga*, *Essex*, *Bunker Hill*, *Independence* and *Princeton* — concentrated on

Bataan (CVL.29) with her flight-deck crammed with P-47N Thunderbolts, on a fighter ferry run during the build-up for the invasion of Leyte (October 1944).

San Jacinto (CVL.30) shows her dazzle-painted port side in July 1944, after serving with TG.58.3 in the Philippine Sea action. This is a good view of the 'Independence' class upperdeck profile: modest island and four stumpy stacks.

111

Bougainville. 'Cherryblossom', Halsey's invasion of Bougainville, went in on 1 November, and on the following night his cruisers and destroyers won the Battle of Empress Augusta Bay, the last night action in the South-West Pacific. The Japanese *riposte* was to rush six heavy cruisers from Truk to Rabaul, but this serious threat to the Bougainville landings was dealt with in short order by the 5th Fleet carriers. In a massive parting shot before returning north to cover the landings in the Gilberts, *Saratoga* and *Princeton* launched a joint strike against the cruisers as they lay refuelling at Rabaul. The attack force of 22 dive-bombers and 23 torpedo-carrying Avengers, escorted by a fighter screen 52 strong, damaged five of the six cruisers and caused the entire force to withdraw at once to Truk.

2: The Gilberts, 6–22 November 1943

After their final triumph at Rabaul, *Saratoga*, *Essex*, *Bunker Hill*, *Independence* and *Princeton* returned north to join *Enterprise*, *Yorktown*, *Lexington*, *Belleau Wood*, *Cowpens* and *Monterey* in the bombardment programme scheduled for 'Galvanic', the landings in the Gilberts. The main targets for the invasion force, which went in on 20 November 1943, were Tarawa and Makin atolls.

Half the work of Spruance's carriers in covering 'Galvanic' had already been done in the battering dealt out to the Japanese cruisers at Rabaul two weeks before; and no naval challenge came from the Combined Fleet at Truk. In the pre-invasion carrier strikes and fighter sweeps the main targets were the Japanese air bases on Nauru and on Mili in the Marshalls group, respectively 450 miles west and 300 miles north of Tarawa. This time, the Japanese aircraft managed to hit back to some effect. On 20 November the Southern Carrier Task Group, TG.50.3, was surprised by an attack of torpedo aircraft out of Nauru, and *Independence* was badly hit. Nevertheless, though she lost all power on three of her four shafts, she managed to limp on one screw into Funafuti in the Ellice Islands. Moreover, her place in TF.50 was taken almost at once by the next 'Essex' class carrier to join the Fleet, *Intrepid*.

Ant-like activity aboard the 'Independence' class *Monterey*, as Avengers are bombed-up during the assault on the Gilberts in November 1943.

Nothing if not jubilant after another successful trip to Rabaul: Commander Joseph C. Clifton passes out the cigars to his pilots in *Saratoga*.

The only other carrier casualty of 'Galvanic' was the escort carrier *Liscome Bay*, which was attacked on 24 November by the submarine *I-175*. The torpedo detonated the contents of *Liscome Bay*'s bomb store, and over 700 officers and men perished as she blew up and sank — a horrifying casualty rate of over 81 per cent of her complement. Though the gallant and invaluable work of the American escort carrier forces does not form part of the fleet carrier story, the escort carriers nevertheless contributed significantly to the survivability of the fleet carriers. As none of the classes of escort carrier had a maximum speed greater than 18–19 knots with a following wind, they presented much easier targets than the 30-knot fleet carriers. From their appearance in 1943 to the end of the Pacific War, the escort carriers remained a magnet for Japanese air and submarine attacks.

The awesome sight of the assembled Fast Carrier Task Force: TF.58 at anchor in Majuro Lagoon, after the break-in to the Central Pacific with the capture of the Marshall Islands.

Relaxation for some: on the hangar deck of *Yorktown*, ordnancemen work on bombs amid wing-folded Hellcats while their luckier shipmates take in a movie. The space of the hangar deck was ideal for shipboard relaxation during weeks at sea without a break — even for sporting activities.

3: The Marshalls, January 1944

After the capture of the Gilberts no time was wasted in preparing for the attack on the Marshalls, 'Flintlock'. This operation represented a radical departure from previous American strategy. Taking into account the fanatical resistance put up by every Japanese garrison since Guadalcanal, Nimitz in the Central Pacific and MacArthur in SoWesPac now proposed to concentrate only on the capture of essential Japanese bases. Other garrisons would be isolated, bypassed and kept neutralised by land-based and carrier air attacks 'to wither on the vine'. The first bypassed Japanese strongpoint in SoWesPac was that of Rabaul and New Ireland, isolated by landings on western New Britain on 26 December 1943, and the Admiralty Islands on 29 February 1944. In the Marshalls, Nimitz overrode Spruance's initial objections and ordered that the island airfields ringing Kwajalein — Jaluit, Mili, Maloelap and Wotje — would not be taken by seaborne assault. Instead, they would be neutralised by air attack while the invasion forces concentrated on Kwajalein.

For 'Flintlock', the Fast Carrier Force underwent a change of number and commander. Now designated Task Force 58, it was taken over by Rear-Admiral Marc Mitscher. This time the pre-invasion task of the fleet carriers was given massive assistance from Hoover's TF.57, whose land-based bombers were now operating from Tarawa in the Gilberts as well as from the Ellice Islands. The suppression of Eniwetok, 350 miles north-west of Kwajalein and designated as the next objective after 'Flintlock' had taken Kwajalein, was entrusted to battleship/cruiser bombardment.

The pre-invasion bombardments began on 29 January 1944, with Hoover's bombers concentrating on Jaluit and Mili, one carrier task group attacking Maloelap and another Wotje, the other two combining to attack Kwajalein, and the battleships and cruisers hitting

Eniwetok that night. This was the most breathtaking and versatile display of modern sea power yet seen in the Pacific — 'offensive in high gear', as the US Marine Corps historian later put it. On 30 January, Majuro Atoll, 350 miles south-east of Kwajalein, fell without resistance, giving Spruance an excellent new lagoon anchorage for his supply and maintenance fleet. On 1 February the invasion forces landed on Roi and Namur and on Kwajalein, the latter lying 50 miles south-south-east at the opposite end of the world's largest lagoon.

4: Truk/Marianas, 17–25 February 1944

Kwajalein atoll was declared secure after six days' vicious fighting, with American casualties half those suffered on Tarawa and Japanese casualties proportionally doubled, a heartening testimony to the fast-growing expertise of the American amphibious forces. With Kwajalein secure it was time to prepare for 'Catchpole', the reduction of Eniwetok. The air interdiction programme required of Mitscher's carriers was the most demanding yet. Only one fleet carrier task group — *Saratoga*, *Princeton* and *Langley* — was to accompany the expeditionary force to Eniwetok. The other three were to suppress first Truk and then, 600 miles away to the north-west, the main Japanese bomber fields on Saipan, Tinian and Guam in the Marianas.

No less than nine carriers took part in the Truk raid: *Enterprise, Essex, Yorktown, Intrepid, Bunker hill, Belleau Wood, Cabot, Cowpens* and *Monterey*. The aptly-chosen codename for the operation was 'Hailstone', and it was timed to coincide with the landings on Eniwetok: 17 February.

Never had the Japanese been caught so completely on the wrong foot. Spruance arrived off Truk on 17 February, his nine carriers accompanied by six battleships, ten cruisers and 28 destroyers. Admiral Koga, however, had withdrawn all heavy units of the Combined Fleet westward to Palau as soon as the American reconnaissance aircraft appeared over Truk, thus rendering the Eniwetok invasion force safe from naval intervention. Between 17 and 19 February, Mitscher's carrier aircraft flew 1250 sorties against Truk. Though there were no heavy warships, TF.58 managed to sink three destroyers, seven fleet auxiliaries, six tankers and seventeen freighters. The real achievement at Truk was the massacre of the Japanese air group left behind to defend the Combined Fleet's main base: over 250 Japanese aircraft were destroyed on the ground or shot down, in exchange for only 35 American aircraft shot down. Once again, however, a handful of

Target Truk: reconnaissance photograph of the Japanese Combined Fleet Base taken nine days before TF.58's massed attacks of February 1944.

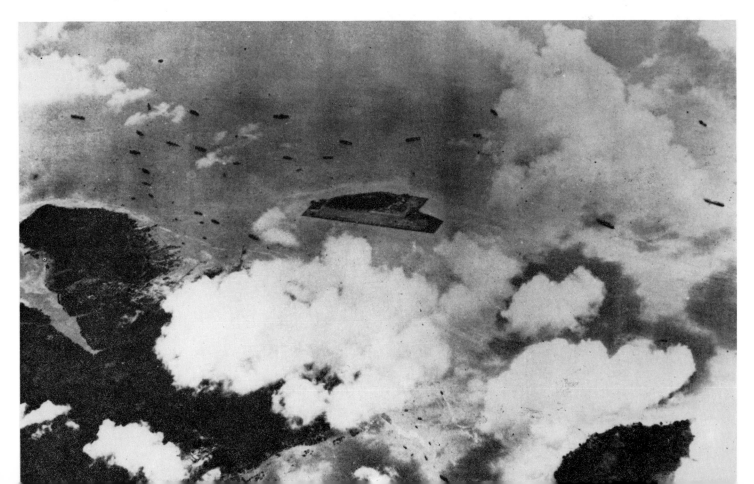

Dauntlesses survey their handiwork after attacking Param Island at Truk. The faithful SBD remained in production until 22 July 1944.

Opposite above
Near-miss from a 1000 lb bomb aimed at two Japanese transports in Truk Lagoon. This picture was taken by aircraft from *Intrepid* (CV.11).

Opposite
Day Two of the Truk Raid, 17 February 1944: a Japanese warship engulfed in smoke after being plastered with hits.

The heartening sight of Japanese shipping burning at Truk on 16 February 1944, the first day of Mitscher's mass attack by TF.58.

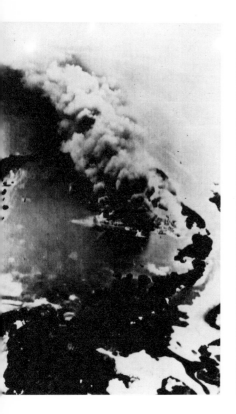

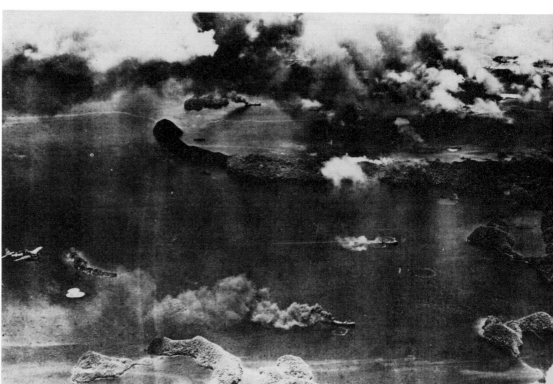

Japanese torpedo-bombers managed to get through and score a hit on the American carriers. This time the victim was *Intrepid*, but again the damage was contained and she managed to reach base. Mitscher's carriers then headed back to Kwajalein, refuelled and set off for the Marianas, wiping out a large force of bombers which had just flown in from Japan.

In the four months since November 1943, 5th Fleet's carriers had provided air cover and pre-invasion bombardment for three major amphibious invasions — Bougainville, the Gilberts and the Marshalls. They had covered an arc of operations over 4000 miles long, from the Solomons to the Marianas. In addition, the American carriers had not only deterred the Japanese Fleet from sailing to contest the American break-in to the Central Pacific, they had forced Admiral Koga to make a 2000-mile strategic retreat, withdrawing the Combined Fleet from Rabaul to Truk and from Truk to Palau. Nor was any respite granted after the fall of Eniwetok, declared secure on 23 February.

After taking the Marshalls, Central Pacific Force gathered its strength for the next major invasion: the Marianas, from where the Japanese homeland itself could be subjected to land-based bombing by the new B-29 Superfortresses. The operation was scheduled to begin in mid-June 1944, leaving Truk and the major part of the Caroline archipelago neutralised and isolated. MacArthur was meanwhile to complete the conquest of New Guinea in time for the invasion of Mindanao, southernmost of the Philippine Islands, in mid-November. From late March 1944, MacArthur's 'coast-hopping' advance westward along the New Guinea coast received the weighty assistance of the 5th Fleet's carriers.

5: New Guinea, March–April 1944

MacArthur's resumed offensive in New Guinea of April 1944 was preceded by another fleet carrier smash at the Combined Fleet's bases by TF.58, which sailed from its new anchorage of Majuro Atoll in the Marshalls on

22 March. Repeated strikes at Yap and the Palaus in the last four days of the month prompted Koga to order another fleet withdrawal, 800 miles further west to Tawi Tawi in the Sulu Islands, east of Borneo's northern tip. Koga, however, did not live to see this redeployment completed; he was killed in an aircraft crash on 31 March, and was replaced by Admiral Soemu Toyoda.

Having accomplished their now-familiar task of hustling the Combined Fleet off base before getting down to the job in hand, Mitscher's carriers sortied out again on 13 April, nine days before the scheduled landings by MacArthur's invasion troops. TF.58 dealt faithfully with the Japanese positions at Hollandia, Tanahmerah Bay and Aitape, intensifying their attacks on D-1, 21 April. On their return to the Marshalls, they hit Truk again before replenishing and training for the next offensive in the Central Pacific, the invasion of the Marianas. This second attack on Truk left only a handful of Japanese aircraft after a desperate air battle which cost TF.58 26 aircraft, but 28 of the 43 downed airmen were recovered, 22 of them in a daring 'snatch' by the submarine *Tang* which penetrated Truk lagoon to bring the airmen out.

Battle of the Philippine Sea

By the end of April 1944 both commanders in the Pacific, Nimitz and Toyoda, knew that a decisive fleet action could not be far away. American planners were rightly convinced that the Japanese Fleet, despite its Fabian tactics and continued withdrawals over the past six months, must come out and fight for the Marianas. This was territory which Japan could not afford to lose, nor the Americans dare to bypass. The situation was thus similar to the eve of Midway two years before — with the difference that in June 1944 the prime American objective was to secure the Marianas, not bring on a naval 'battle without a morrow'. To defend the Marianas in 1944, Admiral Toyoda had devised 'A-Go' — a plan which, like Yamamoto's 'MI' plan two years before, was aimed at nothing less than the destruction of the American Pacific Fleet.

Philippine Sea: The rival forces

Toyoda's 'A-Go' plan relied on catching the American carrier task groups between the hammer of land-based air attacks from the Marianas, reinforced from the southern

Philippines and the Carolinas, and the Japanese carrier fleet coming up from the west. As explained in the operational plan issued on 3 May 1944, the Japanese carriers would be attacking an enemy fleet already reduced by 'at least one-third' by land-based air raids. This would enable the Japanese carriers to engage on equal and hopefully on advantageous terms. 'A-Go' had all the compound logic which had betrayed 'MO' and 'MI' back in 1942. Its most obvious flaw was that it took no account of the proven ability of the American carrier fleet, roaming and striking at will, to destroy any concentration of Japanese land-based air power it chose. This fundamental miscalculation brought about the wreck of 'A-Go' in the last and greatest carrier clash of the Pacific War: the Battle of the Philippine Sea.

By the spring of 1944 the Japanese Combined Fleet had been re-formed as the '1st Mobile Fleet', in a deliberate aping of the American Fast Carrier Force. The Mobile Fleet consisted of three carrier task groups, deploying a total of 430 carrier aircraft:

Van force   Light carriers *Chitose*, *Chiyoda*, *Zuiho*; battleships *Yamato*, *Musashi*, *Haruna*, *Kongo*; five cruisers; nine destroyers.
Force A   Fleet carriers *Shokaku*, *Zuikaku*, *Taiho*; three cruisers; nine destroyers.
Force B   Light carriers *Ryuho*, *Junyo*, *Hiyo*; battleship *Nagato*; one cruiser; ten destroyers.

Commanding the Mobile Fleet in June 1944 was Vice-Admiral Jisaburo Ozawa, who had relieved Nagumo as commander of the Japanese carrier arm in November 1942. (Nagumo was now commanding the exiguous naval flotilla and naval land forces on Saipan.)

Ozawa's opposite number, Mitscher, had four carrier task groups under his command in June 1944 — fifteen fleet carriers in all, deploying a total of 891 carrier aircraft:

TG.58.1   Fleet carriers *Hornet*, *Yorktown*; light fleet carriers *Belleau Wood*, *Bataan*; three cruisers; two AA cruisers; fourteen destroyers.
TG.58.2   Fleet carriers *Bunker Hill*, *Wasp*; light fleet carriers *Monterey*, *Cabot*; three cruisers; twelve destroyers.
TG.58.3   Fleet carriers *Enterprise*, *Lexington*; light fleet carriers *San Jacinto*, *Princeton*; one cruiser; four AA cruisers; thirteen destroyers.
TG.58.4   Fleet carrier *Essex*; light fleet carriers *Langley*, *Cowpens*; three cruisers; fourteen destroyers.

Battle of the Philippine Sea, June 1944

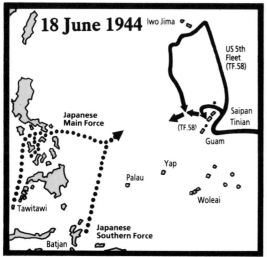

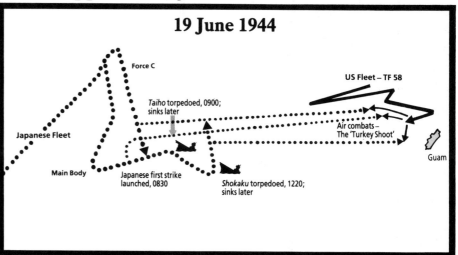

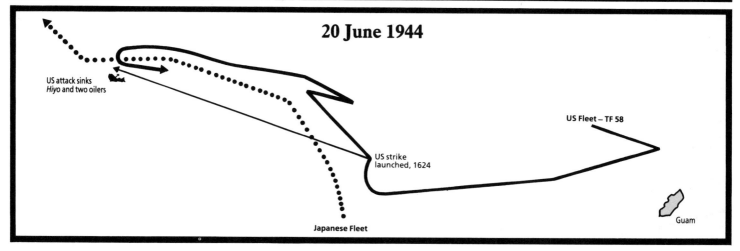

In addition to the carrier force, concentrated against the remote possibility of surface action with Japanese heavy units, there was TG.58.7. This was Vice-Admiral Lee's 'Battle Line', with the battleships *Washington, North Carolina, South Dakota, New Jersey, Iowa, Alabama* and *Indiana*, four cruisers and thirteen destroyers.

To add to the numerical and qualitative superiority of TF.58's carriers and their aircraft was the fact that Japan's 1st Mobile Fleet had never put to sea, *as* a fleet, even for basic aircrew training — and carrier fleets can not exercise at anchor. On the other hand, in the eight months up to June 1944, TF.58 had been perfecting its teamwork and expertise in a steady stream of operations.

11–15 June: The opening moves

For Toyoda, the biggest initial problem with 'A-Go' was the uncertainty, until the American assault troops actually hit the beach, over where the next invasion really would go in.

The enormous range which the American carrier task groups could cover had taught the Japanese, from painful experience, that initial carrier-borne air strikes were not in themselves infallible signs of an imminent invasion at that particular spot. Toyoda was not taken in by the preliminary carrier strikes of May 1944, which hit Marcus and Wake, respectively 1000 miles and 1400 miles from the Marianas. He was determined not to unleash 'A-Go' until it was clear where the next invasion would be, even though this would probably result in the successful lodgement of the invasion force, freeing the American fleet carrier force to deal with Ozawa's Mobile Fleet.

Nor did Toyoda react as soon as he heard of the first American fighter sweep over the Marianas on 11 June (D-4). This destroyed 36 Japanese aircraft out of the 500-odd concentrated in the Marianas, but TF.58 fighter losses were eleven aircraft shot down, with five of the pilots recovered, a disastrous omen against the chances of 'A-Go' succeeding. On

12 June, one carrier group peeled off to hit Guam while the other three concentrated on Saipan and Tinian. On 13 June, Lee's battleships and cruisers moved in to join the pre-invasion programme with radar-controlled gunnery — and that was when Toyoda ordered Ozawa and the Mobile Fleet to prepare for 'A-Go'. Ozawa concentrated his forces in the Guimaras Strait, between Negros and Panay in the western Philippines, where they spent the next two days fuelling. The Mobile Fleet was lacking its strongest battle squadron, Rear-Admiral Ugaki with the battleships *Yamato* and *Musashi*, which had been sent south to bombard MacArthur's forces in the battle for the island of Biak (27 May–2 July). Ugaki's squadron, hastily recalled, was still on its way back when, on hearing of the American landings on Saipan, Toyoda issued the executive order for 'A-Go' on the forenoon of 15 June.

By the evening of 15 June Ozawa and the main body of the Mobile fleet had threaded their way through the central Philippines,

from the north, but it had still been a risk, temporarily reducing TF.58's strength by half. Now the risk turned out to have been well calculated. From the positions reported by *Flying Fish* and *Seahorse*, Spruance knew that even at its best speed the Mobile Fleet would be unable to close within air-strike range before 19 June. He could therefore afford to let the two northern task groups finish their second day's bombardment on the 16th, knowing that they would have rejoined by evening on the 18th.

The first order issued by Spruance in the Battle of the Philippine Sea, on the evening of 15 June, was for all four task groups of TF.58 to rendezvous 180 miles west of Tinian on the evening of 18 June. This would enable Mitscher's aircraft to keep up the good work over the Marianas until first touch was made with the oncoming Mobile Fleet. There was ample scope for taking additional measures to guard against the chance of Ugaki's giant battleships continuing to operate independently from the Japanese main body. Spruance therefore ordered Vice-Admiral Lee to form his Battle Line, with the battleships withdrawn from their close-support role amid the carrier task groups, plus eight cruisers and 21 destroyers drawn from the support groups of Turner's invasion force.

15–18 June: The fleets converge

On 16 June, Ozawa made rendezvous with his replenishment tankers and with Ugaki's battleships some 450 miles east of San Berna-dino Strait. He spent 17 June in refuelling, then resumed his eastward course as night drew on, with Kurita's Van Force pushed forward about 100 miles ahead of the other two carrier task groups. This was the old 'sacrificial goat' ploy, albeit with massive battleship support, with the lightest Japanese carriers nearest to the enemy to distract attention from the main Japanese fleet carrier force.

Spruance only received one sighting report between 15 and 19 June. The submarine *Cavalla* sighted one of the Japanese task groups on the evening of 17 June, 700 miles west of Guam, forging on to the east at 20 knots. In this encounter, circumstances combined to deprive Spruance of the usual excellent service by his long-range air reconnaissance. On 17 June, the American land-based scout planes were still 60 miles short of the Mobile Fleet when they reached the limit of their fuel range

emerging into the Philippine Sea via the San Bernadino Strait, and a rendezvous had already been set for Ugaki's battleships coming up from the south. What Ozawa did not know was that both he and Ugaki had already been sighted by patrolling American submarines, Ozawa by *Flying Fish*, Ugaki an hour later by *Seahorse*. This would have come as no particular surprise, and might indeed have served to lure a more incautious American C-in-C to seek premature action. But one piece of vital information did not reached Ozawa: the shattering news that, to all intents and purposes, 'A-Go' had already failed. So far from cutting down the strength of TF.58 by massed land-based air attacks, the Japanese air forces in the Marianas — based on the 'unsinkable aircraft-carriers' of Saipan, Tinian, Guam and Rota — were well on the way to extinction after intense air fighting over the past four days. Not one of the American carriers had even been scratched while Mitscher's fighter strength, virtually unscathed, had established total air su-

premacy over the Marianas. The prospects of enough reinforcements arriving from Yap, the Palaus or Truk was remote, while the island staging-posts of Chichi Jima and Iwo Jima, 650 miles to the north, were already being battered by two American task groups, TGs. 58.1 and 58.4, detached on 12 June. This effectively severed the 'mainline' air reinforcement route to the Marianas from Japan.

None of these dismaying facts were ever signalled to Ozawa by his colleague Vice-Admiral Kukuda, commanding the Marianas air forces. Ozawa was therefore left to press on across the Philippine Sea in the false belief that, as planned, the efforts of his carriers would finish the job begun by the 500 Japanese aircraft striking from the Marianas.

For his part, Spruance was greatly relieved to receive such early sightings of the Mobile Fleet from the patrol submarines to the west. Detaching two task groups to bombard Iwo Jima and Chichi Jima had been essential to prevent a flow of reinforcing Japanese aircraft

Poised to continue the job of softening-up Saipan's already battered defences: Avengers ranged forward aboard *Lexington* on 15 June 1944, the day of the invasion of the Marianas.

The new fire-power of the US carriers claims another victim during an attempted night attack on TG.58.3. Tracers can be seen flying over the aircraft on *Lexington*'s flight-deck, converging onto the Japanese aircraft crashing astern.

and had to turn for home, nor was any contact made on 18 June. American ship-borne air reconnaissance was entirely carried out by carrier aircraft by June 1944, instead of by long-range floatplanes catapulted from battleships and cruisers. Though this certainly made life safer aboard the battleships and cruisers, not to mention for the float-plane aircrew, it did not improve the gathering of fleet intelligence. However, not only did the Japanese Fleet still use catapult floatplanes, but an enduring virtue of its otherwise obsolescent carrier aircraft was a slightly longer range. In June 1944, this

advantage enabled the Japanese to sight the Americans first.

By late afternoon on 18 June, Ozawa's scout planes had located units of TF.58 420 miles to the east. The carrier commander of the Van Force, taking it for granted that Ozawa would waste no time in attacking, launched a strike force 67 aircraft strong, timed to approach TF.58 out of the light of the setting sun. Ozawa, however, decided to launch an all-out strike on the following morning at the maximum range for his aircraft, which would give the Mobile Fleet a temporary advantage until the range shortened enough to permit the launching of the first American strike. To keep the range open he therefore turned the Mobile Fleet south for the night of 18–19 June, and Obayashi's strike was recalled. Ozawa resumed course to the north-east at 0300 on 19 June, with Kurita's Van Force still leading by 100 miles.

By the evening of 18 June, TF.58 was back at full strength after the return of TG.58.1 and TG.58.4 from their attacks on Iwo Jima

and Chichi Jima. Lee's Battle Line was deployed with TG.58.4 lying 12 miles off its northern flank; the other three task groups were deployed 15 miles to the east of the Battle Line, their sequence from north to south being 1, 3, and 2. Spruance, however, still had no fresh news of the Mobile Fleet. His primary duty being to defend the invasion forces lying off Saipan, Spruance therefore withdrew east at nightfall on 18 June, only turning back to the west at first light on the following morning. A communications breakdown during the night robbed him of the information he so urgently required. A PBY searching 600 miles west of the Marianas located two groups of hostile ships on its radar, but flew back to its base with the information when no radio acknowledgment of the contact was received. Spruance did not receive this information until 0900 on 19 June, but by then it was valueless. It was hoped that a patrol-line of submarines deployed across the anticipated path of the Mobile Fleet would have more luck. So indeed it proved. But it was this lack of early

airborne reconnaissance warning which prompted Spruance to 'lie back on the ropes' during the coming battle, ever-mindful of his vital defensive role, and let the Japanese carrier strike forces shatter themselves against the American fighter superiority.

Phase 1: First Japanese strikes launched

Daybreak on 19 June saw Ozawa's luck apparently still holding. Two groups of search planes — sixteen catapult floatplanes launched at 0445 and fourteen carrier-based Zeros launched at 0515 — located TF.58. The Zeros reached the picket destroyers of Lee's Battle Line, although half of them were shot down by *Langley*'s Hellcats. The floatplanes missed Lee's force on their way out, but on their return flight sighted TG.58.4 at 0730.

Philippine Sea, Day 1, 19 June 1944 — a near-miss alongside *Bunker Hill*. The attacking Japanese aircraft, with its tail sheared off, is about to crash into the sea at left.

Opposite
Rear-gunner's viewpoint from one of *Lexington*'s Avengers, at the moment of launch.

A fine view of TG.58.3 ploughing into wind while Hellcats are launched, as seen from *Lexington*.

The first Japanese strike force was launched by Obayashi's Van Force carriers shortly before 0830: 45 Zero fighter-bombers, eight torpedo aircraft and sixteen Zeros as fighter escort. Ozawa's Force A fleet carriers began launching shortly before 0900: 53 dive-bombers, 27 torpedo aircraft and 48 Zeros, followed half an hour later by a third strike force, 47 aircraft strong, from Force B.

The first blow fell while Ozawa's big carriers were still launching aircraft. From 0816, the Force A carriers had been stalked by one of Spruance's four patrol submarines, *Albacore*. Her skipper, Commander Blanchard, found himself presented with a perfect beam shot at *Taiho*, and fired a full salvo of six torpedoes shortly after 0900. Of these one was detonated by a heroic Japanese torpedo-bomber pilot who spotted the incoming menace and blew it up by crashing his aircraft on to it; but another torpedo hit *Taiho*. At first it seemed that the damage was slight.

Blast from the explosion jammed the nearest elevator in the 'up' position, and all 42 of *Taiho*'s first-strike aircraft were therefore able to get airborne safely. But another, unseen menace was soon at work. *Albacore*'s torpedo had released explosive fumes from the poorly-refined aircraft oil storage — with supreme irony, the very Borneo oil for which Japan had gone to war in December 1941. With her hangar sealed shut and the fumes stealthily spreading, *Taiho* became a floating bomb with less than six and a half hours to live.

Phase 2: First Japanese strikes repelled

TF.58's first air operations on 19 June continued the good work of the previous eight days: grinding down the already heavily-depleted Japanese air force based on the Marianas. Only a trickle of reinforcement aircraft had struggled through from Truk, and by 19 June the total air strength on

Guam, over whose Orote Field the first air battle of the day took shape, had been reduced to 50. From dawn to 1000, when the first strike forces from the Mobile Fleet were detected on radar, Mitscher's Hellcats were engaged in dogfights over Guam in which over 30 more Japanese aircraft were shot down.

Mitscher's reaction to the approach of the Japanese carrier aircraft was an expansion of the classic *riposte*. He ordered the launch of every available aircraft in TF.58, to make certain of keeping the upper hand over the islands while maintaining the strongest possible fighter combat air patrols to meet the carrier attacks from the west. All told, TF.58 was shielded by an 'umbrella' of some 300 Hellcats on 19 June, maintained by successive landings to refuel and re-arm. It was this element which proved decisive in completing the ruin of 'A-Go'.

Launched half an hour before the main strike force, the aircraft of Obayashi's Van

Force were the first to pass through the fire. They were intercepted shortly after 1030, still 45 miles short of their objective: Lee's Battle Line and TG.58.4. Hellcats from *Essex*, *Langley* and *Cowpens* tore the Japanese formation to pieces, shooting down 42 aircraft out of 69 and sending 27 battle-damaged survivors straggling empty-handed back to their carriers by 1100.

The boon of radar, used to full advantage, enabled Mitscher's carriers to inflict even heavier punishment on the Japanese second wave. This was detected at 1107, at a range of 115 miles — ample time to reinforce the Hellcat CAPs, and vector them to intercept the incoming Japanese west of Lee's Battle Line. The Hellcats engaged over 100 of the Japanese strike force of 128 aircraft. About twenty others broke through to attack the rearmost carrier task groups, with wholly innocuous results. In TG.58.2, *Wasp* received minor damage and so did *Bunker Hill*. In TG.58.3, a torpedo narrowly missed *Enterprise*, exploding in her wake as she zig-zagged. There were a few casualties among gunners and crewmen injured by splinters and blast from near-misses close alongside, but that was all. Every carrier in TF.58 remained fully operational. One of the new 'Jill' torpedo aircraft crashed into the battleship *Indiana*, the only one of Lee's heavy ships to suffer an actual attack, but the armoured belt stood up well to the impact, and the torpedo warhead failed to explode. Only about 30 survivors returned to Ozawa's carriers — unhappily for him, with exaggerated tales of American carriers left burning and crippled.

Phase 3: *Shokaku* and *Taiho* lost

Ozawa did not even have time to learn that his all-important first strikes had met with 75 per cent losses before the Mobile Fleet suffered its next disaster. It happened at 1220 as Force A was steaming into wind, recovering aircraft. Since sighting the Mobile Fleet on the evening of 17 June, Commander Kossler had driven his submarine *Cavalla* in pursuit at full speed. By noon on 19 June he had caught up, as a result of the Mobile Fleet's course changes to operate aircraft. Working his way in to virtually point-blank range, Kossler fired six torpedoes at *Shokaku*. Three hit at 1220. The result was a holocaust of petrol fires, with the veteran Japanese carrier going the way of the first *Lexington* at Coral Sea: fires, explosions, more riven pipes and tanks, more explosions. After an unavailing three-hour struggle she was torn apart by an exploding bomb magazine shortly after 1500, sinking at 1524.

Shokaku had hardly vanished below the surface when *Taiho* blew up. It need not have happened but for the inept damage-control techniques which bedevilled the Japanese Fleet in its last eighteen months of existence. The cause was the inflammable petroleum fumes released by the explosion of *Albacore*'s torpedo. These should have been contained — not spread throughout the ship by turning on the forced ventilation system in an unthinking attempt to clear them. The inevitable spark did its work at 1532 and the results were horrific. Side and bottom plating was blown out by the blast, resulting in mass flooding, and the flight-deck was buckled upwards. Ozawa had time to shift his flag and transfer his staff to the cruiser *Haguro*, but another huge explosion sank *Taiho* at 1628 with most of her complement. Only about 500 of *Taiho*'s crewmen were saved out of 2150. This double disaster to *Taiho* and *Shokaku* left *Zuikaku* as the Japanese Navy's last operational heavy fleet carrier.

Phase 4: The last Japanese strikes — 'The Great Marianas Turkey Shoot'

The explosions which sank *Shokaku* and *Taiho* were fitting accompaniments to the ruin which befell the last Japanese air strikes launched late in the forenoon of 19 June. Force B's first strike had been launched at 0930, 47 strong, against TG.58.4, but it was directed too far north, with dire results. Over 30 aircraft of the strike force found nothing and turned back to their carriers. The remainder, about twelve, found TG.58.4 and gallantly tried to attack, only to be set upon by a Hellcat CAP double their own number in strength. No more than five got through to drop their bombs in hasty, inaccurate passes before breaking free for home, while seven fell to the Hellcats.

The last Japanese attack on TF.58 on 19 June, 82 aircraft strong, was launched by *Zuikaku*, *Hiyo*, *Junyo* and *Ryujo* at 1000. Once again the direction was bad, and the strike force again lost cohesion during the search for the target. One group of 34 aircraft sighted and attacked TF.58.2, but nearly all were shot down. The other 49, finding no targets, headed for Orote Field on Guam, ignorant that this haven now lay churned and pitted by the American carrier bombers flown off to give Mitscher's Hellcats a free hand. Most of them, 30 in all, were shot down by a force of 27 Hellcats before reaching Guam. No accurate count was ever taken of surviving Japanese aircraft which tried to land on Orote and the other Marianas airfields on 19 June, but only 130 of the 373 aircraft launched that day by Ozawa's carriers had returned by the end of the day.

Passing into US Navy legend as 'The Great Marianas Turkey Shoot', the air battles of 19 June 1944 were the Hellcat fighter's finest hour. The shattering total of Japanese naval aircraft destroyed, counting aircraft 'splashed' because of battle damage or empty tanks, was about 315 — in exchange for only 29 American aircraft lost that day. The 'Turkey Shoot' completed the ruin of 'A-Go', aimed as this had been at destroying the American carrier fleet by the interplay of land-based and carrier-based air power. However, it did not mark the end of the Battle of the Philippine Sea. Ozawa was left with 102 operational carrier aircraft at the end of the day. In total ignorance of the true state of affairs on the Marianas airfields, he believed that most of his missing aircraft had made landfall there and would be ready for action on the morrow. Ozawa also believed that the day's losses had been repaid at least in part with three and maybe four American carriers crippled if not sunk, leaving him with seven intact carriers against eleven American carriers. He therefore ordered a withdrawal to the north-west, permitting the Mobile Fleet to replenish out of range of American attack before returning to renew the battle.

Phase 5: Spruance attacks the Mobile Fleet

For the know-alls not saddled with Spruance's responsibilities, it was at the time and has always been easy to condemn him for over caution in refusing to pursue and annihilate the Mobile Fleet after the losses suffered by the Japanese in the 'Turkey Shoot' on 19 June. Spruance did not know, on the late afternoon of 19 June, of the fates of *Taiho* and *Shokaku*, nor did he know the full extent by which the Japanese air strength had been reduced, but he did know that over-zealous pursuit could have disastrous consequences, as after the successes of 4 June 1942 at Midway. His prime task remained ensuring the security of Turner's invasion fleet and the interdiction of Japanese air reinforcements to Guam (yet to be invaded) and from that he never wavered. He spelled it out in a concise signal to Mitscher: 'DESIRE TO ATTACK ENEMY TOMORROW IF WE KNOW HIS POSITION WITH SUFFICIENT ACCURACY'. To remove any doubts over 5th fleet's over-riding priority, Spruance added: 'IF NOT, WE MUST CONTINUE SEARCHES TOMORROW TO ENSURE ADEQUATE PROTECTION OF SAIPAN'.

The resumption of the battle on 20 June therefore turned on the effectiveness of American air reconnaissance, land-based and carrier-based; and Ozawa's north-westerly withdrawal to meet his tankers carried him out of

Fighter contrails in the sky over
TG.58.3, seen from the AA cruiser
Birmingham, mark the ruin of
Japanese hopes by Mitscher's
Hellcats.

American air reconnaissance range over the
night of 19–20 June: Mitscher's dawn search,
launched at 0530 on the 20th, found nothing.
After a 200-mile run to the west, TF.58
turned north and flew off a second search at
1330. By this time the range between the two
fleets had been reduced to 300 miles. It therefore took until 1605 before an Avenger from
Enterprise sighted the Mobile Fleet.

Chafing at the delays in the pursuit, Mitscher decided to launch an all-out strike, even
though this would mean returning aircraft
having to land in the dark; and by 1635 this
was on its way: 77 Helldivers and Dauntlesses, 54 Avengers with torpedoes and an
escort of 85 Hellcats. They sighted Ozawa's
tanker fleet first, at 1840, with the warships
of the Mobile Fleet in its three divisions
30 miles beyond. Though the strike force was
the most powerful yet launched against an
enemy fleet — 131 dive-bombers and torpedo
aircraft all told — it still had to cope with a
triple target deployed over more than 30 miles
of sea, and results in terms of ships sunk were
disappointing. *Zuikaku*, a prime target, was
set ablaze with multiple bomb hits; her fires
almost forced her crew to abandon ship, but

Another victim of the 'Great Marianas
Turkey Shoot', as a Japanese bomber
goes down in flames.

127

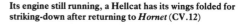

were brought under control at the last moment. *Chiyoda*, set afire, and with a wrecked flight-deck, was also saved, but *Hiyo* was torpedoed and sunk, while damaging hits were also scored on the cruiser *Maya* and battleship *Haruna* in the 20 minute attack.

If Mitscher's strike of 20 June left the Japanese with a carrier fleet battered but still in being, it was again the air battle which counted. The Americans only lost fourteen aircraft in the attack while the Hellcats liquidated the Zero CAPs. Added to the aircraft lost in *Hiyo*, *Zuikaku* and *Chiyoda*, the cumulative losses suffered under TF.58's attack left Ozawa with only 35 of the 102 aircraft with which he had intended to renew the battle for the Marianas.

The returning American aircraft, however, still had to face the ordeal of landing-on in the dark. Largely as a result of Mitscher's courageous order to disregard possible submarine or bomber attack and illuminate flight-decks, 80 aircraft were lost in the return alone, 'splashing' with empty tanks, or crashing on deck. Excellent rescue work, however, made the losses in trained aircrew gratifyingly light: a total of sixteen pilots and 33 aircrew.

So ended the two-day Battle of the Philippine Sea, the most momentous carrier battle since Midway, and the biggest carrier battle of all time. Spruance ordered a pursuit for 21 June, but this time, unlike the aftermath of Midway, there were no Japanese cripples to finish off and sink, and Ozawa had too great a lead to be overhauled in his headlong withdrawal to Okinawa. After fruitless searches on 21 June, Spruance returned to resume his watch over the invasion forces on Saipan. Here the land battle was again severe, with the conquest of the island not completed until 19 July. In the month after the Philippine Sea battle, there was no respite for TF.58, which had to complete the neutralisation of Tinian, invaded on 24 July, and Guam, invaded on 21 July. The land battle for the Marianas did not end until the first week of August, with Tinian declared secure on 1 August and Guam on 10 August. During the fight for the Marianas after the Philippine Sea, repeated carrier strikes and warship bombardments not only prevented the launching of a Japanese airborne counter-offensive from Iwo Jima, but wiped out the last vestige of an organised

A light-hearted moment aboard *Monterey* during the Marianas operations, as the carrier notches up her 5000th landing. The lucky pilot, Ensign Robert W. Zemke, is greeted by the reception committee.

Relaxation after battle: a strenuous basketball game on a carrier's forward elevator. The fair-haired player in the middle is future President of the United States, Lieutenant Gerald Ford.

Veterans of the Philippine Sea battle, the US fleet carriers' greatest triumph: *Enterprise*, the only carrier to serve right through the Pacific War from Pearl Harbor to Tokyo Bay, with *Lexington* in the background.

air defence of the island. The American carriers dominated the Central Pacific.

Philippine Sea: The action assessed

The Battle of the Philippine Sea was a resounding victory for the 'Essex' and 'Independence' class carriers in their first fleet action; but this victory went far beyond merely seeing-off the Japanese fleet and ensuring the conquest of the Marianas. The vital American achievement was the infliction of unprecedented Japanese losses in carrier aircraft, pilots and aircrew in a single action, leaving the last operational Japanese carriers impotent. The Battle of the Philippine Sea

had effectively liquidated the Japanese naval air arm; it was the last action of the Pacific War in which carrier fleets traded blows with each other.

The achievement of the American fleet carriers in the Marianas campaign exploded the myth — depressingly reborn since the end of World War II—that carriers have no chance against land-based air forces. At the Philippine Sea, Spruance and Mitscher proved that a sufficiently strong carrier fleet can not only neutralise land-based air strength with one hand, but fight and win a fleet action with the other.

Another myth — or at least popular misunderstanding — was also dispelled by the

Another addition to the Fast Carrier Task Force: *Franklin* (CV.13) in August 1944.

Battle of the Philippine Sea. This was the axiom that enjoying superior strength demands offensive tactics. Throughout the crucial phase of the Philippine sea, Spruance, refusing to be diverted from his prime objective, was content to let the Japanese fleet come to him and fight on his terms — against overwhelming American fighter supremacy. Once Ozawa's attacks had been made and broken, Spruance was ready to unleash his own attack, again with overwhelming fighter supremacy. The triumph of the Philippine Sea was the triumph of the Hellcat fighter.

6
Kamikaze Ordeal

After the capture of the Marianas in June-August 1944, the American Central Pacific drive on Japan was suspended for six months to permit the reconquest of the Philippines. Admiral Spruance handed over command of 5th Fleet to Halsey, relieved of his duties as ComSoPac on 15 June 1944, and came ashore with his staff to begin planning for the conquest of Iwo Jima and Okinawa when the Central Pacific offensive was reopened in early 1945. Under Halsey's command, the 5th Fleet which had won the Battle of the Philippine Sea was redesignated 3rd Fleet. Its next task was to support MacArthur and the 7th Fleet in the forthcoming Philippine campaign.

As the cutting edge of Halsey's 3rd Fleet, the Fast Carrier Task Force was now redesignated TF.38. Mitscher remained in overall command of the carrier force, but new admirals took over the carrier task groups. Among them was the recently promoted Rear-Admiral Frederick C.Sherman, last Captain of the first *Lexington* at Coral Sea, who took over TG.38.3. The other new task group commanders were Vice-Admiral John S. McCain (TG.38.1), Rear-Admiral Gerald F. Bogan (TG.38.2) and Rear-Admiral Ralph E. Davison (TG.38.4). Apart from the immensely respected and popular Mitscher, continuity with 5th Fleet command was maintained with the retention of Vice-Admiral Lee as commander of the Battle Line, flying his flag in *Washington*, his flagship since Guadalcanal.

By October 1944, two new 'Essex' class carriers, *Franklin* and *Hancock*, with the 'Independence' class light carrier *San Jacinto*, were serving with TF.38. *Franklin* and *San Jacinto* were assigned to TG.38.4, working with the veteran *Enterprise* and *Belleau Wood*; *Hancock* joined *Wasp*, *Hornet*, *Monterey* and *Cowpens* in TG.38.1. *Franklin*'s arrival in time for the invasion of Guam had permitted

Yorktown to be withdrawn from the Fleet for her first dockyard overhaul. This change was soon followed by the arrival of the new 'Essex' class *Ticonderoga* and also of *Saratoga*, returning to Fleet service after a long-overdue spell in dockyard hands.

Operations with the Royal Navy

Saratoga had had a particularly demanding year, covering more ocean than any other American carrier in the first half of 1944.

After supporting the assault on Eniwetok in February, *Saratoga* had been loaned to the British Eastern Fleet, based on Ceylon, proceeding thither by way of Australia. This transfer was mainly due to TF.58's prowess in hustling the Japanese Fleet westward from its bases in the Carolines and the Palaus to seek temporary refuge in Singapore. Such a startling and sudden concentration of Japanese naval strength on Ceylon's doorstep, apparently part and parcel of the latest Japanese offensive in Burma though in fact nothing to do with it, seemed to presage a Japanese grand offensive into eastern India

In the wake of the *kamikaze*s: the blazing after flight-deck of *Belleau Wood* (CVL.24) after a *kamikaze* crashed into the aircraft ranged for take-off during operations off Leyte on 30 October 1944. A fire crew is hosing the intact Avengers at left to stop them from fuelling the blaze, which caused no vital damage to the ship.

On the eve of the Leyte invasion: cleaning a 5-inch gun in an 'Essex' class carrier. Flak of the highest possible density, to blast the aircraft out of the sky before it could hit, proved the best answer to the *kamikazes*.

supported by the Combined Fleet in the Bay of Bengal. The carrier-starved British Admiralty therefore reciprocated the American request of a fleet carrier which had sent *Victorious* to the Pacific in early 1943, and *Saratoga*'s transfer was the result. Her spell of duty with the Eastern Fleet was the Royal Navy's second object lesson in American carrier technique, *Victorious*'s visit to the South Pacific in the previous year having been the first.

After a long detour through the SoPac area to Australia, *Saratoga* and her escort of three destroyers were met at sea by the British fleet carrier *Illustrious*, the battle-cruiser *Renown*, and the old battleships *Queen Elizabeth* and *Valiant* in the eastern Indian Ocean on

27 March 1944. At Ceylon, *Saratoga* came under the command of Admiral Somerville, C-in-C, Eastern Fleet — the most polyglot Allied fleet in the world. Apart from the predominantly British element, comprising one fleet carrier, a battle-cruiser, two old battleships, four cruisers and seven destroyers, there were *Saratoga* and her three destroyer escorts, the French battleship *Richelieu*, a Dutch cruiser and destroyer, a New Zealand cruiser and four Australian destroyers.

With two fleet carriers, *Illustrious* and *Saratoga*, now at his disposal, Somerville planned a carrier-borne strike at the Japanese naval base of Sabang in Sumatra. Though two years had passed since the US Pacific Fleet's carriers had launched their first such attacks in the Pacific, this was the first such venture for the Eastern Fleet. The stirring British sense of identification with Pacific operations was increased by a request from the American COMINCH, Admiral King, for the Sabang

raid to be timed for mid-April. Sabang was an important link in the Japanese air reinforcement route from southern Malaya to New Guinea, where MacArthur was preparing for his assault on Hollandia. Somerville willingly complied and the Eastern Fleet sailed from Trincomalee on 16 April 1944, reaching its launch-point 100 miles south-west of Sabang early on 19 April. The strike force was launched at 0530: seventeen Barracuda torpedo-bombers and thirteen Corsair fighters from *Illustrious*, eleven Avengers, eighteen Dauntlesses and 24 Hellcats from *Saratoga*.

The British and American air groups achieved complete surprise when they swept in to attack at 0700. The fighters knocked out 22 Japanese aircraft caught on the ground; the strike aircraft went for the big oil storage tanks, the harbour installations and the insignificant handful of shipping found in the harbour. One small merchantman was sunk, another beached and three of the four oil storage tanks were set ablaze. Only one aircraft was shot down, a Hellcat from *Saratoga*, and its pilot was rescued under fire by a British submarine pushed close inshore to carry out such air-sea rescue work ('lifeguard' submarines, as they were known in the Pacific).

By the time the Eastern Fleet returned to Ceylon after this thoroughly satisfactory operation, it was clear that the crisis which had led to *Saratoga*'s transfer had passed. The pressure was off the Eastern Fleet; the Japanese Combined Fleet had moved back east to Tawi Tawi, while on the Burma front the Japanese 'March on Delhi' was already bogging down at Kohima and Imphal. *Saratoga* was therefore recalled to the United States for refit, and Admiral King suggested that as she went she should take part in another Eastern Fleet carrier strike, on Surabaya. The Fleet sailed on 6 May and reached its flying-off position at 0630 on 17 May. By 0730 *Illustrious* and *Saratoga* had together launched 45 Avengers and Dauntlesses, escorted by 40 Hellcats and Corsairs.

Once again complete surprise was achieved over the target, but the results obtained at Surabaya did not match those of the Sabang raid. No crucial damage was caused to the most important target, the oil refinery, which was Java's only source of aviation fuel. Damage to the refinery, as to the harbour installations, looked good from the air but was in fact superficial, and only one small ship was sunk in the harbour. Once again only one aircraft was shot down, but this time with no possibility of 'life-guard' work by friendly submarines, as had been achieved at Sabang.

On the following afternoon, 18 May, *Saratoga* parted company with the Eastern Fleet on the first stage of her long voyage back to the United States. Her flight-deck operating techniques had been a revelation to the less experienced British, as had the superiority of her strike aircraft. By the end of the year, the British Fleet Air Arm, preparing at last for full-scale carrier operations under American command in the Pacific, had phased out the Barracuda in favour of the Avenger, or 'Tarpon', as it was briefly called in British service. All in all, *Saratoga*'s brief tour with the Eastern Fleet — 'a profitable and very happy association', as Somerville put it in his valedictory signal to the departing American veteran on 18 May — was the best of omens for the future formation and deployment of the British Pacific Fleet.

Apart from the fighter replenishment of Malta by *Wasp* in April-May 1942, only one other American fleet carrier served under British command down to 1945, *Ranger*. After covering the American landings in the Fedala-Casablanca sector during 'Torch' in November 1942, *Ranger* had returned to training duties with the US Atlantic Fleet. In the late summer of 1943, however, she was transferred to the British Home Fleet, and it was there, under the command of Admiral Sir Bruce Fraser, that she carried out her one and only strike at an enemy shore target (page 31). This was *Ranger*'s sole moment of glory, but her contribution was by no means over. Relegated to training duties in 1944–45, *Ranger* was the invaluable 'spare carrier' on which advanced trainee pilots could practice at sea after completing basic flying school and carrier training on the converted paddle-steamers *Wolverine* and *Sable* on the Great Lakes. It was most fitting that, having contributed so much to American carrier development before the war, *Ranger* should still be in service at the war's end, helping to increase the flow of superbly-trained aircrew to the carrier fleet in the Pacific.

The Battle of Leyte Gulf

In early August 1944 the end of Japanese resistance on the Marianas coincided with MacArthur's clearance of western New Guinea. It was now time to clear the decks for the temporary convergence of the Central and South-Western Pacific offensives in the liberation of the southern Philippines. MacArthur intended to guarantee the invasion land-based air cover by taking Morotai in mid-September and the Talaud Islands a month later. Nimitz

demanded the final isolation of the Japanese bases in the Carolines, and the seizure of a new advanced fleet base west of the Carolines, by the conquest of the Palaus, Yap and Ulithi.

Halsey broke his flag as C-in-C, 3rd Fleet on 26 August and immediately prepared for the softening-up attacks with which TF.38 would support both invasions. This began with neutralising strikes from east to west along the Carolines, ending with the Palaus between 6 and 8 September, then shifting to the southern Philippines. MacArthur's men had no trouble when they landed on Morotai on 15 September, but the Central Pacific attack on the Palaus was a very different matter. It strongly resembled the Gilberts/Marshalls campaign, with vicious fighting on Peleliu which continued until the end of the year; but the vital objective of Ulithi with its fine fleet anchorage was taken without opposition on 23 September. The day before the landings on Morotai and Peleliu the Joint Chiefs had, on Halsey's urging, made a momentous decision. TF.38 had encountered so little opposition in its sweeps over the Philippines that Halsey had deduced that Japanese air power in the islands was on its last legs. He therefore recommended bringing forward the invasion of the Philippine island of Leyte by two months, diverting invasion forces earmarked for other preliminary landings; and the Joint Chiefs agreed. The invasion of Leyte, MacArthur's long-promised 'return' to the Philippines, was set for 20 October.

Leyte: Halsey's preliminary strikes

Before moving in to cover the Leyte landings, TF.38's preliminary operations — this time had the hopeful objective of luring out part of the Japanese fleet. These operations were the furthest into Japanese waters so far attempted. The actual strikes were flown between 10 and 13 October. They amounted to the familiar task of slicing at the chain of airfields along which the Japanese would attempt to reinforce the Philippines: the Nansei Shoto islands from Okinawa south to Formosa. During these strikes TF.38 discovered that Halsey's dismissal of Japanese air strength in September had been decidedly premature, for Mitscher's carriers found themselves subjected to the heaviest air attacks since the formation of 5th Fleet in the previous year. About 1000 Japanese aircraft were committed to the attacks on TF.38 between 10 and 16 October. American morale, however, was sustained by two factors: intercepted Japanese broadcasts boasting of how the American fleet was being decimated (nothing is quite so cheering as to hear

the enemy announce that he has destroyed you), and the savage losses inflicted on the Japanese by the task groups' fighters and AA fire. At least 500 of the 1000 attackers were destroyed, for the loss of 110 American aircraft. As ever, prompt 'life-guard' work kept the aircrew losses minimal, while there was no shortage of replacement aircraft. Though two American cruisers were crippled by torpedoes during these attacks on TF.38, both were retrieved and towed back to Ulithi for repairs.

Indeed, it was the crippling of the two cruisers, *Canberra* and *Houston*, which gave TF.38 most cause for mirth, boosting the broadcast Japanese claims to a total of two American battleships and eleven carriers sunk, and many more damaged. For a while Halsey let the cripples dangle as bait, and the Japanese Vice-Admiral Shima did make a tentative sortie against them with two heavy cruisers before realising that he was heading into a trap and turned back. As Halsey withdrew on 19 October with both cruisers safely in tow, he took the opportunity to signal that he was 'RETIRING TOWARDS THE ENEMY' after all ships reported sunk by Radio Tokyo had been salvaged!

The strikes at Okinawa and Formosa were only the prelude to concentrated bombardments of the Japanese airfields on the northern and largest Philippine island of Luzon between 16 and 19 October. These attacks temporarily reduced the Japanese 1st Air Fleet, charged with the air defence of the Philippines, to an operational strength of twenty Zeros and 30 bombers by 17 October — the day that MacArthur's invasion fleet was sighted on the last leg of its voyage to the invasion beaches in Leyte Gulf.

'Sho-Go': The Philippines defence plan

Toyoda's immediate reaction to the invasion fleet was to issue the executive order for his Philippine defence plan: 'Sho-Go'. This astounding operation, involving every major unit of the Japanese Fleet able to put to sea, embodied every major Japanese mistake committed since Midway. These mistakes included excessive reliance on battleship firepower in the teeth of enemy air superiority; excessive reliance on land-based against massed carrier-based air power; and the old ploy of pushing forward a decoy force to lure the Americans off their guard. 'Sho-Go' also set at nought all the proven American experience and expertise in launching and protecting seaborne invasions, and all the American superiority in land, sea and air manpower and *matériel*. It should never have stood a chance — and yet it came very close to success.

The scene in *Ticonderoga*'s Ready Room before a dawn attack on Japanese airfields near Manila. Halsey's estimate of TF.38's attrition of Japanese air strength in the Philippines proved, after the Leyte campaign began, to have been over-confident.

Opposite
Enterprise preparing to launch Hellcats on 15 October 1944 — 'D-5' for the Leyte invasion.

Lexington recovering aircraft after one of the softening-up strikes at the Philippine airfields before the landings on Leyte.

'Sho-Go' was a tacit admission that the rump of the Japanese carrier fleet no longer had any offensive potential after the Philippine Sea battle. On the other hand, it could still present an irresistibly tempting target. Ever since the Coral Sea it had been axiomatic, in every Pacific naval action, that enemy carriers be attacked at the earliest opportunity. 'Sho-Go' relied on this axiom — and on the fact that the Americans could not know for sure that the Japanese carriers were toothless tigers. For the first time in the war, a Japanese carrier fleet was to sail with only enough aircraft to attract attention to itself, sufficient, in fact, for only one attention-demanding air strike. This would lure TF.38 away from the invasion area in pursuit, letting through the Japanese battleships to wreak havoc amid the defenceless transports off the invasion beaches. With a sufficiently bloody repulse on the beaches of Leyte, months must pass before the Americans resumed their assault on the Philippines — which it was essential that the Japanese held if they were to be able to continue to ship the all-important oil of the East Indies and Borneo to the homeland.

To this end the 'Sho-Go' naval forces were divided into four task groups:

Carrier Decoy Force (Vice-Admiral Ozawa) Carriers *Zuikaku* (52 Zeros, 28 fighter-bombers), *Chitose* (25 torpedo-bombers), *Chiyoda* (seven bombers), *Zuiho* (four torpedo aircraft, two reconnaissance float-planes); battleship-carriers *Ise*, *Hyuga*; three light cruisers; eight destroyers.
Task: To sail from Japan, approach the Philippines from the north-east, get sighted and take as long as possible in getting sunk by TF.38.

Force A (Vice-Admiral Kurita) Battleships *Yamato*, *Musashi*, *Nagato*, *Kongo*, *Haruna*; twelve cruisers; fifteen destroyers.
Task: To sail from Lingga Roads, Singapore via Brunei, refuel and traverse the Sibuyan Sea to run San Bernadino Strait by night; descend on Leyte Gulf from the north at daybreak and massacre the American invasion fleet, with Force C.

Force C (Vice-Admiral Nishimura) Battleships *Fuso*, *Yamashiro*; one cruiser; four destroyers.
Task: To part company with Kurita off Borneo, traverse the Sulu Sea to run Surigao Strait by night, and enter Leyte Gulf from the south at daybreak. It formed the southern jaw of a pincer attack on the

American invasion fleet, carried out in collaboration with Kurita.

2nd Striking Force (Vice-Admiral Shima) Three cruisers; four destroyers.
Task: To sail from Okinawa, traverse the Sulu Sea in Nishimura's wake and reinforce his drive through Surigao Strait.

Birth of the *kamikazes*

The task groups of the 'Sho-Go' operation were dependent throughout on land-based air support which, though reduced to a strength of 50 aircraft by 17 October by the American pre-invasion attacks, was boosted to about 200 by reinforcements from Japan between the 17 and 22 October. These reinforcements were additional proof of Halsey's tendency to under-estimate Japan's remaining air strength. They gave Vice-Admiral Ohnishi, commanding 1st Air Fleet, conventional attack forces as well as the revolutionary new measure for which he had gained Toyoda's startled approval on 19 October, and which was used for the first time in the ensuing battle. This was the formation of the *Shimpu* Special Attack Corps, of volunteers prepared to expend themselves as human bombs by

The blistered hulk of *Princeton*, still afloat but burned out after the bomb from the 'Judy' plunged through her flight-deck and exploded amid fuelled and armed aircraft in the hangar. The cruiser *Birmingham* lies close alongside, providing power for fire-fighting. The final horror came when *Princeton*'s exploding bomb store swept the upper deck of *Birmingham* with blast and steel splinters. It is painfully easy to imagine the fate of the men in this picture; the bomb store explosion killed 233 men outright and wounded over 400 more.

Aboard *San Jacinto* a torpedo, with its warhead still to be fitted, is wheeled towards an Avenger during Halsey's pursuit of Ozawa's carrier decoy force off Cape Engaño.

deliberately crashing their aircraft onto American warships and transports. *Shimpu* was an alternative reading of the Japanese characters for the word describing the 'divine wind' which had shattered Kubilai Khan's invasion fleet off the Japanese coast in the late thirteenth century. The word was *kamikaze*.

Kamikaze mentality has been earnestly expounded by Western as well as Japanese writers, all of whom are quick to explain that the catchphrase 'suicide attack' hardly applies. Suicide is born of despair, and *kamikaze* pilots were not despairing men. The Corps never lacked volunteers, all eager to be remembered for having died inflicting shattering damage on the enemy, rather than perishing ingloriously in a sky filled with enemy fighters without having struck a blow in Japan's defence. Far less often explained is the fact that *kamikaze* theory, regardless of the pilots' undoubted zeal, was immensely hard to put into practice. By taking out one American warship with each aircraft, *kamikaze* attacks were intended to solve Japan's problem of having insufficient aircraft and skilled pilots to stop the Americans with conventional air attacks. Yet, by the autumn of 1944, higher-than-average flying and combat skills were needed merely to dodge the swarming American fighters and arrive intact over an American carrier task group. However, even more advanced skills were needed to be sure of hitting a fast-moving warship with a diving aircraft, especially if the pilot was hit or his controls were shot away as he made his death dive. Mere will-power, in short, was not enough to overcome the practical difficulties.

Taking all possible circumstances into account, there was no chance of every *kamikaze* pilot living long enough to be certain of choosing his point of impact and crashing in the most damaging place. In the first three months, 25 October 1944 to 25 January 1945, about 447 *kamikaze* missions were flown. Of these, 179 pilots returned to base having failed to find worthwhile victims, and 67 more had been chopped out of the sky by fighters or AA fire. From the 201 *kamikaze* missions actually completed, the net American loss came to two escort carriers and three destroyers sunk. The all-important American fleet carriers suffered aggregate damage of varying degrees in seven 'Essex' class and two 'Independence' class ships — well over 50 per cent of the total fleet carrier force — yet all carriers hit by *kamikazes* survived to take part in the campaigns of 1945. Damage to other fleet units was considerable — 23 cruisers, five battleships, 23 destroyers and 27 other ships — yet of these there were replacements to spare. The only American fleet carrier sunk was the victim of a conventional bombing attack.

The survivability of the American fleet carriers was helped by the fact that they were never the sole targets for *kamikaze* attacks. The slower, more vulnerable escort carriers, of which there were also plenty to spare, were naturally more popular targets. Later *kamikaze* attacks usually began with attempts to take out the radar picket destroyers operating on the fringes of the fleet, which would hopefully improve the chances of the main attack force getting through. One of the favourite *kamikaze* aircraft was a bomb-laden Zero, which had to be escorted on its approach to the target by other fighters; losses of fighters shot down while escorting *kamikazes* only accelerated the wastage of Japan's last skilled fighter pilots. All these considerations meant that the American carrier fleet remained unbroken even when the *kamikaze* assaults reached zenith, which occurred off Okinawa in April 1945. The first *kamikaze* attacks, launched in the final stages of the battle of Leyte Gulf in October 1944, did nothing to reverse the course of that titanic struggle.

The American strength

In the Leyte invasion of October 1944 the Americans deployed two fleets for the first time, with Halsey's 3rd Fleet supposedly permitting Kinkaid's 7th Fleet to concentrate on getting the troops ashore and giving them the closest possible support.

To add to the weight of pre-invasion bombardment and enable 7th Fleet to see off any surprise Japanese surface attack, Kinkaid had been given a powerful Battle Line under Rear-Admiral Jesse B. Oldendorf: six old battleships, eight cruisers and 21 destroyers. Torpedo-boats and another seven destroyers had been pushed forward to patrol the likeliest Japanese approach-route to 7th Fleet's left flank, Surigao Strait. Close air cover was provided by the escort carrier force under Rear-Admiral Thomas L. Sprague: eighteen carriers in three groups of six, each screened by six or seven destroyers. The northernmost of these three escort carrier groups was commanded by another Rear-Admiral Sprague, Clifton A., flying his flag in the escort carrier *Fanshaw Bay*. Clifton Sprague's 'Taffy 3' (officially CG.77.4.3) covered 7th Fleet's right flank, confident that any heavy Japanese forces coming through San Bernadino Strait to the north would be stopped in its tracks by Halsey's 3rd Fleet.

There was, however, a significant difference between the Leyte invasion and that of

The end of *Zuikaku*, last of Japan's 'Pearl Harbor' fleet carriers and accordingly singled out for special attention in the American carrier attacks off Cape Engaño. This is the second American strike at Ozawa's carriers on 25 October. *Zuikaku*'s speed had been cut to 18 knots by a torpedo hit scored in the first attack, and this time *Lexington*'s aircraft easily scored three more torpedo hits, one of them captured by this photograph. *Zuikaku* finally rolled over and sank at 1410.

the Marianas back in June. Before the latter operation, Spruance had been categorically told that 5th Fleet's priority was ensuring the safety of the invasion fleet. At Leyte, however, the invasion fleet was covered by the most powerful escort carrier fleet then assembled in the Pacific. Halsey's orders were that 3rd Fleet should co-operate with 7th Fleet in covering the invasion, but also that — if the opportunity arose *or could be created* — 3rd Fleet was to attack and destroy the Japanese Fleet. Such a flexible brief was typical of Nimitz, who preferred never to truss his subordinate admirals into a rigid operational framework. This flexible approach had paid rich dividends at Midway and the Philippine Sea. Nimitz assumed that if Halsey did attempt to pursue the Japanese with TF.38, he would leave at least Lee's Battle Line and maybe one or more carrier task groups to extend the cover of 7th Fleet's northern flank. This was the type of canny insurance which Nimitz had come to expect from Spruance as a matter of course. Never for one moment did Nimitz imagine that Halsey would take off after Ozawa with the whole of 3rd Fleet, leaving 7th Fleet unsupported and wide open to surface counter-attack from the north.

20–23 October: Opening moves

On 20 October, the day on which the Leyte landings prompted the 'Sho-Go' executive order from Toyoda, Kurita arrived off Brunei from Lingga Roads and began refuelling; Shima sailed from the Ryukyus; and Ozawa left Japan's Inland Sea with his carrier decoy force. Kurita sailed from Brunei early on 22 October having detached Nishimura's squadron, which followed that evening.

By nightfall on 22 October, Kurita was heading for the Palawan Passage and the Mindoro Strait entrance to the Sibuyan Sea; Nishimura was approaching the Balabac Strait entrance to the Sulu Sea; Shima was approaching Koron in the western Philippines, where he planned to refuel his cruisers and destroyers; and Ozawa was still heading south from Japan, dog-legging westward to stay out of range of reconnaissance aircraft based on the Marianas and thus avoid being spotted until the time was ripe.

Day 1, 23 October: US submarines attack

On the morning of the 23 October the American submarines *Darter* and *Dace*, patrolling the Palawan Passage, opened the three-day Battle of Leyte Gulf in resounding style. They caught Kurita's force proceeding in two columns at a leisurely 16 knots, ideal for a surprise attack, which was duly pressed at

0620. *Darter* torpedoed and sank Kurita's flagship, the cruiser *Atago*, leaving Kurita and his staff swimming for their lives, and crippled the cruiser *Takao*. *Dace* meanwhile fired four torpedoes which blew the cruiser *Maya* clean out of the water.

The submarines' reports gave Halsey and Kinkaid their first warning that something big was afoot; but the Japanese forces were still out of range of American carrier-borne scout planes, and no further contact with the widely-dispersed Japanese forces were made that day. Halsey decided to detach TG.38.1, comprising *Wasp*, *Hornet*, *Hancock*, *Monterey* and *Cowpens*, to replenish at Ulithi. He also ordered groups 2, 3 and 4, which had been patrolling about 260 miles north-west of Samar, to move closer inshore and fly off air searches in the morning. This brought Group 4 east of Leyte Gulf, Group 2 east of San Bernadino Strait, and Group 3, furthest north, east of the Polillo Islands off Luzon by daybreak on 24 October.

Day 2, 24 October: Loss of *Princeton*

On the morning of 24 October all three carrier groups launched air searches to the westward, and Group 3 flew off a strike on the airfields around Manila. Group 2's aircraft found Kurita's force at 0812, Group 4 found Nishimura at 0905, and Halsey immediately signalled Group 1 to return. But before the oncoming Japanese battle squadrons could be attacked 'the bear blew first', with massive Japanese air attacks informing Halsey how wrong his estimate of Japanese air strength in the Philippines had been.

The brunt of the Japanese attacks fell on Sherman's Group 3, which only had twelve Hellcats up to counter the first of three attacking forces, which totalled some 200 aircraft. Moreover, Sherman's carriers were caught with bombers and torpedo aircraft ranged on deck. These were hastily struck below and every available Hellcat was launched as a furious air battle developed overhead. By sheer luck and the prowess of the Hellcat pilots, not to mention the inexperience of the ill-trained Japanese airmen, the damage to Group 3 was not as serious as it could have been; but what happened was grim enough.

At Santa Cruz it had been shown that a sneak attack by one or two aircraft could get through where more powerful strike forces were intercepted. Nearly two years later, a solitary 'Judy' dive-bomber avenged the crippling of *Zuiho* in the American sneak attack at Santa Cruz. At 0938 Group 3's carriers were recovering and refuelling their Hellcats when the 'Judy' roared out of a low cloud and dropped a 550 lb bomb fair and square on

Princeton's flight-deck. The bomb set ablaze the hangar-deck, packed with armed and fuelled Avengers, six of which were engulfed in blazing aviation fuel. From 1002 the Avengers began to explode, sending *Princeton*'s fires out of control. Destroyers moved in to take off her crew while the cruiser *Birmingham* moved close alongside to help *Princeton*'s fire-fighters, followed soon after by the cruiser *Reno*. Both cruisers had to cast off when a submarine alert was raised, but after several hours' fight only one big fire aft remained to be quelled. *Birmingham* came back in to rejoin battle with the flames and take *Princeton* in tow — and that was when *Princeton*'s after bomb store exploded, blowing off her stern. *Birmingham* escaped fatal structural damage but her packed upper decks were swept by blast and wicked steel splinters, killing 233 outright and wounding over 400. Her last survivors taken off, *Princeton* was abandoned and sunk by torpedoes from *Reno*.

Princeton's long ordeal had been accompanied by further Japanese air attacks, all of which were beaten off. One of these strikes consisted of Ozawa's carrier-borne strike aircraft, 76 strong, launched in an attempt to reveal the Japanese decoy force. However, Ozawa's carriers were not sighted before Kurita's battleships had come under ferocious attack in the Sibuyan Sea.

Day 2: Battle of the Sibuyan Sea

With Group 3 fighting off Japanese air attacks to the north and Group 4 launching its first search-and-strike missions against Nishimura in the south, Bogan's Group 2 was left to open the attack on Kurita's battleships in the forenoon of the 24th, with Group 3 and 4 weighing in that afternoon. Between 0910 and 1530 five separate strikes were launched at Kurita's force, which was bereft, after the morning's air battles, of the promised Japanese fighter cover The American aircraft naturally concentrated on the super-battleships *Yamato* and *Musashi*, almost legendary giants which no American force had ever sighted before. Far too large a proportion of the strike forces, however, consisted of dive-bombers, which the big Japanese battleships proved well able to survive. Against such ships, torpedoes were the master-weapon, and it was torpedoes which settled *Musashi*'s fate. Around noon the second attack from Group 2 merged with the first strike from Group 3, hitting *Musashi* with

Revelation of the new menace which broke on 7th Fleet while Halsey was chasing Ozawa. *Kamikaze* diving on the escort carrier *Suwanee* (top). The moment of impact—the victim is *St Lô* (right). *St Lô* burning after the attack (*far right*).

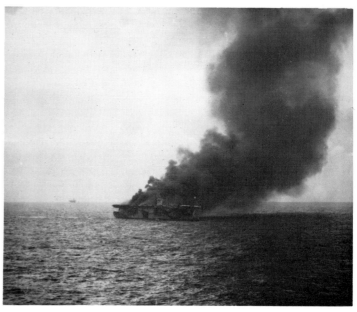

eight torpedoes and four bombs. Settling in the water, *Musashi* dropped astern with the cruiser *Tone* standing by. Superb damage control kept her on an even keel until her forecastle deck was awash, but the *coup de grace* was administered by another joint attack by Group 4 and Group 2, from *Essex, Enterprise, Intrepid, Franklin* and the light carrier *Cabot*. The Avengers hit her with another ten torpedoes at 1520. Even then, *Musashi* lingered for another four hours, kept afloat by devoted efforts by her crew, before she capsized and sank at 1935. Here at last was the ultimate proof that fleet carrier strike aircraft were a match even for super-battleships specifically designed and built as 'unsinkable gun platforms'.

Apart from the sinking of one of the most powerful battleships in the world, the Battle of the Sibuyan Sea had two other immediate consequences. It threw the *Sho-Go* programme badly off balance, making it impossible for Nishimura and Kurita to make a simultaneous break-in to Leyte Gulf; and it led Halsey to make a fatal miscalculation which remains one of the most controversial decisions in modern naval histroy.

The repeated American attacks led Kurita to the decision that if he pressed on he risked losing his entire battleship force long before it got anywhere near Leyte Gulf. At 1550 Kurita turned back to the west, intending to resume his eastward course after dark. At this point, Halsey's attention was still concentrated on the problem of fighting and destroying Kurita's battleships and at 1512 he ordered Lee to form the Battle Line, which was to operate separately from the carriers as Task Force 34. So far so good; if the carrier aircraft of TF.38 failed to stop the Japanese battleships, it made sense to have TF.34 formed and ready to finish the business with a gun action. By 1600, however, it seemed to Halsey that the position had changed dramatically. TF.38's returning aircraft were reporting four to five Japanese battleships torpedoed and bombed, with one probably sunk; at least three heavy cruisers torpedoed and others bombed; one light cruiser sunk, a destroyer probably sunk and four others damaged. With all these over-optimistic claims of Japanese battle damage came the news that Kurita had turned in his tracks. Then, at 1640, came the sighting of Ozawa's carriers away to the north.

Weighing all these premises, the false and the true, Halsey immediately marked down Ozawa's force as his primary objective. To a large extent it is hard to blame him. If MacArthur had always been driven by his vow to return to the Philippines, Halsey had always yearned to annihilate the Japanese

Fleet in revenge for what it had done at Pearl Harbor. Now, in his first battle as a fleet commander at sea, just such an annihilating victory lay within Halsey's grasp. But he should have revised his plans when, at 1935, one of his scout planes reported that Kurita had turned back to the east. He should have left TF.34 to block San Bernadino Strait instead of leading it, with all three carrier task groups, against Ozawa. Above all, Halsey should have told Kinkaid precisely what he was doing, instead of signalling, at 2000: 'AM PROCEEDING NORTH WITH THREE GROUPS TO ATTACK ENEMY CARRIER FORCE AT DAWN.'

It could also be said that Kinkaid might have asked his fellow fleet commander if the 'three groups' mentioned included TF.34; but he did not. Instead Kinkaid *assumed* that TF.34 had remained on guard duty off San Bernadino Strait. In this belief, the 7th Fleet commander prepared to tackle the Japanese threat heading through Surigao Strait for his left flank, ignorant of the far greater threat about to be hurled at his right.

Day 2/3: Surigao Strait and Samar

Though Nishimura's battleship squadron had been sighted advancing across the Mindanao Sea at 0905 on 24 October 1944, the ensuing attacks by TG.38.4 had neither inflicted serious damage on it nor caused Nishimura to imitate Kurita and retire until nightfall. (Some of the most famous photographs of the carrier war were taken by *Enterprise*'s aircraft that morning, showing *Fuso* and *Yamashiro* with their towering 'pagoda' fighting tops being drenched by columns of spray from near-misses.) Nishimura was undeterred when one of his cruisers' scoutplanes reported that six battleships and a powerful cruiser-destroyer force were waiting for him on the other side of Surigao Strait. He might, however, have reacted differently if he had known that Kurita's temporary retirement had left the Nishimura force to take on odds of over three to one, with no prospect of help from Kurita for four hours at least.

The story of the Battle of Surigao Strait is soon told. It was the last battleship-versus-battleship action in naval history, and was a shattering Japanese defeat. Nishimura's squadron stood boldly on in line-ahead, its progress monitored and harried by American torpedo-boat and destroyer attacks from 2250 on 24 October. *Fuso* was torpedoed at 0309 and sank half an hour later, but still Nishimura kept coming. The rest of his force was then battered to extinction by Oldendorf's battleships and cruisers in a totally one-sided gunnery action lasting from 0351 to 0409. Nishimura was lost when *Yamashiro* capsized

and sank at 0419. Shima, arriving on the scene of the disaster, took one look and wisely decided that there was nothing to be gained by adding to the tally of American kills; he turned in his tracks and withdrew. By first light on 25 October, 7th Fleet's Battle Line had liquidated the southern jaw of the pincers which had been intended to crush MacArthur's invasion fleet to extinction in Leyte Gulf.

Oldendorf's cruisers were still finishing off the last Japanese cripples in Surigao Strait when electrifying news came from the north: an SOS from the escort carriers of Clifton Sprague's 'Taffy 3', which was running for its life with Kurita's battleships and cruisers hard on its heels and rapidly overtaking. If Sprague had had the faintest idea that TF.34 was not patrolling San Bernadino Strait he would have had search planes aloft with the first hint of dawn. As it was, practically the first warning received by his lumbering escort carriers was the arrival in their midst of 18-inch and 16-inch shells from Kurita's battleships at 0659, fired from barely 20 miles away. Oldendorf's victorious Battle Line, low on ammunition after prodigious expenditure in Surigao Strait, was 100 miles or more to the south. Lee's TF.34 was even further away: some 300 miles to the north, still in company with TF.38's carriers which had just launched their first strike at Ozawa's decoy carriers. 'Taffy 3' was on its own, with no option but to run for it at its lagging top speed of $17\frac{1}{2}$ knots, calling vainly for help from every 3rd Fleet and 7th Fleet unit on the air.

Clifton Sprague later attributed the escape of most of his force to 'the definite partiality of Almightly God'. Japanese mistakes were a considerable help. Kurita did much to snatch defeat from the jaws of certain victory, first by ordering a confused general chase in which many of his ships unwittingly obscured the range of others, then by losing his nerve and withdrawing at the very moment when, at 0915, his leading cruisers were overtaking the fleeting escort carriers. With equal certainty, if the Americans escaped by virtue of divine help they certainly earned it, with the escorting destroyers of 'Taffy 3' gallantly drawing the Japanese fire at the cost of three of their number sunk. Sprague also deliberately allowed the gunnery range to shorten by turning into wind to launch every strike aircraft which could be put into the air, aided by aircraft from Rear-Admiral Stump's 'Taffy 2' to the south. As the running Battle off Samar rose to its height, 7th Fleet aircraft sank the Japanese heavy cruisers *Chokai* and *Chikuma*. However, when Kurita called off the fight and withdrew at 0915, one of Sprague's carriers, *Gambier Bay*, had already been sunk and the

other five seemed likely to follow within minutes.

Kurita's decision to withdraw would be incomprehensible without putting it into its fair context. As he saw it, 'Sho-Go' had been a disaster from the outset. There had been the traumatic submarine attacks early on 23 October, with his own flagship 'shot from under him'; virtually non-stop carrier attacks throughout the 24th, sinking the mighty *Musashi*; Nishimura's force destroyed only hours before — and now an apparently easy victim leading him straight for a southern horizon stacked with yet more carrier silhouettes, Stump's 'Taffy 2', launching aircraft. As Kurita saw it, he was being led by the nose straight towards the main American carrier force, which could only mean that Ozawa's decoy mission had failed; and, as had happened at the Philippine Sea, the promised support of the land-based air forces had never

materialised: enough was enough. Without detracting in any way from the achievement of the 7th Fleet escort carriers on the morning of 25 October 1944, Kurita recoiled less from their puny substance than from the giant shadow of TF.38's fleet carriers — none of which was anywhere near him.

Day 3, 25 October: Cape Engaño

After the Battle of the Sibuyan Sea on 24 October and the night Battle of Surigao Strait, the running Battle off Samar on the morning of 25 October overlapped with the final phase of the Leyte Gulf epic: the Battle of Cape Engaño, Luzon's north-eastern tip, in which TF.38 destroyed Ozawa's carrier decoy force.

By 0700 on 25 October, Halsey was confident that his decision to pursue Ozawa with all 3rd Fleet's carriers and battleships had

A Helldiver is launched from *Hancock* against the Manila airfields on 25 November 1944. Despite strenuous efforts by American land-based and carrier-based aircraft, the *kamikaze* offensive against 7th and 3rd Fleets which began on 25 October 1944 did not peter out until January.

been the right one. He had heard of 7th Fleet's annihilation of Nishimura in Surigao Strait; Kurita seemed to have vanished; and now Ozawa's carriers were less than 200 miles away. Lee's Battle Line was now fully formed, including Halsey's flagship, *New Jersey*, and TF.38's first strike was already in the air and searching. At 0710, just as the air began to ring with 7th Fleet's appeals for help, Ozawa's ships were located at a range of 145 miles. At 0830, a minute after Kinkaid had reported 7th Fleet's situation as critical, Mitscher's first strike fell on the Japanese decoy force.

After launching his strike against TF.38 on

Langley (CVL.27) taking a heavy swell over the bows while operating with TG.38.3 in December.

the previous day, Ozawa was left with only nineteen Zeros against 120 American strike aircraft and powerful fighter opposition. As at the Philippine Sea, however, the American strike force achieved comparatively little with its first blow. *Chitose* was the only Japanese carrier to suffer mortal damage, overwhelmed with multiple hits from the dive-bombers and sinking an hour later. *Zuiho* was hit but not crippled by a single bomb and *Zuikaku*'s speed was cut to 18 knots by a single torpedo hit. Apart from these casualties the only other victims of the first American attack were a destroyer sunk and the light cruiser *Tama* crippled by a torpedo.

All this time signals had been pouring in from 7th Fleet where, until Kurita's sudden withdrawal at 0915, a disaster was clearly imminent. Unable to send immediate help, Halsey grimly stuck to the immediate task of destroying Ozawa, but TF.38's second attack at 1000 achieved no more than leaving the carrier *Chiyoda* dead in the water and ablaze. By this time it almost seemed that 3rd Fleet was hell-bent on letting Kurita get clean away, and Nimitz made a rare tactical intervention — bluntly demanding of Halsey 'WHERE IS TASK FORCE 34?' Utterly frustrated — 'I turned my back on the opportunity I had dreamed of since my days as a cadet' — Halsey finally called off TF.34 and TG.38.2 at 1115, and set off to intercept Kurita, but it was too late. By the time the fast battleships reached San Bernadino Strait that evening, Kurita had already passed through to the west three hours before.

Meanwhile, TG.38.3 and TG.38.4 had car-ried on with the liquidation of Ozawa's force, accomplished on the afternoon of 25 October with another massive combined strike, 200 aircraft strong, attacking from 1300. *Lexington*'s air group finished off *Zuikaku* with three more torpedoes; the last of the 'Pearl Harbor carriers' capsized and sank at 1410. *Zuiho* was set on fire by *Essex*'s dive-bombers from TG.38.3, but her fires were contained and another attack was required by the TG.38.4 aircraft. In notable contrast to the speed with which her sister-ship *Shoho* had been overwhelmed at the Coral Sea, *Zuiho* survived repeated hits until she finally sank at 1526. This left only the burning *Chiyoda* to be finished off by TF.38's cruisers at 1700. The two hybrid battleship-carriers, *Ise* and *Hyuga*, escaped, together with the light cruiser *Oyodo* and five destroyers.

Predictably, Halsey's belated attempts to

142

destroy Kurita's retreating battleships with long-range air strikes on 26 October achieved little. These were carried out by Bogan's TG.38.2 and McCain's TG.38.1, the latter entering the battle for the first time after returning from its premature diversion to Ulithi. The attacks of 26 October achieved no more than the sinking of the light cruiser *Noshiro*, Kurita escaping to Brunei with *Yamato, Kongo* and *Nagato*.

Leyte Gulf: The action assessed

Even allowing for the fateful results of Halsey falling for Ozawa's decoy, the three days of Leyte Gulf achieved a decisive victory for the US Navy. The Leyte invasion force was secured, and the Japanese Fleet was destroyed as a coherent fighting force. Carrier had fought carrier for the last time.

A frequently overlooked result of Halsey's famous pursuit of Ozawa is that it almost certainly saved TF.38 from damaging losses from the first *kamikaze* attacks flown against 7th Fleet on the forenoon of 25 October. As if Sprague's 'Taffy 3' had not already suffered enough from Kurita's battleships and cruisers, 7th Fleet's escort carriers now became the guinea-pigs for Japan's latest airborne strategy. The *kamikaze*s struck just after 1050 when 'Taffy 3' was recovering aircraft. The first caromed off the port side of *Kitkun Bay*'s flight-deck and crashed in the sea, its bomb exploding as it disappeared; the second and third were shot down as they dived on *Fanshaw Bay* and *White Plains*; but the fourth smashed through the flight-deck of *St Lô* and exploded in the hangar, blowing the ship apart and sinking her in less than 30 minutes. A further attack on 'Taffy 3' badly damaged

Kalinin Bay. Further south, 'Taffy 1' had also suffered, with extensive damage inflicted on the escort carriers *Santee* and *Suwannee*. The net result was one escort carrier sunk and four damaged in less than two hours. It was fortunate indeed that this novel and disconcerting tactic was first used against the expendable escort carriers and not the fleet carriers of the Fast Carrier Task Force.

Even with the casualties inflicted by these first *kamikaze* attacks, the losses of 7th and 3rd Fleets at Leyte Gulf were negligible. Japanese loss totalled one heavy carrier, *Zuikaku*, three light carriers, *Chitose, Chiyoda* and *Zuiho*, three battleships, *Musashi, Fuso* and *Yamashiro*, ten heavy and light cruisers, and nine destroyers. In comparison, the Americans lost one light carrier, *Princeton*, three destroyers, and two escort carriers.

After its savaging at Leyte Gulf, the Japanese Fleet was reduced to rage and tatters and the only effective weapon left to slow the remorseless American advance was the full-scale use of *kamikaze*s. The next major *kamikaze* attacks were hoarded until the American landings on Luzon in the first week of January 1945, but before then TF.38 caught the full fury of a natural 'divine wind'. A typhoon hit the Fleet on 18 December, while it was covering MacArthur's intermediate invasion of Mindoro Island, and was a timely reminder that the Japanese were not the only enemy. The typhoon killed nearly 800 officers and men, blew 186 aircraft over the side, capsized and sank three destroyers, and badly damaged seven other ships. Halsey was blamed by a Court of Enquiry for having taken inadequate precautions, but was reatined in command of 3rd Fleet for the invasion of Luzon, which went in at Lingayen Gulf on 9 January 1945.

Kamikaze victims, Leyte-Luzon campaign, October 1944– January 1945

The first *kamikaze* attack on an American fleet carrier had taken place before Ohnishi had formally requested Toyoda to agree to the formation of the corps. It happened on 15 October off Luzon, when TG.38.4 was attacking Japanese airfields on the eve of the Leyte landings. Flown by the commander of the Japanese 26th Air Flotilla, Rear-Admiral

Arima, a lone 'Judy' dive-bomber had immolated itself and its 500 lb bomb on the flight-deck of *Franklin*. Prompt fire and damage control limited the effects to three men killed and twelve wounded and *Franklin* stayed on station with TF.38, which did not experience its first multiple *kamikaze* attack until 30 October. It was a sharp awakening to the new menace: *Enterprise* was narrowly missed and both *Franklin* and *Belleau Wood* were now obliged to withdraw for repairs, with the loss of 158 men and 45 aircraft. There were four other casualties before the end of the Leyte campaign: *Lexington* damaged on 5 November and *Cabot*, *Essex* and *Intrepid* on 25 November, when six bomb-carrying Zeros and two 'Judies' attacked TGs.38.2 and 38.3.

However, neither these first *kamikaze* attacks nor the effects of the typhoon in December 1944 prevented Halsey from sweeping into the South China Sea in support of the Luzon landings. In this operation, the closest American carriers had come to Japan since the Tokyo Raid of April 1942, TF.38's aircraft hit targets on Formosa and the Chinese mainland from Hong Kong and Hainan north to Amoy and Swatow. The only casualty of a *kamikaze* attack was the 'Essex' class *Ticonderoga*, badly damaged off Formosa on 21 January. This was only four days before the last *kamikaze* mission was flown from the Philippines. Only two escort carriers had been sunk by *kamikaze*s since 25 October: *St Lô* on that day and *Ommaney Bay* on 3 January, on the eve of the Luzon landings. Of the 23 carriers damaged since October, only seven had been fleet carriers of the Fast Striking Force, which now returned to Ulithi to rest and replenish before undertaking the next campaign.

Iwo Jima and Okinawa, February–June 1945

After leading 3rd Fleet back to Ulithi on 25 January on completing the naval contribution to the Philippines campaign, Halsey handed over to Spruance, and 3rd Fleet became 5th Fleet again, and TF.38 became TF.58. Halsey now went ashore to begin planning the final assault on Japan, while Spruance prepared to implement the conquest of Iwo Jima and Okinawa which he had been planning since the previous August.

Iwo Jima was invaded on 19 February 1945 after being bombed and shelled day and night for the previous three weeks, with TF.58 launching carrier strikes against the nearest airfields on the Japanese mainland. As the decision had been made to save the next major

On the voyage out to the Pacific for the 1945 campaigns: the 'Essex' class *Bon Homme Richard* (CV.31) in the Gulf of Paria, Venezuela, on 7 February 1945.

Opposite
'Murderers' Row' at Ulithi. From foreground: *Wasp, Yorktown, Hornet, Hancock, Ticonderoga; Lexington* at left of picture.

kamikaze effort for the American attempt to take Okinawa in the Ryukyus, there was only one sizeable *kamikaze* attack during the Iwo campaign. This was launched on 21 February by 32 aircraft which broke through the radar picket screens and intensified CAPs. In an unusually effective attack, measured in terms of number of targets hit per number of aircraft attacking, the escort carrier *Bismarck Sea* was sunk, and *Saratoga* and four other ships were badly damaged.

In the slaughter of the campaign on Iwo, which had to be conquered foot by foot, only 216 Japanese prisoners were taken out of a garrison of 22,000. American casualties were 5931 dead and 17,272 wounded. Fighting on Iwo continued until the last week of March, by which time the 5th Fleet had already begun its preliminary strikes for 'Iceberg', the invasion of Okinawa.

'Iceberg' marked the debut of the British Pacific Fleet (BPF), based on Sydney under the supreme command of Admiral Sir Bruce Fraser, RN, with Vice-Admiral Sir Bernard Rawlings, RN, commanding at sea. The BPF's initial strength was no more than that of an American task group: two battleships, four fleet carriers, with a total of 218 aircraft, five cruisers and eleven destroyers. After

much politicking behind the scenes, Admiral King's reluctance to allow the BPF to participate in the final defeat of Japan was overcome, and the BPF joined Nimitz's command on 15 March. The BPF was generously allocated task force status, despite its modest 'front-line' strength, as the all-British TF.57. Its greatest weakness was its makeshift Fleet Train, starved of fast carriers and always dependent on American generosity at the bases of Manus, Ulithi and Leyte. However, the BPF's strength, the armoured flight-decks of its carriers, paid rich dividends in the crisis-ridden weeks of the Okinawa campaign. On orders from Washington, the BPF under Spruance, and later under Halsey, was deliberately kept well away from Japanese fleet base targets — the destruction of Japan's last warships was jealously preserved as an all-American duty of revenge. For its first stint in 'Iceberg', following the landings on Okinawa on 1 April, the BPF was tasked with bombarding the Japanese airfields on the Sakishima Gunto islands between Formosa and Japan.

TF.58's pre-invasion strikes were launched on 18 March with carrier-borne attacks on the airfields of Kyushu, Japan. This close-range bombardment of the Japanese mainland underlined the failure of the pre-emptive *kamikaze* strike on 5th Fleet at its Ulithi anchorage on 11 March. This was carried out by 24 Yokosuka P1Y1 'Frances' twin-engined bombers, each carrying a 2000 lb bomb. Over half the pilots got lost and turned back; only eleven found Ulithi and attacked, and only one scored a hit, causing a modest damage to the 'Essex' class carrier *Randolph*. But it was a very different story when 5th Fleet moved within range of the *kamikazes* and bombers poised to defend Okinawa.

To repel 'Iceberg', the Japanese had planned a frightening new *kamikaze* plan: *Kikusui* ('Floating Chrysanthemum'), swamping attacks by a total of 2100 aircraft hoarded for the purpose. There were 300 with the 1st Air Fleet on Formosa, 800 with the 3rd Air Fleet in the Tokyo district, 600 with the 5th Air Fleet on Kyushu and 400 with the 10th Air Fleet on south-west Honshu. The *Kikusui* plan included a one-way seaborne *kamikaze* mission by the 'Special Sea Attack Force', using the last reserves of fuel oil in what was left of the Japanese Fleet. As soon as the Americans had landed on Okinawa, *Yamato* would head for the invasion beaches at full speed, with a skimpy screen of the light cruiser *Yahagi* and six destroyers. There *Yamato* would beach herself and go out in a blaze of glory, murdering the invasion fleet with her guns.

The first air attacks hit 5th Fleet when it attacked the Japanese naval bases at Kobe and Kure on 19 March. Bombers damaged *Wasp* and *Franklin*, the latter terribly. It was the old story: two bombs penetrated the flight-deck and exploded to cause a holocaust amid the armed and fuelled aircraft in the hangar below. Explosions rocked the ship for five hours but she did not sink. After two days, she was able to make enough steam to limp back to Ulithi. One look at the photographs taken of the inferno aboard *Franklin* shows what an amazing performance this was — perhaps the most impressive testament to the hardiness of the 'Essex' class carriers — but *Franklin* never saw action again.

The main weight of the *Kikusui* offensive, however, had yet to fall. The first blow came on 6 April, from no less than 355 *kamikazes*. Two picket destroyers, two ammunition ships and a tank landing-craft were sunk, and 22

The awesome armada gathered at Ulithi in
February 1945 for the assault on Iwo Jima. Eleven fleet
carriers can be counted in this picture.

A close-up of 'Murderers' Row', with (left to right)
Wasp, *Hornet*, *Hancock* and *Yorktown*.

On station for D-Day, Iwo Jima, 19 February 1945. The tied-down Hellcats seem to be hunched against the gale-driven spray sweeping over the bows.

Preparing to launch a brace of Hellcats from the forward catapults of *Lexington* on 25 February 1945. Though all aircraft of the later war months could take off unassisted and normally did so, catapult launching helped reduce congestion on the flight-deck and enabled other aircraft to be brought up and ranged aft.

The incredible toughness of the Avenger airframe. This Avenger from *Bennington* (CV.20) was flying in formation when it was hit by the aircraft above it, shot down over Chichi Jima. With the outer port wing gone and the fuselage buckled, the aircraft nevertheless stayed in the air on a 100-mile return flight to its task group before ditching in the sea. All three crewmen were saved.

Below and Opposite
Emergency lighting assists fire-fighting in *Randolph* (CV.15) after a Japanese attack on 11 March 1945.

other ships were damaged. On the same day, the doomed 'Special Sea Attack Force' sailed on its one-way mission to the Okinawa beaches. It never stood a chance. Sighted at 0822 on 7 April, 250 miles from Okinawa, *Yamato*, *Yahagi* and their escorting destroyers came under the hammer of no less than 380 strike aircraft launched from Mitscher's carriers at 1000. The attacks began shortly after noon. *Yahagi* sank at about 1400, *Yamato* 25 minutes later after taking ten torpedo hits — nine of them on the port side, causing damage beyond all control — and six bombs. This brutal execution is usually dignified with the title 'Battle of the East China Sea'. It was the last American attack on an operational Japanese task force at sea, and marks the true closing of the circle begun with the Japanese carrier attack on Pearl Harbor in December 1941. Damage to American carriers on 7 April was limited to the carrier *Hancock*. But the airborne *Kikusui* attacks continued.

On 11 April, the *kamikaze*s made a determined effort to attack TF.58, whose carrier fighters were exacting a heavy toll. *Bunker Hill* was badly damaged, and *Enterprise* lightly so by a near-miss. *Enterprise* was damaged again, more heavily, on 13 April and *Intrepid* on the 16th. The rising toll of damage suffered from the *kamikaze*s obliged Spruance to re-form TF.58 in three task groups instead of four. He gladly accepted Admiral Rawlings' offer to keep the BPF on station for another week, although its parlous supply problems required a return to Leyte to replenish. So far the only damage suffered by the British force was a *kamikaze* hit on the flight-deck of *Indefatigable* on 1 April. The armoured flight-deck stood up well to the impact and blast, and *Indefatigable* stayed on station. After a

final attack on the Sakishima Gunto on 20 April, TF.57 set off for Leyte having earned the admiration and gratitude of its 5th Fleet allies. The British were back on station by 4 May, having fully earned their place on the team. On their first day of resumed operations both *Formidable* and *Indomitable* were hit by *kamikaze*s but were soon back in action, with impressed American liaison officers taking copious notes. 'When a *kamikaze* hits a US carrier', reported one of them, 'it's six months repair in Pearl. In a Limey carrier, it's "Sweepers, man your brooms!"'

By the end of the first week in May, it was clear that the *Kikusui* attacks were losing their edge but there was one more mass attack, on 11 May. For the cost of 72 *kamikaze*s shot down on their way to attack, two got through, sending *Bunker Hill* back for extensive repairs and forcing Mitscher to shift his flag to *Enterprise*. On 12 May, however, while attacking the Kyushu airfields, *Enterprise* was hit again and Mitscher once more shifted his flag, this time to *Randolph*. Never before had the carriers had to take punishment on this scale, but the end was in sight. From 12 May no more *Kikusui* attacks were launched. The last *kamikaze* attacks of the campaign were launched on 21–22 June, but caused little damage. After an exhausting land battle, Okinawa was finally declared secure on 2 July.

The 5th Fleet's carriers had not only stood up to, but had been instrumental in breaking, the most intense *kamikaze* attacks ever launched: 1809 *kamikaze* sorties flown, and 930 aircraft shot down. A total of seventeen ships had been sunk and 198 damaged, including twelve fleet and escort carriers and ten battleships. It is fair to point out — as was recognised at the time by both Spruance and Nimitz — that without the portion of the load shouldered by the British Task Force 57, American carrier losses would almost certainly have been heavier. For what proved to be the last time, the Fast Carrier Task Force had maintained air superiority until the ground forces could purchase enough real estate for the land-based air forces to occupy. The fall of Okinawa had carried the war to Japan's doorstep.

Halsey had relieved Spruance for the final stage of the Okinawa campaign on 27 May, with Vice-Admiral McCain taking over the Fast Carrier Force. Their task was now to achieve the neutralisation of Japan's remaining air strength before the invasion of Kyushu, 'Olympic', scheduled for November 1945. On 1 July 1945, Halsey led 3rd Fleet out of Leyte to begin this penultimate task: ten fleet carriers, six light carriers, eight battleships, nineteen cruisers, and over 60 destroyers. A week after its first strikes on the

Essex launches a strike of Corsairs in support of the Okinawa invasion. The forward aircraft is spotted for launch from the starboard catapult.

Franklin was the worst single carrier casualty of the Okinawa campaign. On 19 March 1945 she was hit by two bombs which, as with Princeton at the time of Leyte Gulf, set fire to armed and fuelled aircraft in the hangar. This is what Franklin looked like after the first explosions, which lasted for five hours.

The cruiser *Santa Fe* edges alongside the burning *Franklin* to provide rescue and firefighting services.

First signs of progress as the worst of the fire begins to be contained aft. Though fires continued to break out for days, *Franklin* was eventually able to raise steam and return to Ulithi, but she had lost 832 dead and 270 wounded, and was so badly damaged that she was never returned to service.

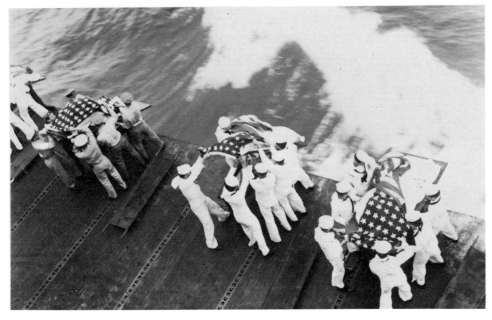

Burial at sea for four of the 28 men killed in *Hancock* in a bombing attack on 7 April 1945. Okinawa marked the zenith of the Japanese air offensive against the American carrier fleet, in which 1465 *kamikaze* aircraft took part.

Top and centre right
The ultimate symbol of American air supremacy: US Navy Avengers over the fields of Ie Shima and the sacred cone of Fujiyama itself.

Opposite left
Taken from *Independence*: *Langley*, with screening cruisers in close attendance, during a sweep against air bases on the Japanese mainland.

Opposite below
A Hellcat spotted for launch on the port catapult of *Randolph*. Even allowing for the fact that she is on the starboard zig-zag, the escorting destroyer seems perilously close. But the closer to the Japanese bases TF.38 operated during the last weeks of the war, the tighter the rings of escorts round the carriers had to be.

When Japan's naval bases came under constant American carrier attack in July 1945, the wheel had indeed come full circle since the attack on Pearl Harbor in December 1941. This is Kure, photographed at the height of Halsey's blitz on the naval bases (24 July) by one of *San Jacinto*'s aircraft. The main target is the carrier *Amagi*, at left. With her sister-ships *Aso* and *Ikoma*, Amagi was left a total wreck by these attacks.

Japanese airfields in the Tokyo district on 10 July, TF.38 was joined by the BPF, now redesignated TF.37: three fleet carriers, one battleship, six cruisers and fifteen destroyers. The last month of the Pacific War was abruptly cut short by the atomic bombs on Hiroshima and Nagasaki, dropped on 6 and 9 August respectively, and the Japanese surrender, on 15 August, signed in Tokyo Bay on 2 September.

The worst enemy was the weather, which restricted air operations to thirteen American and eight British strike days. There was no opposition at sea and very little in the air; the *Kikusui* attacks of April and May did not rematerialise, with the last reserves of Japanese aircraft being hoarded for mass attacks as soon as the invasion of the homeland began. Halsey and McCain, however, took no chances, and maintained TF.38's

Another view of Kure during the attacks on 24 July, with the last minutes of the cruiser *Tone* recorded at centre. This was the ship whose belated seaplane launch on the morning of Midway, over three years before, had failed to reveal the presence of American carriers until too late.

How the American occupation forces found her: the burned-out wreck of the carrier *Junyo* at Sasebo.

three-group deployment adopted by Spruance during the Okinawa campaign. This permitted a stronger picket-line of destroyers and cruisers to be deployed to protect the carriers, and concentrated the fighter strength of CAPs.

In those last thirteen days of air operations, however, the carriers of 3rd Fleet achieved the mission which had become of supreme propaganda value, and from which the British were still jealously excluded: the final destruction of the Japanese Fleet. This was achieved in three days of attacks on naval bases, on the 24, 25 and 28 July, which sank the carrier *Amagi*, battleship-carriers *Ise* and *Hyuga*, battleships *Haruna* and *Nagato*, five cruisers, and many smaller warships.

Full vigilance against the *kamikaze* threat was maintained to the end, even after Japan's announcement of capitulation. This was expressed by Halsey's famous signal that 'THE WAR WITH JAPAN WILL END AT 1200 ON 15TH AUGUST. IT IS LIKELY THAT KAMIKAZES WILL ATTACK THE FLEET AFTER THIS TIME AS A FINAL FLING. ANY EX-ENEMY AIRCRAFT ATTACKING THE FLEET IS TO BE SHOT DOWN IN A FRIENDLY MANNER'. The last carrier strike by 3rd Fleet was carried out at dawn on 15 August, Nimitz cancelling all further attacks at 0700; but there were a few attempted *kamikaze* attacks, all of them shot down. The closest call was at 1120 on 15 August, when two bombs fell close to the British carrier *Indomitable*. The last massed carrier air operation of 3rd Fleet was Operation 'Tintype' on 22 August 1945: a victory flypast over the Fleet by over 1000 aircraft. The long voyage from Pearl Harbor was over.

7

The New Giants

Eight days after the Instrument of Japan's surrender was signed under MacArthur's ponderous stage-management in Tokyo Bay, the greatest American carrier yet completed was commissioned. This was USS *Midway*, first of the new generation of American 'battle carriers' (CVBs), designed when it still seemed that it would be at least 1946 before the final assault on Japan could be pressed, and long before the Japanese Fleet had been neutralised at Philippine Sea and Leyte Gulf. The class was designated the successor to the 'Essex' class carriers, a few of which had seen action when *Midway* was laid down. The name-ship of her class, *Midway* was therefore the first American fleet carrier designed and built from the lessons of actual combat experience.

The first imperative derived from the bitter lessons of the 1942 carrier battles was the need for survivability. Coral Sea, Midway, the Eastern Solomons, Santa Cruz — all these desperately-fought carrier actions had proved that there could never be enough fighter aircraft to keep off enemy air attacks on a carrier. Hence the need for the largest possible air group to guarantee protection both to the carrier and its strike aircraft; the bigger the carrier, the bigger the air group and hence the bigger the standing CAP and the fighter escort for each strike. *Midway* was designed to operate a maximum of 137 aircraft, with the accent on fighters, 37 more than in the 'Essex' and 'Yorktown' classes. Though greater aircraft accommodation had to be provided, this was not purchased at the price of lesser performance (see Table 5).

Along with greater aircraft capacity and the need for speed and manoeuvrability went the need for greater AA fire-power. Eighteen 5-inch AA guns in single mountings, nine per side, and 21 quadruple 40 mm mountings compared favourably with twelve 5-inch mountings and sixteen less 40 mm guns in the 'Essex' class, but a great improvement in *Midway* was the positioning of the AA gun mountings in outboard sponsons below the level of the flight-deck. This not only greatly reduced the danger from lateral blast when the guns were firing, but freed the entire area

of the flight-deck for ranging and spotting aircraft on deck. The highly successful outboard elevator and pronounced overhang of the flight-deck on the port side, both features of the 'Essex' class, were retained.

Midway and her two sisters, *Coral Sea* and *Franklin D. Roosevelt* — her name adopted after the President's death in April 1945, seventeen days before the ship was ready for launching — were not the result of hasty planning or panic measures, as in the case of the last Japanese carriers designed and built in the war. An enlarged 'Essex' class, CV.44, was envisaged, but this was cancelled in January 1943 in preference to the more ambitious 'Midway' class design. *Midway* (CVB.41) was laid down on 27 October 1943, *Coral Sea* (CVB.42) — renamed *Franklin D.*

Laid-up veterans in November 1945: *Saratoga, Enterprise, Hornet* and *San Jacinto. Saratoga* was expended in the Bikini atom bomb tests of July 1946 (it took two blasts to sink her); *Enterprise* was scrapped in September 1958, all efforts to save her as a national monument having failed; *San Jacinto* was retained as an aircraft transport (AVT). Only *Hornet* survived for peacetime reconstruction and retention in service as a jet-age fleet carrier.

TABLE 5

COMPARATIVE DATA TABLE OF AMERICAN FLEET CARRIER CLASSES, 1943 AND 1945

	'Essex'	'Midway'
Displacement (tons)	27,100	45,000
Length overall (ft)	872.00	986.00
Max. beam (ft)	147.50	136.00
Draught (ft)	28.50	32.75
Machinery (ft)	4-shaft turbines	4-shaft turbines
S.H.P.	150,000	212,000
Max. Speed (kts)	33	33
Armament	12 × 5-inch	18 × 5-inch
	68 × 40 mm	84 × 40 mm
Aircraft	100	137
Complement	3500	4085

Opposite above
Hornet transformed as an ASW (anti-submarine warfare) carrier, recovering a Grumman S-2E Tracker in the Pacific (December 1968).

Opposite below
Fine shot of the late 'Essex' class *Princeton* (launched July 1945), operational at last in May 1946. After 15 years' service she was converted as an amphibious assault ship (APH).

Too late for the Pacific War but still very much in service 35 years after, transformed for the needs of the missile age: *Coral Sea* in June 1981, returning at Pearl Harbor.

The ultimate statement of the fleet carrier's superb value for taxpayers' money. Originally built to embody all the hard-won lessons of World War Two, the 'Midways' proved able to accommodate all the radical changes to carrier design over the ensuing three decades. This is *Midway* in June 1971, with angled flight-deck and fully-enclosed 'hurricane' bow, off the South-East Asian mainland during the Vietnam War.

Roosevelt — on 1 December 1943. A third ship, CVB.43, was laid down on 10 July 1944. Two, CVBs.56 and 57, were cancelled in March 1945.

The result was three magnificent fleet carriers, the greatest fighting ships in the world which, though just too late for service in World War II, set the pattern for the postwar fleet of giant American carriers. Rarely if ever has a class of warship given its nation's taxpayers such value for money. Astonishingly, in early 1983 it was announced that *Coral Sea*, last of the trio in service, had been ordered a fifteen-month, $200 million refit to enable her to serve on for another ten years into the early 1990s.

Index

Page numbers in *italics* refer to illustrations